PSYCHOLOGICAL PERSPECTIVES
ON SELF AND IDENTITY

Psychological Perspectives on Self and Identity

Edited by Abraham Tesser, Richard B. Felson, and Jerry M. Suls

AMERICAN PSYCHOLOGICAL ASSOCIATION
WASHINGTON, DC

Published by
American Psychological Association
750 First Street, NE
Washington, DC 20002

Copies may be ordered from
APA Order Department
P.O. Box 92984
Washington, DC 20090-2984

In the U.K., Europe, Africa, and the Middle East, copies may be ordered from
American Psychological Association
3 Henrietta Street
Covent Garden, London
WC2E 8LU England

Typeset in Goudy by Monotype Composition, Baltimore, MD
Printer: Sheridan Books, Ann Arbor, MI
Cover Designer: Nini Sarmiento, Ni Design, Baltimore, MD
Technical/Production Editor: Eleanor Inskip

The opinions and statements published are the responsibility of the authors, and such opinions and statements do not necessarily represent the policies of the APA.

Library of Congress Cataloging-in-Publication Data

Psychological perspectives on self and identity / editors, Abraham Tesser, Richard B. Felson, Jerry M. Suls.
    p. cm.
    Includes bibliographical references and indexes.
    ISBN 1-55798-678-9
    1. Self. 2. Self—Social aspects. I. Tesser, Abraham. II. Felson, Richard B. III. Suls, Jerry M.

BF697 .P765 2000
155.2--dc21   00-021139

British Library Cataloguing-in-Publication Data
A CIP record is available from the British Library.

Printed in the United States of America
First Edition

CONTENTS

CONTRIBUTORS

Sunaina Assanand, PhD, University of British Columbia

Roy F. Baumeister, PhD, Case Western Reserve University, Cleveland, Ohio

Jennifer D. Campbell, PhD, University of British Columbia

Adam Di Paula, PhD, University of British Columbia

Richard B. Felson, PhD, Pennsylvania State University

Eddie Harmon-Jones, PhD, University of Wisconsin-Madison

John G. Holmes, PhD, University of Waterloo, Ontario, Canada

Ziva Kunda, PhD, University of Waterloo, Ontario, Canada

Penelope Lockwood, PhD, University of Toronto at Lethbridge, Alberta, Canada

Sandra L. Murray, PhD, State University of New York, Buffalo, New York

Andrzej Nowak, PhD, Florida Atlantic University & University of Warsaw, Poland

Beth A. Pontari, PhD, University of Florida

Barry R. Schlenker, PhD, University of Florida

Constantine Sedikides, PhD, University of Southhampton, England

John J. Skowronski, PhD, Ohio State University at Newark, Ohio

Jerry M. Suls, PhD, University of Iowa

Abraham Tesser, PhD, Ohio State University

Robin R. Vallacher, PhD, Florida Atlantic University

PREFACE

For the last three decades or so, one edge of social psychology has grown tremendously. The growth has been continuous and punctuated occasionally by exhilarating breakthroughs. The edge of social psychology to which we refer is, of course, research on the self.

We now know a lot about the consequences of self-awareness and of having self-schemas. We have a good idea of the pervasiveness of self-serving biases and the occasions for self-presentation. And, we know about self-motives such as self-verification, self-assessment, and self-enhancement. Graduate students from a variety of disciplines coming of age during this period have been attracted by the allure of this research area. In short, the self has established itself as an important area of research with a growing cadre of scientists.

The expanding growth of knowledge on the self-edge and the expanding number of scientists interested in this area created a need for organization. In the mid-1990s, a group of researchers (Constantine Sedikides, Dianne Tice, Roy F. Baumeister, Rich Felson, and Mark Leary) discussed the possibility of creating an organization that would foster communication and interdisciplinary research among researchers of the self and identity. The first meeting of the International Society for Self and Identity (ISSI) was held in the fall of 1996 in Sturbridge, MA. The meeting was well attended, and the society was off to a good start.

In short order, the executive committee of the ISSI recognized the need for greater and more coherent dissemination of research related to the self and identity. Exciting research programs on the self and identity are pushing the limits of knowledge, but they remain scattered and not easily accessible. A published volume summarizing programs of scholarship on the forefront would help. Such a volume could put at least some of the work in a single, accessible place. If the work were carefully edited, it would capture some of the most engaging and productive research programs. Such a volume could inform researchers as well as students. It could be of interest across disciplinary boundaries including sociology, communication, and clinical psychology as well as social psychology. Moreover, there was a precedent, namely the successful and important series of volumes under the title *Psychological Perspectives on the Self*, edited by Jerry Suls. Suls had no plans for an additional volume but generously agreed to help the new ISSI with its efforts. Mark Leary spearheaded the search for an editorial team, and the present volume was born.

The exuberance of the ISSI was infectious. We, the editors, set out enthusiastically and optimistically to capture the productive excitement that characterizes contemporary research on the self. We carefully considered and discussed a variety of research programs. With luck, we were able to recruit a group of researchers that we considered to be among the very best. The scholarship that they present to us in this volume is broad, programmatic, and interesting. Our optimism and enthusiasm was appropriate at the outset. It seems even more appropriate as we bring this project to a close.

Working on this volume has been a pleasure for us (Tesser organized the work. Felson and Suls contributed equally and the order of their names on the masthead is arbitrary). We appreciate the challenge provided by the ISSI. We thank the American Psychological Association for its ready openness to the idea. Most of all, we thank the authors whose work is published here. We learned from them. We hope you do as well.

I

Structure and Dynamics
of the Self

INTRODUCTION

JERRY M. SULS, ABRAHAM TESSER, RICHARD B. FELSON

In a recent review of the literature, Banaji and Prentice (1994) counted more than 5,000 publications on phenomena related to the self, spanning a wide variety of journals, monographs, and books. As the size and scope of this literature attests, the self is a well-established research area in a variety of disciplines including clinical psychology, communication, developmental psychology, social psychology, and sociology. The purpose of this volume is to provide an overview of recent and emerging empirical work in this field, as well as its philosophical and scientific origins. The book should be useful to established scholars and students alike. In order to put contributions to this volume into context for the reader, we first present a brief history of the social psychology of self.

The history of thought on the self dates from the ancient Greeks. Aristotle emphasized the difference between physical and nonphysical aspects of being human. He referred to the soul as the nonphysical or psychic core of each human being that was essential to mental functioning. Much later this concept was labeled as the self. The shift in terminology is important because, with the rise of Christianity, the concept of soul became the domain of theology. The distinction between physical and nonphysical was maintained and subsequently elaborated by René Descartes, the French philosopher. (His famous dictum, "I think, therefore I am," asserts that because thinking is undeniable, so is the existence of the thinker.) The *I*, a thinking, knowing entity was recognized as a key aspect of the self. The nature of experiencing oneself became a major preoccupation of subsequent philosophers such as George Berkeley, David Hume, James Mill, and John Stuart Mill. A point of debate was whether the self represents the process of experiencing or the content of what is known. The ensuing philosophical debate set the stage for the development of psychology in the later part of the 19th century.

Wilhelm Wundt (1897/1902) argued that the sense of self really represents the individual's experiences of his or her own body, particularly muscle tension and other internal states. This view seemed too narrow, however, to the American psychologist William James (1890), who offered a more complex perspective on the self and, in a real sense, created the agenda for future (social) psychological inquiry about self and identity. James made a distinction between the self as knower or *I* (process) and known or *me* (content). According to James, the known self consisted of three domains of self-experience: the *material me*, which included one's body and material possessions, as well as family members and things connected to the self; the *social self*, which involves the recognition one obtains from friends and significant others, and the *spiritual self*, which refers to the psychic faculties or dispositions. Thus, the *me* is the aggregate of things known about self. The *I* is the stream of consciousness that creates this knowing. Because it is a relatively continuous stream, James thought each thought can remember what went before, which was responsible for people's feeling of continuity across time. James had hoped he had (by integrating the known and knower aspects of the self) settled classic philosophical disputes about whether the self was a process or a content. For James, the self was both. These ideas became influential in contemporary theories and research on the self. Discussion of the content and structure of the self figures prominently in chapters by Baumeister, Vallacher and Nowak, and Campbell, Assanand, and Di Paula in this volume.

James contributed many other ideas about the self, but two were especially important. Because the social self relies on what we think other people think or expect of us, James (1890) argued that "a man has as many social selves as there are individuals who recognize him and carry an image of him in their mind" (p. 190). These comments anticipate the importance of self-presentation and social roles in contemporary research. Another of James's ideas was that self-esteem is determined by the ratio of one's successes to one's pretensions or goals. This means that people's objective level of success, wealth, or attractiveness, and so forth, is less important than how well they perceive meeting their strivings. The emphasis on self-esteem and strivings leads directly to consideration of self-motives and self-regulation in contemporary research. The work described by Sedikides and Skowronski and Harmon-Jones are manifestations of this tradition in the social psychology of the self.

George Herbert Mead (1934) was the father of symbolic interactionism, a theory that has had great influence on social psychologists trained in sociology departments. The theory emphasizes the role of symbols and the individual's "definition of the situation." Through symbols, people create a world of objects to which they respond. The self refers to the tendency for people to respond to themselves as symbolic objects.

Mead emphasized that social interaction creates the sense of self. We learn to take the role of others and, in this way, learn who we are and how we should behave. Mead's approach was similar to the approach of Charles Horton Cooley (1902), another important early contributor to the study of self. Cooley is best known for introducing the concept of the looking-glass self. By this, Cooley meant that people obtain a sense of who they are by how others perceive them. Murray and Holme's work on reflected appraisal in this volume builds on this tradition.

As a result of the influence of symbolic interactionism, the study of self has a long tradition in sociology. Some scholars, influenced by Mead's emphasis on subjective point of view and the self as process, rejected quantitative research. Others used survey methods to study the self. For example, Morris Rosenberg (1965) developed a measure of self-esteem—the global judgment of self—and examined its determinants. Manford Kuhn (Kuhn & McPartland, 1954) asked respondents to answer the question "Who am I?" in order to examine the content of people's self-concepts. The first three chapters of this volume on the structure and dynamics of the self fall within this tradition.

One branch of symbolic interactionism emphasized the situational nature of the self and the role of the audience. This branch, associated with Erving Goffman (1959), uses a stage metaphor to understand human behavior. Individuals are identified as actors managing impressions, presenting themselves to others, and devoting considerable effort to avoiding embarassment. Goffman laid the theoretical groundwork for the study of impression management in the experimental laboratory. Schlenker and Pontari's work builds on this tradition. Their examination of impression management for altruistic purposes is grounded in Goffman's analysis of cooperative facework.

Sigmund Freud's concept of the ego also shares many elements in common with the notion of self, and the ego received more attention from the neo-Freudians, such as Erich Fromm, Karen Horney, and Harry Stack Sullivan. These scholars and therapists theorized about the origins of self-love and self-acceptance, which had implications for development and therapy. Baumeister's chapter has clear implications for some of these psychoanalytic ideas.

Theorizing and research on self and identity continued among psychotherapists, such as Carl Rogers (1961) and developmentalists, such as Erikson in the early and middle decades of this century. During this interval, however, limited attention was paid to the self by other parts of the psychological community, in part, because of the dominance of behaviorism, which emphasized constructs that were observable and easily quantified. The self was considered as an anti-scientific concept because it was a cognitive and internal concept. Moreover, early theorizing about the self was only in rare cases tested with rigorous experimental methods.

In the late 1960s behaviorism began to lose some of its influence when social and clinical psychologists used experimental methods to study the self. A particularly important development was the adoption of theoretical concepts and methodologies from cognitive psychology. By borrowing what experimental psychologists had learned about attention, psychologists studying the self began to consider the implications for self-consciousness and self-regulation (Duval & Wicklund, 1965). Adapting the schema concept, which has both structural and functional elements, from cognitive psychology led to research on self-schemata using reaction time, memory, and attention tasks (Markus, 1977). Similarly, as theory and research on mood and emotion advanced, their implications for self-esteem and self-evaluation became clearer. The question of how self-knowledge is obtained has roots in James and the symbolic interactionists, as we have described. By the 1970s and 1980s, however, scholars also recognized that the group dynamics tradition (Festinger, 1954) had something to contribute as social psychologists demonstrated how comparisons with other people define self-knowledge. The work described by Lockwood and Kunda represents a logical descendent of this tradition.

Since the 1970s there has been a continuing stream of research and theorizing about the cognitive, affective, and social aspects of the self (see Baumeister, 1998; Gergen, 1971). Social psychologists have studied the way self-knowledge is organized, the effects of self-awareness on subsequent behavior, how different motives influence how and what self-knowledge is sought or avoided, determinants of self-esteem, and how situational variables and personal characteristics influence which side of the self people show to others.

* * *

The work described in the present volume is clearly related to and builds on what has come before. We have arranged the chapters in this book into three parts. The first part contains chapters with a strong emphasis on the structure and dynamics of the self. Baumeister's work focuses on the dynamics of will power. He argues in chapter 1 that the exertion of will, like the exercise of a muscle, depletes energy and makes subsequent acts of will more difficult. In chapter 2, Vallacher and Nowak view the self as a complex, dynamical, self-organizing system that tends toward its own equilibrium over time. Campbell, Assanand, and Di Paula (chapter 3) emphasize the importance of self-complexity and self-certainty for self-esteem and adjustment.

The two chapters in Part 2 are concerned with motivational properties of the self. Following up on their earlier work, Sedikides and Skowronski (chapter 4) speculate on the evolutionary antecedents of three classes of self-evaluation motives: valence (positive self view), learning (self-improvement), and homeostatic (self-verification). In chapter 5, Harmon-Jones addresses the primacy of self motives. That is, are the phenomena described by dissonance theory simply instances of self-esteem maintenance? They are not, according to Harmon-Jones.

The final three chapters emphasize the self in interpersonal processes. Lockwood and Kunda's research shows that exposure to others that are outstanding is not always threatening (chapter 6). Indeed, under specified conditions, such exposure is self-inspiring. In chapter 7, Murray and Holmes note that intimate relationships can offer a safe haven. Their research suggests, however, that just when the resources of an intimate relationship are most needed, those low in self-esteem tend to distance themselves from the relationship. Finally, common wisdom suggests that people consciously engage in self-presentation and that they do so on special occasions like first dates or conversations with their supervisor. Their motives are selfish and their methods duplicitous. Not so, argue Schlenker and Pontari in chapter 8. They suggest that self-presentation is more frequently under automatic than conscious control; that it is found under ordinary, repeated circumstances; and, that it is often undertaken to benefit another.

* * *

Often there is a positive emotional response associated with seeing something new in what we have often looked at—or, from finding a new and useful way to think about things. Working on this volume has led us to see new things in familiar territory and has taught us to organize some parts of our thinking in new ways. It was a pleasure for us. We invite the reader to share in that pleasure.

REFERENCES

Banaji, M. R., & Prentice, D. A. (1994). The self in social contexts. *Annual Review of Psychology, 45*, 297–332.

Baumeister, R. (1998). The self. In D. T. Gilbert, S. T. Fiske, & G. Lindzey (Eds.), *The handbook of social psychology* (Vol. 1, pp. 680–740). Boston: McGraw-Hill.

Cooley, C. H. (1902). *Human nature and the social order*. New York: Scribner.

Duval, S., & Wicklund, R. (1965). *A theory of objective self-awareness*. New York: Academic Press.

Festinger, L. (1954). A theory of social comparison processes. *Human Relations, 7*, 117–140.

Gergen, K. (1971). *The concept of self*. New York: Holt, Rinehart & Winston.

Goffman, E. (1959). *The presentation of self in everyday life*. New York: Doubleday.

James, W. (1890). *Principles of psychology*. New York: Holt.

Kuhn, M. H., & McPartland, T. S. (1954). An empirical investigation of self-attitudes. *American Sociological Review, 19*, 68–76.

Markus, H. (1977). Self-schemata and processing information about the self. *Journal of Personality and Social Psychology, 35*, 63–78.

Mead, G. H. (1934). *Mind, self, and society*. Chicago: University of Chicago Press.

Rogers, C. (1961). *On becoming a person*. Boston, MA: Houghton Mifflin.

Rosenberg, M.(1965). *Society and adolescent self-image*. Princeton, NJ: Princeton University Press.

Wundt, W. (1902). *Outlines of psychology*. (C. H. Judd, Trans.). New York: Stechert. (Original work published 1897)

1

EGO DEPLETION AND THE SELF'S EXECUTIVE FUNCTION

ROY F. BAUMEISTER

Defining the nature of human selfhood was recognized as a difficult, important problem by some of psychology's founding thinkers (Freud, 1923/1961; James, 1892/1948; Jung, 1971). The difficulty of coming up with a comprehensive definition of self stems not so much from any inaccessibility but rather from its ubiquitous familiarity: Every day people use the concept of self with relative ease, yet it is very difficult for psychologists to encompass all of these usages in a single definition. Issues of cross-cultural variation (e.g., Markus & Kitayama, 1991) versus evolutionary bases (Sedikides & Skowronski, 1997) only complicate the matter further.

I recently proposed that selfhood is rooted in three universal concepts that may help to define it (Baumeister, 1998). The first is *reflexive consciousness*, through which knowledge of the self develops through awareness. The second is *interpersonal membership*, whereby the self develops amid interpersonal relationships and serves to connect the physical organism to social networks. The third is the *executive function*, which encompasses volition: choosing, deciding, initiating action, exerting control over self and world, and altering the self.

9

In recent decades, social psychologists have actively studied phenomena linked to reflexive consciousness: self-knowledge, self-perception, self-awareness, self-schemas, self-esteem, and so forth. The interpersonal aspect of self has also received a fair share of attention, under the rubric of topics such as self-presentation, reflected appraisals, and interpersonal consequences of various self-views. Executive function, however, has received far less study and less systematic attention than the others. It is this neglected aspect of the self that is the focus of the present chapter.

The fact that social psychology has been slower to understand the self's executive function than other aspects of the self is probably due not to its lack of importance, but rather, to the conceptual and methodological difficulties of studying the executive function (which are formidable). The executive function includes acts of choice and initiative, which are crucial features of human life and make the huge variety of human activities possible. The executive function also includes self-regulation, which is tremendously adaptive and vital for the well-being of both society and the individual. Self-regulation failures are central to many social and personal problems in today's societies, including alcohol and drug abuse, smoking, overeating, failure to exercise, crime and violence, teen pregnancy, school failure and underachievement, money and credit problems and failure to save, venereal disease, and domestic violence (see Baumeister, Heatherton, & Tice, 1994). Evidence suggests that children who performed better at delay of gratification at age 4 were found to be more successful socially and academically more than a decade later (Mischel, Shoda, & Peake, 1988; Shoda, Mischel, & Peake, 1990).

In this chapter, I propose that the executive function operates like a muscle. This is essentially an energy model. Although Freud (1923/1961, 1933/1961) proposed that the ego required energy for its operation, recent models of self have emphasized information-processing structures rather than energy processes. It may, however, be necessary to turn back to energy models in order to understand the self's executive function.

SELF-REGULATION

My understanding of the self's executive function began with narrower, although still general, questions: What is the nature of self-regulation? How does the self manage to operate on itself so as to alter itself? Modern self-regulation theory has been heavily influenced by Carver and Scheier's (1981, 1982) important work, which began with their studies on self-awareness. They borrowed a cybernetic model from Powers (1973) to suggest that self-regulation uses a feedback loop, like a thermostat. The acronym TOTE (test, operate, test, exit) captured the simple form of their model: The self *tests* by comparing some feature against a standard of how things should be, *operates* to bring the self into line with standards and goals, *tests* again and, if the goal has been met, it *exits* the sequence.

The importance and use of this model are well recognized. The model describes how the regulatory process is controlled. It does not, however, make clear what happens in the "operate" phase, in which the contents of the self are changed to bring them into line with what is desired or expected. This has become the focus of my work: How is the self-regulatory change actually achieved?

In an initial but extensive survey of research on self-control failure, my colleagues and I (Baumeister et al., 1994) were led to a tentative suggestion that many failures seemed to reflect a weakness of some form of strength or energy, as suggested by the traditional term *willpower* (see also Mischel, 1996). This line of thought began with the inner struggle to control one's impulses. An impulse is understood as the desire to perform a specific behavior on a specific occasion: Thus, it arises when a general motivation (e.g., hunger) encounters a specific stimulus (e.g., a piece of cake). To sustain one's diet, the self must find some way to prevent itself from eating the cake. Research on impulse control did not suggest that the most common problem is that impulses were so powerful and overwhelming that people could not possibly restrain themselves. Rather, the self's capacity for overriding the impulse seemed inadequate.

We began our laboratory work on self-regulatory operations by pitting the willpower theory against several other possible models, including a skill model and an information-processing (schematic) model. We noted that these three ways of thinking about self-control made competing predictions about what would happen to an act of self-control if it followed close on the heels of a different act of self-control. If self-control were matter of strength or energy (as in willpower), then the first act should expend some of that energy (or tire the muscle), and so performance on the second act would be impaired. In contrast, if self-control operated like a master schema in information-processing terms, then the first act of self-control should prime the schema, and so performance should be improved on the second act. Finally, if self-control is essentially a skill, then there should be no change to the second act of self-control as a result of the first, insofar as skill remains essentially constant from one trial to another and improves only gradually across many trials.

A series of studies supported the strength model over the schema and skill models (Muraven, Tice, & Baumeister, 1998). In a first study, people were instructed to regulate their emotional feelings and facial expressivity while watching a sad, upsetting film clip. Their physical stamina was then tested with a handgrip task that required self-control to override the muscular pain and fatigue in the hand from squeezing the grip. Their physical stamina decreased from before to after the movie. In a control condition, people watched the same distressing film without regulating their emotions, and their stamina was unchanged. Thus, the act of trying to control one's emotional response (either by suppressing or amplifying it) depleted some resource that was then no longer available to help them perform well on the handgrip stamina test.

In a second study, people were instructed to control their thoughts. We borrowed the thought suppression task from Wegner, Schneider, Carter, and White (1987), which involved telling people to try not to think about a white bear. After performing this exercise (and recording their thoughts) for several minutes, they were then given the ostensibly unrelated task of solving anagrams. The anagrams were actually unsolvable, and the task was designed to see how long they kept trying before giving up. Persisting in the face of failure requires self-regulation, because one must overcome the discouraging, frustrating feeling of getting nowhere and the resultant impulse to quit. The people who had been given the thought suppression task gave up faster on the anagram task than did people who had not tried to control their thoughts. Thus, trying not to think about a white bear depleted some resource that was then unavailable for persisting on the anagram task.

Impulse control was the focus of another investigation along the same lines (Baumeister, Bratslavsky, Muraven, & Tice, 1998), and indeed impulse control is often what many people regard as the prime focus of self-control. Participants in this study were asked to skip a meal and eat nothing for three hours prior to the experiment so that they arrived hungry. In the laboratory they encountered the mouth-watering aroma of freshly baked chocolate chip cookies, and they sat down at a table in front of a display of these cookies and other chocolate candies. Also on the table was a bowl of radishes. In the crucial condition, the experimenter said that the participant had been assigned to the "radish condition" in which the task would involve eating only radishes. The participant was left alone in the room for five minutes, ostensibly to eat the radishes, but in fact to struggle with the temptation to help himself or herself to the delicious chocolates and cookies. Afterward, the food was cleared away, and the participants were given a pair of (actually unsolvable) geometric puzzles to measure how well they could persist in the face of failure.

Once again, the results suggested that a strength or muscle model fits self-control best. The people in the radish group gave up much faster on the puzzles, as compared to people who were permitted to eat the tempting chocolates, and also compared to a control group in which the participants were not given any food at all. Resisting the chocolate temptation depleted some resource and left them less able to keep working at the puzzle.

These experiments, along with a few others designed to rule out various alternative explanations (see the subsequent section), indicated that self-control seems to operate on the basis of a strength or energy model. Like a muscle that gets tired after exertion, self-control deteriorated in the aftermath of another, seemingly unrelated act of self-control. These patterns contradicted the view of self-control as a master schema or information-processing system, as well as a skill model.

Two further implications were important. First, different acts of self-control appear to draw on a common resource. The different experimental procedures used measures drawn from different spheres of self-control. Thus, apparently, the same resource was used for suppressing thoughts, amplifying or stifling emotions, physical stamina, persistence in the face of failure, and impulse control (resisting temptation). These carryovers suggest that the widely different forms of self-control are all under the influence of a single, unified entity. Freud's (e.g., 1930) concept of the superego proposed that a single psychic agency maintained control over widely different behaviors, and although these findings do not necessarily confirm many of the specific and subtle features of Freud's superego theory, they do support his view of the unity of self-control. Second, the resource that is used in these many acts of self-control is limited. Five minutes of resisting a chocolate temptation and making oneself eat radishes instead was enough to reduce persistence on un-solvable puzzles by more than 10 minutes, or by more than half.

Given the importance of self-control, this limited but versatile resource would already deserve a prominent place in self theory. Whatever it is that enables people to control their thoughts, feelings, impulses, and performance must be regarded as highly adaptive and precious. We were to find, however, that the importance of that resource went even beyond self-control.

CHOICE AND INITIATIVE

Self-regulation is one of the major aspects of the executive function in general, along with choice and initiative (see Baumeister, 1998). The apparent unity of self-control thus raises the broader question of the possible unity of the entire executive function. Was it possible that the same resource or energy used for self-control would also be used in choice, decision making, active (as opposed to passive) responses, and the rest?

We found that acts of choice seem to deplete the same resource used in self-control (Baumeister et al., 1998). We borrowed the choice procedure from one of the best-known and most widely studied topics in social psychology, namely cognitive dissonance (Linder, Cooper, & Jones, 1967). Participants in the crucial condition were asked to make a speech favoring making a large tuition increase, which was clearly contrary to the interests and attitudes of most students. They were told that we would appreciate their cooperation but that the final decision was up to them. In contrast, participants in the low-choice condition were told to make the same speech, but the experimenter said that they did not have any choice about what speech to make.

This manipulation of choice has been used in countless studies of attitude change, but we were not interested in the attitudinal consequences. We wanted to know whether making the choice would have the same effects that resisting temptation or stifling emotions had had in previous studies. Hence the choice manipulation was followed by an ostensibly unrelated task, which in fact was identical to the procedure for the radish and chocolate study described earlier: persistence at unsolvable geometric puzzles. Compared to those in the no-speech control condition, high-choice participants quit working on the puzzles significantly faster. In contrast, people who were assigned to make the same speech under low choice showed no loss of persistence at the puzzles.

There was even a fourth condition in which people were asked to make a proattitudinal speech (favoring keeping tuition hikes to a minimum) under high choice. We wondered whether making a choice to do something one approves would deplete the self, as opposed to merely consenting to do something contrary to one's beliefs. People in this condition quit rather early on the unsolvable puzzles; in fact, they did not differ from the people who agreed to the counterattitudinal (high-choice) speech.

Thus, it was not the behavior to which one consented but rather the act of consenting that depleted the resource. High versus low choice for the same behavior made a large difference in how much the self was depleted. The same level of high choice for a counterattitudinal versus proattitudinal behavior made no difference. The act of choice is apparently itself depleting.

We had thus shown effects of choice on self-regulation. To verify that choice and self-regulation both draw on the same resource, we also wanted to show the reverse, namely, that acts of self-control would deplete the self and thereby alter the nature of choice. What would this effect be? If the self had less energy available for making choices, we reasoned, then it would tend to become more passive in its choosing. Hence we used the distinction between active and passive choice. In many decisions in life, there exists a passive option (of doing nothing). Previous work had attested that active responses leave stronger psychological aftereffects than do passive ones (e.g., Allison & Messick, 1988; Cioffi & Garner, 1996; Fazio, Sherman, & Herr, 1982). One possible explanation is that active responses use the self, whereas passive responses do not. It is in a sense easier to do nothing and remain inert than to take positive action, which suggests that positive action might require the resources of the self. If those resources have been depleted, people should be more passive.

Measuring passive tendencies requires one to have two choice options and to have two conditions that differ only in which of the options is passive (e.g., Cioffi & Garner, 1996; Fazio et al., 1982). We instructed participants to watch a movie as long as necessary until they fully grasped it, and we made the movie as boring as possible. (It showed an unchanging image of a wall in the laboratory.) Half the participants were told they needed to keep pressing a button to continue the movie, because if they did nothing (i.e., failed to press the button) the film would stop automatically. The others were told that the film would continue automatically until they pressed the button to stop it.

Prior to the film, we administered a manipulation of ego depletion. For this study, we took yet another methodological approach to ego depletion, based on the general guideline that self-control consumes resources precisely when the self must override its initial response. In this procedure, we required people to acquire a habit and then to break it repeatedly. They were first instructed to go through a page of text and cross out every letter *e*. This instilled the habit of responding to every *e*. Then we gave them more text and told them to cross out every *e* unless it was next to a vowel or if there was a vowel two letters removed (e.g., the *o* in *removed* would mean that the person would not cross out either *e*). The assumption was that this would require the self to override the habit of responding to every *e*. In a control condition, people worked on three-digit arithmetic problems, which were rated as difficult and effortful but did not require the self to expend its volitional resources. The results showed that people became more passive following the depleting *e* task than following the math problems. Thus, again, self-control and volition (initiative in this case) require the same resource.

After these studies we settled on the term *ego depletion* to describe the pattern rather than *self-regulatory depletion*, which had been all that the first set of studies permitted. Apparently a broad range of the self's functions all draw on the same resource, which is easily depleted. We selected the term *ego* for two reasons. One is in homage to Freud, who was among the first to discuss selfhood in energy terms. Freud (e.g., 1923/1961, 1933/1961) did propose that the ego has its sources of energy and uses them for its acts of volition, although he was not clear about the sources or nature of this energy. The other reason for using the term *ego* is that the prefix *self* often implies a reflexive act, as if it is the self that is doing the depleting rather than being depleted (e.g., self-control, self-fulfilling prophecy). The important point is that the executive function of the self expends some valuable, limited resource in its acts of volition, including self-control, active initiative, and responsible choice.

ALTERNATIVE EXPLANATIONS

Because applying an energy model to the self goes against the trend of recent thought, it is necessary to consider whether our findings can be dismissed based on alternate explanations. If the findings mean what they appear to mean, then the self does in fact operate its executive function on the basis of a limited resource of energy or strength, and it will be necessary to augment the field's recent self theories with some sort of limited-resource or energy model. But undoubtedly the reader has wondered whether several of these findings might not be so conclusive about the need to change self theory.

One problem that concerned us was that the dependent variables in most studies involved persistence on unsolvable problems. Although one can make the argument that effective self-control in life involves making oneself persist after failure, the usefulness of doing so evaporates when the problems are unsolvable, because persistence will not lead to success. In fact, one could argue the opposite, namely, that effective self-regulation would entail withdrawing effort from unsolvable problems, so as to conserve time and effort for more promising endeavors (Janoff-Bulman & Brickman, 1982). In this view, people who quit early on our laboratory tasks were not showing deficits in self-control but rather improvements.

This interpretation was not supported by any indications that people had recognized the tasks as unsolvable, but such self-reports are not entirely reliable. Hence we conducted another study in which the anagrams were solvable (Baumeister et al., 1998). Ego depletion impaired performance on solvable anagrams just as it impaired performance on unsolvable ones.[1] In other words, ego depletion was really an impairment, not a stimulus, to effective self-regulation via strategic withdrawal of effort.

Another explanation is based on mood. Perhaps the first self-control task was frustrating or upsetting in some way, and the result was negative affect that carried over to the second task and, especially on the performance measures, caused people to quit faster than they would have otherwise. This view too fails to gain any support from manipulation checks, in which there were no signs of bad moods. This interpretation also does not readily explain the results of the first study, in which all participants watched the same upsetting film, but subsequent decrements were found only among participants who tried to change their emotional reaction, and, moreover, it did not matter whether they tried to increase or to decrease their emotional state. If bad mood mediated the results, the people who tried to increase their bad mood should have been different from the ones who tried to stifle and suppress it, but they were not.

Still, the concern over possibly unnoticed bad moods led us to conduct another study using a positive mood. In this, participants were given the thought suppression manipulation from Wegner et al. (1987) and then were instructed to try not to smile or laugh while watching a funny videotape of a monologue by comedian Robin Williams. The people who had tried to

---

[1]One might raise the question as to whether solving anagrams is a measure of self-regulation or self-control at all, especially because I proposed elsewhere that arithmetic problems do not require self-regulation. Anagrams do involve overriding responses insofar as one must break one's set to see the letters arranged one way and shuffle them into new combinations. As for arithmetic, numerical problems are often the straightforward, even automatic, application of well-learned rules. In contrast, I suspect that word problems in mathematics may make more demands on the self, in that the self must decide how to translate the words into equations with numbers and variables.

suppress the white bear thought were less able to keep from smiling and laughing than were the people who had not suppressed thoughts. If thought suppression had induced a bad mood, it should have been easier, not harder, for them to avoid smiling and laughing.

Arousal might also be suggested as a mediating factor. Again, our manipulation checks have not consistently shown evidence for arousal resulting from depletion and, if anything, the few studies that show any result show the opposite (self-reported tiredness) resulting from the depletion procedure. More commonly, though, depletion produces neither self-reports of arousal nor tiredness. Probably the strongest evidence against the arousal interpretation comes from the choice study, however, insofar as arousal has been strongly linked to cognitive dissonance in high-choice conditions (Zanna & Cooper, 1974). Arousal should be high in the counterattitudinal condition but low in the proattitudinal speech condition, but these showed identical patterns of ego depletion.

Some might wonder whether mental effort is all that is involved in ego depletion. Mental effort is a vague concept that in some respects is compatible with our theorizing, because it involves the expenditure of precious energy by the self. Still, ego depletion does not reduce to effort expenditure alone. The issue of mental effort was the reason that we included a control group involving arithmetic problems. Most people report that solving arithmetic problems requires more mental effort than suppressing the thought of a white bear (and our pilot data confirmed this), but only thought suppression produced the effect of ego depletion. Solving arithmetic problems is, however, done by following rules that most adults have learned automatically, whereas suppressing thoughts requires the self to override its responses—and overriding its own responses is precisely what constitutes the expenditure of the self's resources in self-control. (We would speculate, however, that solving word problems instead of numerical computations might consume the self's energy, insofar as word problems require some volition to translate the verbal description into numerical terms.) Thus, it is effort involving the self, and not the mere exertion of any mental activity, that produces ego depletion.

Yet another alternative explanation is that the typical research participant thinks in terms of having an implicit contract to do a certain amount of activity, and doing the first task satisfied this contract, causing him or her to quit faster on the second task (or to relax and enjoy the humorous film). The main finding that contradicts this explanation comes from the passive option study, in which depleted participants in the active–quit condition sat there longer watching the boring movie, as compared to those in the nondepleted control condition. If participants felt they had satisfied their implicit contract by the first task, they should have terminated the boring film quicker and left the experiment, but instead they sat there longer.

Although the implicit contract notion does not seem to fit all of our findings, it does raise the broader issue of how motivation might be related to ego depletion. Giving up early on a difficult, frustrating task could be ascribed to motivation. Hence the next section of this chapter addresses the motivation question separately.

Another alternate interpretation is that people had some notion of how they performed on the first self-control task, and this influenced them on the second. In particular, if people failed at self-control on the first task, they might have already been discouraged enough to quit early on the second task. This explanation is problematic in view of the range of outcomes on the first task. In some studies, the first task was sufficiently hard that most people would have failed—for example, almost no one can suppress the white bear thought with complete success for the entire 5 minutes. In contrast, participants exercised self-control successfully in other studies—for example, covert observation verified that no participant in the radish condition ate any of the forbidden cookies or chocolate.

Still, we were sufficiently intrigued by the notion of implicit feedback to conduct another study (Wallace & Baumeister, 1998). We gave people explicit feedback about how well they performed on the first self-control task (the Stroop color-word task) and then measured performance on a second (persistence on unsolvable puzzles). No differences even approaching significance emerged as a function of feedback, even though we did replicate the depletion effect. Success-versus-failure feedback is one of the most common and readily successful manipulations in social psychology, and its inability to alter the course of ego depletion suggests that cognition and affect are not powerful mediators of these effects. Ego depletion is not apparently a matter of attributions about the self or of self-perceived efficacy. Thus, the implication that some expenditure of energy or other limited resource is involved gains further confidence from this finding.

MOTIVATION AND CONSERVATION

I have already suggested that ego depletion cannot be reduced to a simple motivational effect. Still, it is unlikely that motivation is entirely irrelevant to ego depletion. To take one of our experiments, for example, it might be proposed that highly motivated participants would not have quit so quickly on the unsolvable puzzles if they were to be paid a large sum of money for continuing. The hypothesis that some energy is depleted suggests that people are incapable of doing more. Yet intuition suggests that people could do more if they were sufficiently motivated.

There is, however, an important twist to the motivation question. Quitting early does not necessarily reflect an absence of motivation; it could conceivably suggest a different motivation. I have argued that the resource used by the self for self-control and volition is scarce and precious. If so, then it would be highly desirable to conserve it. It is therefore conceivable that when our research participants quit persisting on a difficult task, it is not because their ego resources are entirely empty. It could mean simply that once the resource is partly depleted, the organism knows to conserve what is left. One would never want to reach a condition of total depletion, because if an important or life-and-death decision had to be made, that person would be unable to make it. Conservation motives may therefore oppose motives to persist on certain tasks.

The link between motivation and ego depletion was the focus of a dissertation by Muraven (1998). In a first study, he measured participants' willingness to consume a good- versus a bad-tasting drink. The good drink was Kool-Aid mixed with the proper recipe. The bad drink was Kool-Aid with all the sugar omitted, leaving only the imitation fruit flavor, and with half of the water replaced with vinegar. Motivation was varied by offering people either a penny or 25 cents per ounce of drink they consumed. Muraven replicated the usual depletion effect under low motivation, using a depletion manipulation in which people were instructed to refrain from laughing or smiling while they watched a comedy video. The people who had to stifle their mirth were less successful at making themselves drink a large amount of the bad-tasting drink, as compared with people who had been permitted to laugh. The high motivation (of high pay) overcame this effect, however, and even created a slight reversal of the usual depletion pattern. The conclusion is that when people are sufficiently motivated, they can overcome the effects of depletion.

Or can they? Resisting the effects of depletion might cause more extreme depletion, especially if the energy model is correct. In the other study, people performed a third task after they resisted depletion on the second, and the third showed some signs of increased depletion. This needs replication, but there is some evidence that motivation to exert control overrides the motivation to conserve but does not really counteract depletion in the long run. The depleted but highly motivated person may continue to expend the self's resources, but this is further depleting.

This pattern of results pointed toward an interpretation in terms of conservation rather than exhaustion for all of the ego depletion findings that we have found. That is, the effects in these studies seem attributable to people trying to conserve the self's limited resources rather than being unable to exert any volition or self-control after a first act. Five minutes' worth of resisting the temptation of chocolate and cookies does not reduce the self to a quivering, helpless shell, but it does create a condition in which the person tries to conserve the remaining resources.

The conservation hypothesis was tested in another study by Muraven (1998). After an initial depletion manipulation, he measured self-control on a cold pressor task. (It presumably requires self-control to force oneself to keep one's hand in ice water, because this involves overriding the ever-increasing impulse to withdraw it; still, for some unknown reason we have not found this procedure to provide consistent evidence of depletion effects, possibly because of error variance caused by failure to maintain the proper and consistent temperature in the ice water.) Prior to the task, however, half of the participants were warned that there would be another task afterward that would require them to suppress laughter and smiling in response to a very funny video, and they were told that this would be difficult. Others were told that there was no further task. The people who anticipated further self-regulation showed the usual ego depletion task, even though, as we noted, the cold pressor task has not generally proven to be a sensitive measure for us. The people in the control condition who were not expecting further duration showed only a small, nonsignificant trend toward depletion.

These results support the notion that self-control decrements following initial acts of self-control reflect conservation of a depleted resource rather than exhaustion. People can perform better on a second task if there is a compelling reason to do so, although it seems to deplete them all the more. Meanwhile, an explicit manipulation of the need to conserve the self's volitional resources led people to abandon self-control more quickly on the intervening task, if they had already been depleted by a first task.

BUILDING THE RESOURCE

An exciting question that promises to shed light on the nature of the self's resource is how that resource is increased. We assume that ego depletion effects are temporary and that the person recovers. Sleep is presumably one common way of replenishing the resource. Sure enough, various signs suggest that people who are deprived of sleep exhibit deficits in self-control and volition. The majority of self-control failures occur late in the day, when people are depleted from the day's decisions and self-regulating (see Baumeister et al., 1994).

Does anything beyond sleep help? One possibility is positive, pleasant emotion. Having an episode of good emotional feelings might restore the self's capacity to exert volition and initiative. This possibility would be a potentially useful extension of functional theories of emotion, because functions (especially in terms of activating behaviors, e.g., Frijda, 1986) have long been far easier to specify for bad than for good emotions. Fear makes people flee, anger makes them fight, and other negative affects often have clear behavioral implications, but it is far more difficult to specify behavioral implications of positive emotions. That difficulty raises the question of what function pleasant emotions serve. If positive emotions helped replenish the ego's capacity to exert control over self and environment, the functional question would be partly answered.

In a preliminary pair of studies, Baumeister, Dale, and Tice (1998) examined the potential power of positive affect for offsetting ego depletion. Half of the participants were depleted (using the task of crossing out some but not all instances of the letter *e* in a page of text), and the others were not. Then each person watched one of three films: a funny video featuring a comedian, a sad film depicting a young mother dying of cancer, or an affectively neutral film about communication among dolphins. Following this, performance on anagrams was measured. Ego depletion led to relatively poor performance in the sad and neutral conditions, but depleted people who were happy from watching the amusing film performed as well as those who had not been depleted. In a second study, depletion impaired persistence on a difficult, frustrating physical game (involving rolling a ball on a tilting surface filled with holes)—but not if a happy mood was induced after the depletion manipulation. Thus, again, the happy mood counteracted the effects of the depletion manipulation.

Positive affect may thus be a short-term solution to ego depletion. A longer term solution could involve increasing one's capacity for volition and control. Earlier in this chapter I suggested the metaphor of a muscle, in that self-control seems to lose power after exertion just as a muscle grows tired during exercise. Many bouts of exercise do, however, have the opposite effect of strengthening the muscle. Does self-control likewise become more effective from repeated use?

One longitudinal study has suggested that self-control can be increased (Muraven, Baumeister, & Tice, in press), although the findings need to be replicated. In this study, participants first came to a laboratory session in which they performed the handgrip stamina test, followed by ego depletion (using the thought suppression/white bear task), followed by a second handgrip stamina test. In this way, each person's vulnerability to ego depletion was assessed. Then people were randomly assigned to perform some self-control exercise for two weeks. One group worked on improving their posture, which clearly requires people to exert initiative and volition, as well as overriding any habitual tendency to slump. Two other groups kept diaries of the foods they ate, which presumably requires some self-discipline in order to write down each item they consumed. (We also anticipated that the exercise of recording food would make people alter their eating habits, although we did not explicitly instruct them to eat or not eat any particular food.) A third group was told to try to regulate their affect by improving their mood whenever they could and, of course, affect regulation is an important category of self-control. Unlike these groups, a control group performed no self-control exercise. Then everyone returned to the laboratory for a repeat of the initial procedure: stamina, depletion, and stamina again.

The results suggested that exercise can increase resistance to ego depletion. The groups that had performed the various exercises for two weeks, combined, suffered less depletion on the second than on the first session, relative to those in control groups. To be sure, not all of the exercises worked equally well and, in fact, the people who were assigned the affect regulation exercise showed no improvement in self-control.

Overall, however, there was some reason to think that exercise was helpful in building strength. Incidentally, strength can be improved in different ways, either in terms of increased initial power or resistance to fatigue. Our results indicated the second form of improvement (stamina) rather than the first (power). There was no increase in baseline stamina from the first session to the second, but the change from baseline to postmeasure (i.e., after the ego-depleting thought suppression task) did show improvement. Our results do not thus suggest that exercise can increase capacity to the point at which people might perform heroic single acts of self-control. Rather, exercise seems to enable people to exert self-control and then continue doing so, relatively free from the usual, debilitating effects of their exertions.

The implications of the improvement data are potentially far-reaching, although again it is important to be cautious about generalizing too far from the results of one study. One disturbing implication of our original set of ego depletion studies is that people should perhaps avoid self-control, because it consumes one of the self's important resources. Given the personal and social ills that attend lack of self-control, my colleagues and I were unhappy about producing findings that would deter people from using self-control.

The longitudinal data, however, suggest that exerting self-control on a regular basis can be beneficial in the long run, even if the short-term effect does deplete a valuable resource. If the self does indeed improve its strength through exercise, then we can safely advise people to exert self-control (as well as initiative, choice, and other acts of volition) frequently. When a crisis comes, instead of finding them with resources depleted, it may prove that they can continue to cope better over an extended period of time than they could have otherwise. Having exerted self-control on a regular basis will make it easier for people to resist the debilitating effects of coping with stress, decisions, or other problems.

LINKS TO OTHER WORK

Thus far I have emphasized research by me and my colleagues that was designed specifically to develop and test the theoretical model of the self's executive function as a strength or energy resource. That model can, however, be used to understand a much broader range of findings on a variety of topics (see Muraven & Baumeister, in press, for a review). This section provides a brief overview of some of the prominent sources of converging evidence.

Research on stress is one important source of relevant evidence. Coping with stress often makes considerable demands on the self's executive function. Controllable stressors may often require the self to engage in extensive, difficult coping efforts, including making decisions and initiating action. Coping with uncontrollable stress can be even more depleting, because it requires the individual to adapt himself or herself to the situation, including suppressing futile impulses to fight or escape and engaging in ongoing affect regulation. These responses, corresponding to primary and secondary control (Rothbaum, Weisz, & Snyder, 1982), both could deplete the self's resources.

Consistent with the ego depletion hypothesis, people show substantial impairments in the aftermath of coping with stress. After dealing with uncontrollable stressors, people show decrements in tolerating frustration (often measured as persistence in the face of failure), proofreading, resisting cognitive interference (as in the Stroop task), and solving anagrams (Cohen, Evans, Krantz, & Stokols, 1980; Gardner, 1978; Gatchel, McKinney, & Koebernick, 1977; Glass & Singer, 1972; Glass, Singer, & Friedman, 1969; Hiroto & Seligman, 1975; Percival & Loeb, 1980; Rotton, Olszewski, Charleton, & Soler, 1978). All of these effects suggest some form of ego depletion.

Stress also impairs subsequent self-control in several well-established behavioral spheres. After coping with stress, people are more likely to show impulsive aggression (Donnerstein & Wilson, 1976) and heightened risk taking (Holding, Loeb, & Baker, 1983), which are important categories of behavior that are typically restrained by self-control (see Gottfredson & Hirschi, 1990). They are more likely to break their diets (Greeno & Wing, 1994; Heatherton, Herman, & Polivy, 1991). Relapse rates for smoking and drinking are higher after stress (e.g., Hull, Young, & Jouriles, 1986).

One common interpretive problem with applying ego depletion theory to such findings involves the perennial question of whether self-control fails because of strong impulses or weak restraints (because only the latter indicates ego depletion). Thus, if stress were to increase hunger, then eating might increase, too—but this would indicate nothing about any change in the self's resources. Fortunately, some evidence contradicts this alternative. Stress appears to increase eating among dieters, for example, but not among nondieters (Heatherton et al., 1991). If stress fostered impulses to eat, then it should have that effect on everyone. In contrast, if stress undermines self-control, then it should increase eating mainly among dieters, because their eating is normally subjected to restraints. Nondieters are not habitually restraining their eating, and so even if their self-control is depleted by having to cope with stress, the reduction in self-control would not remove any blocks against eating.

The study of vigilance is another place to look for ego depletion, because vigilance requires one to force oneself to continue watching for the target stimulus, and if this self-control over attention gradually depletes the self's volitional resource, performance should gradually deteriorate. It is in fact well established that performance at vigilance declines steadily over time as one performs continuously (for reviews, see Davies & Parasuraman,

1982; See, Howe, Warm, & Dember, 1995). The relevance of ego depletion is also suggested by the fact that exertions of self-control impair subsequent volition. Dieting, which is a standard and familiar exercise in self-control, impairs performance on vigilance tasks, and this effect cannot be attributed to mood or arousal effects (Green & Rogers, 1995; Green, Rogers, Elliman, & Gatenby, 1994).

Many theories have been proposed to account for the gradual deterioration in vigilant performance, but the evidence has gradually refuted them all. For example, loss of motivation has been proposed as a reason to account for deteriorations in laboratory performance, but loss of motivation does not readily explain the deterioration in vigilance aboard ships during wartime when the consequences of error can include the death of the watcher. Commenting on the failure of various theories to explain the decline, Parasuraman (1984) suggested that deterioration in vigilance must be attributed to the inability to maintain processing resources, and this conclusion fits well with the suggestion of ego depletion.

Many researchers who study vigilance on laboratory tasks are familiar with a second pattern: After showing gradual deterioration across many trials, vigilance improves just before the anticipated end of the task. This is regarded by many researchers in the field as merely an annoying problem that distorts the data, and it has resulted in standard procedures that include removing the participant's wristwatch before the study (so the person will not know when the end of the allotted time is impending) and not informing the participant of how many trials there will be. What is a trivial annoyance to vigilance researchers may, however, be meaningful to ego depletion theory, because it, too, points to a conservation response rather than full exhaustion to account for the decrements. It suggests that the self naturally and perhaps automatically starts to conserve its volitional resources when they have become partly depleted. When the end of the task is impending and the need to conserve is therefore diminished, people may abruptly be able to perform better again. Sleep deprivation researchers have told me informally that they encounter the same pattern, which provides valuable converging evidence. If the self's resources are restored during sleep, then lack of sleep would exacerbate the effects of ego depletion. But improvement when the end of the study (or of the sleepless period) approaches suggests that the person feels free to expend resources that he or she has been conserving.

Bad moods and emotional distress have also been shown to lead to self-control failure. At present, there are several theories about why this happens, and several of them may be correct. Still, ego depletion is one possible explanation. When people feel upset or distressed, they often try to regulate their emotional state and make themselves feel better. These self-regulatory efforts could deplete the self and hence cause the well-documented subsequent failures of self-control in such spheres as dieting, smoking, drinking, aggression, and spending. Determining whether the consequences of bad moods flow directly from the mood or from the person's efforts to change the mood is a familiar problem in the study of negative affect (e.g., Isen, 1984, 1987), and I shall not try to resolve it here, but it is plausible that many of these effects do indicate ego depletion.

IMPLICATIONS

The research on ego depletion suggests that self theory be expanded to add an energy or strength (i.e., limited resource) model to account for the executive function. That is, the often neglected aspect of self theory concerns how the self makes decisions, exerts control, initiates action, and controls itself. These operations all appear to draw on a common resource that is reduced after use but may become stronger after repeated exercise and recovery. I am not proposing that the existing theories about the self need to be discarded or radically revised—merely that a new dimension be added alongside them.

The potential implications of ego depletion theory are wide-ranging. One set of implications concerns how people make choices and, indeed, move from information processing to behavior. Whatever their metaphysical beliefs regarding free will versus determinism, many psychologists have based their work on an assumption that most human behavior is either consciously directed through active choice processes or, at the other extreme, is the result of mechanistic, determined causes that flow inexorably from external stimuli. If my account of the executive function is correct, however, then human behavior may often be determined mechanistically, whereas a small yet crucial and influential set of behaviors comes from conscious, deliberate choice.

This two-process theory corresponds fairly well to the recently popular and influential distinction between automatic and controlled processes. In my view, the self is the controller of controlled processes and, in a sense, that is what the executive function amounts to—and so this active part of the self is not used or needed in automatic processing. People may be creatures of routine, but they are able to override habit, impulse, and cue on occasion.

Surveying recent studies of automaticity, including much work in his own laboratory, Bargh (1997) proposed that the sphere of conscious, deliberate behavior has steadily shrunk as evidence for automatic processing increases. He wondered whether the eventual outcome would be to eliminate the concept of conscious control altogether and ascribe all human behavior to automatic processing. If everything is automatic, then my work on ego depletion has little to contribute. If, however, the final outcome is more consistent with what Bargh and others can currently propose—namely, that most behavior follows from automatic causal processes and lawful determination, but a small corner does still depend on conscious, deliberate, controlled choice—then ego depletion can explain this pattern. The self's resources for exerting control and volition are severely limited, and it is therefore necessary not to use them for most behavior. Rather, they are to be conserved for important and influential behaviors, when they can do the most good. In plain terms, if you used up your executive function's volitional resources deciding which socks to wear and which hand to open doors with and what route to take to work, you would not be able to make the hard decisions that may arise during the day.

Even if 90% or 95% of behavior should turn out to be automatic, it would not be safe to dismiss the remaining 5% or 10% that might involve volition and controlled processes. This seemingly small segment of behavior may exert a disproportionately large influence over human life. As an analogy, Baumeister and Sommer (1997) noted that the steering wheel of a car may not be needed for most driving, insofar as cars are probably driven straight ahead about 90% of the time. Still, to ignore the remaining few percent (such as by building cars without steering wheels) would seriously compromise the car's value in terms of its ability to get to a variety of destinations. Just as those few turns are disproportionately decisive in reaching a journey's goal, the occasional acts of volition, choice, and self-control may shape and define the course of a life to a profound degree.

The fact that the same resource is used for such a wide variety of the executive function's activities allows us to predict interrelations among seemingly unrelated behaviors and explain seemingly paradoxical correlations. The sexual abuse, substance abuse, and other misdeeds of powerful, influential people may reflect a pattern indicating that self-control cannot be maintained when the self expends its resources making important, far-reaching decisions. Meanwhile, at the other end of the sociopolitical scale, the relatively powerless people who must expend most of their resources just trying to get by and cope with uncontrollable circumstances may also find themselves sufficiently depleted as to succumb to substance abuse, overeating, gambling, and other impulsive patterns. On a more ordinary scale, the multifaceted breakdowns in self-control during stressful times (e.g., when students overeat, smoke too much, become crabby and irritable, and neglect personal hygiene during exam periods) show what happens when the self's limited resources are consumed by extraordinary situational demands.

Several important phenomena on the social–clinical interface may be relevant, although it is important to recognize thses as speculative steps that attempt to infer long-term patterns based on short-term laboratory findings. Changing oneself can place considerable demands on the self, and so its resources may have to be withdrawn from other sources. Folk wisdom claims that attempting to quit smoking will lead to overeating and weight gain, whereas dieting is sometimes accompanied by a resumption of smoking. Although sometimes these patterns are explained by substitution of oral gratifications, they could also reflect ego depletion. More generally, changing oneself during therapy will require considerable self-regulation, and this is likely to cause peripheral problems.

The protracted difficulty of recovering from severe trauma may reflect an extreme of ego depletion. Coping with trauma can expend the self's resources to an extraordinary degree, with the possible result that it may take an unusually long time to recover. (In other words, a good night's sleep may be far from adequate.) Social support is well known to aid in the recovery from trauma, but it is not entirely clear how it accomplishes those effects. Baumeister, Faber, and Wallace (in press) proposed that social support typically removes volitional demands on the self, in at least two crucial ways. First, supporters provide practical assistance with basic life tasks such as obtaining food and paying bills, and so the traumatized self does not have to deal with these. Second, supporters try to cheer up the person, so the possibly substantial effort needed for affect regulation is at least partly taken over by the others instead of being left up to the traumatized self. By freeing the self from these volitional demands, social support allows the self's radically depleted resources time and opportunity to recover.

The procedure is analogous to putting a broken bone in a cast so that it can heal without the further small damages caused by ordinary movement. Social support thus operates like an "ego cast," immobilizing the volitional self so that it does not suffer further depletions from the ongoing, seemingly small demands of everyday life.

Burnout is another social–clinical phenomenon that may involve ego depletion. Symptoms of burnout include loss of will, substance abuse and addiction, absence from or lateness to work, and feelings of helplessness (Maslach, 1982; Perlman & Hartman, 1982; Pines, Aronson, & Kafry, 1981). These suggest that the self's executive function is not operating properly. Burnout may develop when an idealistic person strives repeatedly to make a positive difference but finds that his or her efforts come to naught and hence gradually abandons the struggle. This is not unlike the participants in our studies who are assigned to solve difficult (actually unsolvable) problems and gradually give up.

The struggle with unsolvable problems, and the resulting tendency to give up too easily, is reminiscent of one of psychology's most fascinating and provocative theories, namely, learned helplessness (Seligman, 1975). Indeed, some readers may wonder whether ego depletion is simply a form of learned helplessness. It is not: In particular, ego depletion occurs even when people are successful and efficacious in their initial exertions of self-control, such as in the radish–chocolate study or in the dissonance–choice study (Baumeister et al., 1998).

It may be, however, that the phenomena of learned helplessness sometimes involve ego depletion, at least among human beings. (Learned helplessness was first identified in research with dogs, but attempts to replicate the pattern with human beings quickly began to show different response patterns; see Overmier & Seligman, 1967; Roth & Bootzin, 1974.) That is, the person who struggles with uncontrollable situations may expend his or her resources and subsequently be unable to learn and choose in other situations, not unlike the victim of burnout.

To recast the phenomena of learned helplessness in terms of ego depletion would require some modification of the theory, but the essential phenomena and patterns identified by Seligman and others (e.g., Seligman, 1975) would remain intact. In the original theory of learned helplessness, the essential step involved the learning of noncontingency: The animal or person discerns that outcomes are not contingent on actions and then generalizes this lesson to other situations. One problem with this theory is that noncontingent success, which in principle should teach the same lesson of noncontingency and hence should produce the same effects as noncontingent failure, has not generally succeeded in producing learned helplessness (e.g., Eisenberger, Park, & Frank, 1976; cf. Eisenberger, Kaplan, & Singer, 1974).

In contrast, ego depletion theory would predict that noncontingent failure would produce far more detrimental effects than noncontingent success. The latter can be accepted readily, whereas the former requires the person first to expend resources in fruitless struggling and then consumes more resources in affect regulation and secondary control as the person (or animal) tries to adjust to the aversive, uncontrollable situation and accept it. The sequence of exposure to aversive, uncontrollable experiences followed by debilitation and passivity would be the same as identified in learned helplessness research, but the mediating mechanism would involve depleted resources rather than the perception of noncontingency.

CONCLUSION

The executive function is probably the least studied and least understood aspect of the self, but its importance is undeniable. It is the mechanism by which people make decisions, exert control in controlled processes, override impulses and other responses, initiate behavior in active instead of passive responses, and perform other acts of self-control and volition. It may affect only a small portion of human behavior, but that portion is disproportionately important.

At present, it appears that the executive function operates like muscle strength or energy. When this strength or energy is expended through one act of volition or self-control, people are less able to exert volition or self-control subsequently. The depletion is not permanent, and rest, positive emotion, and possibly other factors seem to promote recovery.

The exact nature of this resource is not known. Two important facts are that it seems rather limited and that the same resource is used for a wide variety of seemingly unrelated tasks. Although it is limited, its limits are not as severe as first suspected, because the decrements in self-control and volition that are observed following seemingly minimal exertions in the laboratory may reflect more an effort to conserve the remaining resources than a genuine exhaustion of the resource. Still, the fact that a few minutes' exertion of self-control or that making a single major choice can impair subsequent behavior, even because of conservation, suggests that the resource is fairly limited.

The self must thus accomplish a great deal with a limited resource. No doubt the need to conserve this resource for important acts of choice, initiative, and self-control explains why people seek to avoid using the self to guide much of their daily behavior, preferring instead to rely on habit, routine, automatic processing, heuristics, cues, and the like. Yet overreliance on these short cuts may also be costly, if indeed this resource becomes strengthened by exercise. Spiritual exercises such as attention control (in meditation), mindful action, and virtuous behavior may be ways to strengthen this vital aspect of self.

Undoubtedly, though, the executive function is one of the most powerful and adaptive features of human selfhood. The gap in achievement and diversity of behavior between the human race and our evolutionary forebearers is exceptional, and much of this can be ascribed to the special, complex capabilities of human selfhood. The human capacity to make ourselves happy and miserable, both directly and through our activities in the complex social world, sets us apart from all other known species. The control over action that the self exerts plays a central role in shaping the uniqueness of human experience. If psychology can understand how the executive function accomplishes control over action, that understanding will shed light on one of the defining aspects of the human condition.

REFERENCES

Allison, S. T., & Messick, D. M. (1988). The feature-positive effect, attitude strength, and degree of perceived consensus. *Personality and Social Psychology Bulletin, 14,* 231–241.

Bargh, J. A. (1997). The automaticity of everyday life. In R. S. Wyer (Ed.), *The automaticity of everyday life: Advances in social cognition* (Vol. 10, pp. 1–61). Mahwah, NJ: Erlbaum.

Baumeister, R. F. (1998). The self. In D. T. Gilbert, S. T. Fiske, & G. Lindzey (Eds.), *Handbook of social psychology* (4th ed., pp. 680–740). New York: McGraw-Hill.

Baumeister, R. F., Bratslavsky, E., Muraven, M., & Tice, D. M. (1998). Ego depletion: Is the active self a limited resource? *Journal of Personality and Social Psychology, 74,* 1252–1265.

Baumeister, R. F., Dale, K. L., & Tice, D. M. (1998). Replenishing the self: Effects of positive affect on performance and persistence following ego depletion. Unpublished Manuscript, Case Western Reserve University, Cleveland, OH.

Baumeister, R. F., Faber, J. E., & Wallace, H. (in press). Coping and ego depletion. In C. R. Snyder (Ed.), *Coping: The psychology of what works*. New York: Oxford University Press.

Baumeister, R. F., Heatherton, T. F., & Tice, D. M. (1994). *Losing control: How and why people fail at self-regulation*. San Diego, CA: Academic Press.

Baumeister, R. F., & Sommer, K. L. (1997). Consciousness, free choice, and automaticity. In R. S. Wyer (Ed.), *Advances in social cognition* (Vol. 10, pp. 75–81). Mahwah, NJ: Erlbaum.

Carver, C. S., & Scheier, M. F. (1981). *Attention and self-regulation: A control theory approach to human behavior*. New York: Springer-Verlag.

Carver, C. S., & Scheier, M. F. (1982). Control theory: A useful conceptual framework for personality-social, clinical and health psychology. *Psychological Bulletin, 92*, 111–135.

Cioffi, D., & Garner, R. (1996). On doing the decision: The effects of active vs. passive choice on commitment and self-perception. *Personality and Social Psychology Bulletin, 22*, 133–147.

Cohen, S., Evans, G. W., Krantz, D. S., & Stokols, D. (1980). Physiological, motivational, and cognitive effects of aircraft noise on children. *American Psychologist, 35*, 231–243.

Davies, D. R., & Parasuraman, R. (1982). *The psychology of vigilance*. London: Academic Press.

Donnerstein, E., & Wilson, D. W. (1976). Effects of noise and perceived control on ongoing and subsequent aggressive behavior. *Journal of Personality and Social Psychology, 34*, 774–781.

Eisenberger, R., Kaplan, R. M., & Singer, R. D. (1974). Decremental and nondecremental effects of noncontingent social approval. *Journal of Personality and Social Psychology, 30*, 716–722.

Eisenberger, R., Park, D. C., & Frank, M. (1976). Learned industriousness and social reinforcement. *Journal of Personality and Social Psychology, 33*, 227–232.

Fazio, R. H., Sherman, S. J., & Herr, P. M. (1982). The feature-positive effect in the self-perception process: Does not doing matter as much as doing? *Journal of Personality and Social Psychology, 42*, 404–411.

Freud, S. (1930). *Civilization and its discontents*. (J. Riviere, Trans.). London: Hogarth Press.

Freud, S. (1961). The ego and the id. In J. Strachey (Ed. and Trans.), *The standard edition of the complete psychological works of Sigmund Freud* (Vol. 19, pp. 12–66). London: Hogarth Press. (Original work published 1923)

Freud, S. (1961). New introductory lectures on psycho-analysis. In J. Strachey (Ed. and Trans.), *The standard edition of the complete psychological works of Sigmund Freud* (Vol. 22, pp. 7–182). London: Hogarth Press. (Original work published 1933)

Frijda, N. H. (1986). *The emotions.* Cambridge, England: Cambridge University Press.

Gardner, G. T. (1978). Effects of federal human subjects' regulation on data obtained in environmental stressor research. *Journal of Personality and Social Psychology, 36,* 628–634.

Gatchel, R. J., McKinney, M. E., & Koebernick, L. F. (1977). Learned helplessness, depression, and physiological responding. *Psychophysiology, 14,* 25–31.

Glass, D. C., & Singer, J. E. (1972). *Urban stress: Experiments on noise and social stressors.* New York: Academic Press.

Glass, D. C., Singer, J. E., & Friedman, L. N. (1969). Psychic cost of adaptation to an environmental stressor. *Journal of Personality and Social Psychology, 12,* 200–210.

Gottfredson, M. R., & Hirschi, T. (1990). *A general theory of crime.* Stanford, CA: Stanford University Press.

Green, M. W., & Rogers, P. J. (1995). Impaired cognitive functioning during spontaneous dieting. *Psychological Medicine, 25,* 1003–1010.

Green, M. W., Rogers, P. J., Elliman, N. A., & Gatenby, S. J. (1994). Impairment of cognitive performance associated with dieting and high levels of dietary restraint. *Physiology and Behavior, 55,* 447–452.

Greeno, C. G., & Wing, R. R. (1994). Stress-induced eating. *Psychological Bulletin, 115,* 444–464.

Heatherton, T. F., Herman, C. P., & Polivy, J. (1991). Effects of physical threat and ego threat on eating. *Journal of Personality and Social Psychology, 60,* 138–143.

Hiroto, D. S., & Seligman, M. E. P. (1975). Generality of learned helplessness in man. *Journal of Personality and Social Psychology, 31,* 311–327.

Holding, D. H., Loeb, M., & Baker, M. A. (1983). Effects and aftereffects of continuous noise and computation work on risk and effort choices. *Motivation and Emotion, 7,* 331–344.

Hull, J. G., Young, R. D., & Jouriles, E. (1986). Applications of the self-awareness model of alcohol consumption: Predicting patterns of use and abuse. *Journal of Personality and Social Psychology, 51,* 790–796.

Isen, A. M. (1984). Toward understanding the role of affect in cognition. In R. S. Wyer & T. K. Srull (Eds.), *Handbook of social cognition* (Vol. 3, pp. 179–236). Hillsdale, NJ: Erlbaum.

Isen, A. M. (1987). Positive affect, cognitive processes, and social behavior. In L. Berkowitz (Ed.), *Advances in experimental social psychology* (Vol. 20, pp. 203–253). New York: Academic Press.

James, W. (1948). *Psychology.* Cleveland, OH: World. (Original work published 1892)

Janoff-Bulman, R., & Brickman, P. (1982). Expectations and what people learn from failure. In N. Feather (Ed.), *Expectations and actions: Expectancy-value models in psychology* (pp. 207–237). Hillsdale, NJ: Erlbaum.

Jung, C. G. (1971). Extracts from Aion: Researches into the phenomenology of the self. In J. Campbell (Ed.), *The portable Jung* (pp. 139–162). New York: Viking Press.

Linder, D. E., Cooper, J., & Jones, E. E. (1967). Decision freedom as a determinant of the role of incentive magnitude in attitude change. *Journal of Personality and Social Psychology, 6*, 245–254.

Markus, H. R., & Kitayama, S. (1991). Culture and the self: Implications for cognition, emotion, and motivation. *Psychological Review, 98*, 224–253.

Maslach, C. (1982). Understanding burnout: Definitional issues in analyzing a complex phenomenon. In W. S. Paine (Ed.), *Job stress and burnout: Research, theory, and intervention perspectives* (pp. 29–40). Beverly Hills, CA: Sage Publications.

Mischel, W. (1996). From good intentions to willpower. In P. Gollwitzer & J. Bargh (Eds.), *The psychology of action* (pp. 197–218). New York: Guilford Press.

Mischel, W., Shoda, Y., & Peake, P. K. (1988). The nature of adolescent competencies predicted by preschool delay of gratification. *Journal of Personality and Social Psychology, 54*, 687–696.

Muraven, M. (1998). *Mechanisms of self-control failure: Motivation and limited resources.* Unpublished doctoral dissertation, Case Western Reserve University, Cleveland, OH.

Muraven, M., & Baumeister, R. F. (in press). Self-regulation and depletion of limited resources: Does self-control resemble a muscle? *Psychological Bulletin.*

Muraven, M., Baumeister, R. F., & Tice, D. M. (1999). Longitudinal improvement of self-regulation through practice: Building self-control through repeated exercise. *Journal of Social Psychology, 139*, 446–457.

Muraven, M., Tice, D. M., & Baumeister, R. F. (1998). Self-control as limited resource: Regulatory depletion patterns. *Journal of Personality and Social Psychology, 74*, 774–789.

Overmier, J. B., & Seligman, M. E. P. (1967). Effects of inescapable shock upon subsequent escape and avoidance learning. *Journal of Comparative and Physiological Psychology, 63*, 23–33.

Parasuraman, R. (1984). Sustained attention in detection and discrimination. In R. Parasuraman & D. R. Davies (Eds.), *Varieties of attention* (pp. 243–271). Orlando, FL: Academic Press.

Percival, L., & Loeb, M. (1980). Influence of noise characteristics on behavioral aftereffects. *Human Factors, 22*, 341–352.

Perlman, B., & Hartman, E. A. (1982). Burnout: Summary and future research. *Human Relations, 35*, 283–305.

Pines, A. M., Aronson, E., & Kafry, D. (1981). *Burnout: From tedium to personal growth.* New York: Free Press.

Powers, W. T. (1973). *Behavior: The control of perception.* Chicago, IL: Aldine.

Rothbaum, F., Weisz, J. R., & Snyder, S. (1982). Changing the world and changing the self: A two process model of perceived control. *Journal of Personality and Social Psychology, 42*, 5–37.

Roth, S., & Bootzin, R. R. (1974). Effects of experimentally induced expectancies of external control: An investigation of learned helplessness. *Journal of Personality and Social Psychology, 29*, 253–264.

Rotton, J., Olszewski, D., Charleton, M., & Soler, E. (1978). Loud speech, conglomerate noise, and behavioral aftereffects. *Journal of Applied Psychology, 63,* 360–365.

Sedikides, C., & Skowronski, J. A. (1997). The symbolic self in evolutionary context. *Personality and Social Psychology Review, 1,* 80–102.

See, J. E., Howe, S. R., Warm, J. S., & Dember, W. N. (1995). Meta-analysis of the sensitivity decrement in vigilance. *Psychological Bulletin, 117,* 230–249.

Seligman, M. E. P. (1975). *Helplessness: On depression, development, and death.* San Francisco, CA: Freeman.

Shoda, Y., Mischel, W., & Peake, P. K. (1990). Predicting adolescent cognitive and self-regulatory competencies from preschool delay of gratification: Identifying diagnostic conditions. *Developmental Psychology, 26,* 978–986.

Wallace, H. M., & Baumeister, R. F. (1998). Effects of success and failure feedback regarding self-control on ego depletion. Unpublished findings, Case Western Reserve University.

Wegner, D. M., Schneider, D. J., Carter, S. R., & White, T. L. (1987). Paradoxical effects of thought suppression. *Journal of Personality and Social Psychology, 53,* 5–13.

Zanna, M. P., & Cooper, J. (1974). Dissonance and the pill: An attribution approach to studying the arousal properties of dissonance. *Journal of Personality and Social Psychology, 29,* 703–709.

2

LANDSCAPES OF SELF-REFLECTION: MAPPING THE PEAKS AND VALLEYS OF PERSONAL ASSESSMENT

ROBIN R. VALLACHER
ANDRZEJ NOWAK

Thoughts about oneself are arguably the most recurrent and salient elements in the stream of consciousness. In light of the ubiquity and subjective importance of self-reflective thought, one would think that the underlying nature of this process would long ago have been captured within a single theoretical perspective. This does not seem to be the case, however. Indeed, the process of self-reflection is open to two mutually contradictory characterizations—both of them equally valid. The first perspective emphasizes the potential for turbulence and constant change in understanding as people reflect on themselves. Thoughts about oneself are drawn from every aspect of one's experience and span an enormous range of content, from the nuances of

Preparation of this chapter was supported by NSF Grant SBR 95-11657. We thank Wojciech Borkowski, Michael Froehlich, and Matthew Rockloff for their assistance with the simulations and experiments described in this chapter. The comments of Richard Felson and three anonymous reviewers on an earlier version of the chapter are highly appreciated.

physical appearance and diverse episodic memories to broad generalizations concerning one's personal aspirations, obsessions, and self-perceived character flaws. Such diversity in self-relevant thoughts, combined with their frequency and salience, establishes considerable potential for turbulence, with highly varied cognitive elements popping in and out of consciousness in a chaotic fashion.

The other perspective emphasizes the potential for—indeed, the inevitable tendency toward—coherence and stability in self-reflection. Despite the wide range of thoughts and feelings made available during introspection, people typically experience integration and continuity in their self-understanding, so much so that this domain of phenomenal experience qualifies as a cognitive structure (e.g., Higgins, Van Hook, & Dorfman, 1988; Linville, 1985; Markus, 1980; Showers, 1992). The organization of self-relevant information is sufficiently stable and coherent to provide a platform for action and self-regulation (e.g., Carver & Scheier, 1981; Duval & Wicklund, 1972; Higgins, 1987; Markus & Nurius, 1986). Thus, people are said to have a firmly anchored view of their self-defining characteristics and values, and they actively resist incorporating new information that would call into question or otherwise undermine this self-concept.

How is it that an integrated sense of self can arise and be maintained when the specific elements surfacing in the stream of thought are so disparate in their content and implications for self-understanding? In this chapter, we suggest that insight into this issue can be gleaned from theory and research on nonlinear dynamical systems (cf. Schuster, 1984) and the recent extension of this paradigm to social psychological phenomena (e.g., Nowak & Vallacher, 1998a; Vallacher & Nowak, 1994a, 1997). Broadly defined, a nonlinear dynamical system is a set of interconnected elements that evolves over time. The primary task of dynamical systems theory is to describe the connections among the system's elements and the changes in the system's behavior to which these connections give rise. Research conducted within this perspective is explicitly concerned with characterizing the relationship between structure and dynamics in a wide variety of phenomena, from brain function to demography. There is reason to think that the lessons derived from this work are useful in establishing the links between the structural and dynamic properties of self-reflection. Our basic assumption is that the flow of cognitive and affective elements in self-reflection, although often complex and seemingly idiosyncratic, conforms to one of a small number of reliable temporal patterns, each associated with an underlying organization of self-relevant thought. By the same token, the identification of reliable patterns of change in self-reflective thought provides insight into the organization of the underlying system of cognitive and affective elements.

We begin by explaining the concept of self-organization, a phenomenon central to the behavior of complex systems in many areas of science, and showing the relevance of this phenomenon to the self system. We then illustrate how specific structural configurations of the self are revealed in the temporal patterns of self-relevant thought. In so doing, we describe research showing how basic structural configurations and their associated dynamic properties map onto basic dimensions of individual variation in self-concept. We conclude by discussing the benefits, both theoretical and methodological, of conceptualizing the self as a complex self-organizing system.

SELF-ORGANIZATION

In recent years, numerous computer simulations, as well as analytical considerations, have established that global order in complex phenomena such as meteorology and economics may emerge from local interactions among lower level elements, without any higher order supervisory mechanism (e.g., Lewenstein, Nowak, & Latané, 1992; Weisbuch, 1992). Perhaps the simplest example of such *self-organization* is provided by ferromagnetic phenomena. In a ferromagnet, each magnetic particle tries to align itself with its neighboring particles. Each particle assumes an orientation that parallels the majority of its neighbors. As a result of this local mechanism, an initially disorganized array of particles becomes progressively organized. First, the particles in a small local neighborhood become aligned, forming separate domains of magnetism. These domains increase in size as the integration process progresses. Finally, all the particles in the system (i.e., the magnetic material) point in the same direction, resulting in global magnetism.

Integration and Differentiation in Self-Structure

There is ample reason to suggest that evaluation does for self-reflection what magnetic orientation does for ferromagnets. Evaluative consistency provides a primary basis for organizing judgments of social objects (cf. Abelson et al., 1968; Eiser, 1990; Fiske & Taylor, 1991; Heider, 1944; Wegner & Vallacher, 1977), including the self (e.g., Duval & Wicklund, 1972; Showers, 1992; Tesser & Campbell, 1983). In providing a common yardstick for otherwise diverse thoughts, evaluation allows people to integrate self-relevant information that is highly disparate in its cognitive content and means–ends relations. Although helping someone in need and resisting the temptation to cheat on one's taxes are clearly distinct phenomena, for example, they are similar with respect to their positive self-evaluative implications. By the same token, cognitive elements that form a logically consistent structure may have contrasting implications for self-evaluation. Being helpful to a stranger, for example, has a far different evaluative connotation than does being helpful to a criminal. To the extent that evaluative consistency provides the basis for integration, these two elements may be hard to reconcile with respect to one's sense of self. In short, although elements of self-relevant information can be related to one another in many ways, the degree to which they are effectively integrated is signaled by their evaluative consistency.

Because of the press for evaluative integration, specific elements of self-relevant information are open to reversals in evaluation as they are considered in juxtaposition with other elements. Expressing one's feelings, for example, may be viewed as a sign of honesty when considered in the context of other positive elements such as paying back a loan or admitting a mistake, but as a sign of poor self-control when considered in the context of elements with negative valence such as cheating in a sports match or interrupting someone during a conversation. To the extent that the stream of self-reflective thought is populated by actions identified in relatively low level, mechanistic terms (e.g., detailed episodic memories), integrative processes are likely to promote the emergence of higher-level, superordinate act identities (e.g., consequences, implications) that provide a comprehensive understanding of these actions. The integration of low-level act identities in service of comprehensive understanding of one's behavior enables one to forge and maintain an evaluatively consistent sense of self (e.g., Vallacher & Wegner, 1989; Wegner, Vallacher, Kiersted, & Dizadji, 1986).

The press for evaluative integration can also be understood in terms of well-documented self-defense mechanisms. Processes such as denial, discounting, selective recall, confirmatory bias, defensive attribution, and dissonance reduction allow people to maintain evaluative consistency in the face of potentially incongruent information. Consider, for example, an act of lying by someone who considers him- or herself to be a moral person. To maintain evaluative consistency in this aspect of his or her self-concept, the person may deny the act, discount the act as unimportant, forget the act over time, justify its occurrence in terms of a larger moral concern, or even change his or her view about the morality of lying. Although these mechanisms are clearly distinguishable and may occur under different circumstances, each reflects an underlying concern with maintaining evaluative consistency in an important region of the self system and may substitute for one another under certain conditions (Tesser, Martin, & Cornell, 1996).

Despite the potential for emergent action identification and the availability of various self-defense mechanisms, global integration is probably an infrequent occurrence in self-understanding. As with complex systems generally, only specific subsets of elements are destined to become integrated. Differentiation as opposed to global integration occurs for two general reasons. The first concerns conflicting demands for integration. Some elements of the self may simply be incompatible. Friendly and competitive, for example, may be equally positive characteristics for a person, but the expression of one may negate the expression of the other. Elements of the self may also be in conflict because of their social definition. When two people are antagonistic toward each other, for example, a person's friendliness toward one may be viewed as unfriendliness toward the other (cf. Heider, 1958). The second reason for differentiation as opposed to global integration concerns limitations on the interactions among elements. Given the sheer size of the self-structure, it is virtually impossible to relate each element to every other element. Especially if one's behavior is segregated by roles and social contexts, there may be no occasion for considering a given pair of elements in relation to one another. How well one performs as a parent, for example, may never be considered in relation to one's performance on a racquetball court.

Evaluative differentiation may be achieved at the expense of differentiation with respect to other dimensions (e.g., Linville, 1985; Showers, 1992). One may be able to make subtle distinctions within a given substructure of the self, generating a mix of positively and negatively valenced elements concerning that aspect of the self. Although cognitive differentiation of this type might be considered evidence of sophisticated self-knowledge, it signals a lack of internal coherence and may provide conflicting guides to action with respect to that domain. Heightened sensitivity to one's potential for both success and failure in a particular role, for example, may promote indecision regarding the performance of action within that role. Evaluative consistency in a substructure of the self system may obscure specific distinctions in an informational sense, but this very quality provides a basis for unequivocal action (cf. Jones & Gerard, 1967). It is the press for evaluative consistency that enables people to act in spite of their intrinsic capacity for seemingly unlimited cognition.[1]

Modeling Self-Organization

We recently performed a series of computer simulations to demonstrate the emergence of evaluative differentiation in self-understanding (Nowak, Vallacher, Tesser, & Borkowski, 2000). The simulations were based on a cellular automata model that has proven useful in modeling the emergence of substructures in social systems (e.g., Nowak & Lewenstein, 1996; Nowak, Lewenstein, & Szamrej, 1993; Nowak, Szamrej, & Latané, 1990). We assumed that the self system is composed of n elements, each reflecting a basic

---

[1]This does not mean that people cannot act when there is evaluative inconsistency in a given region of self-structure. Knowing one's strengths and weaknesses in a particular domain enables one to make decisions concerning one's behavior and thus provides an effective guide for action in that domain. A racquetball player with a strong forehand but a weak backhand, for example, is likely to run around his or her backhand whenever possible during a match. One's overall confidence regarding performance in that domain, however, is likely to be diminished in proportion to the degree of evaluative incoherence. The racquetball player with a strong forehand and weak backhand, for example, may experience ambivalence about entering a tournament. It is also the case that compensating for one's weaknesses is more difficult for some domains than it is for others. A person may have second thoughts about driving a car, for example, if he or she is proficient at steering, braking, and the like, but has questionable depth perception.

piece of self-relevant information. The elements are represented as cells arranged on a two-dimensional grid, as depicted in Figure 2.1. The physical proximity between any two elements corresponds to their degree of relatedness. Each element can be either positive (denoted by light gray) or negative (dark gray). The elements also differ with respect to their relative

Start

End

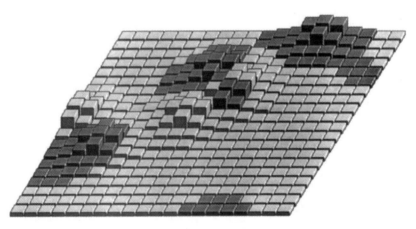

Figure 2.1. Computer simulation of the emergence of self-organization. Light cells represent positive elements of self-relevant information; dark cells represent negative elements. Salience is represented by the height of cells; relatedness of elements is represented by physical proximity.

salience or centrality for self-definition. An element's centrality, which does not change during the course of simulation, is denoted by its height in Figure 2.1 (the greater the salience, the greater the height). Six areas of high centrality were created for each simulation. These areas were created by choosing six elements at random and assigning the maximum value of centrality to them. In each case, the surrounding elements were assigned values of centrality that decreased in proportion to their distance from the respective maximally central element.

In the course of simulation, a randomly chosen element tries to adjust to its eight neighboring elements (four on the adjacent sides and four on the connecting diagonals). Specifically, the elements checks how much influence it receives from the positive as opposed to the negative neighbors. This involves weighting the valence of each neighbor by the neighbor's centrality. The resultant computation is the weighted sum of evaluations of the neighboring elements. This input is then compared to the current state (positive vs. negative) of the element. If the sign of the element agrees with the overall evaluation resulting from the computed influence of the neighboring elements, the element's current evaluation does not change. If the sign of the element differs from the overall evaluation suggested by its neighbors, however, the element changes evaluation—but only if the combined weight of evaluation from other elements is greater than the element's own weighted evaluation. In other words, it is relatively easy to change the evaluation of a relatively unimportant piece of self-relevant information, but it is difficult to change the evaluation of a more central aspect of self.

After the element's state is adjusted, another element is randomly chosen and the process just described is repeated. This continues until each element has been chosen. In the next simulation step, each element has a chance to adjust its state again. The entire process is repeated until the state of the system reaches an asymptote, reflecting no further change in the states of elements or a stable pattern of changes in the system. The achievement of static equilibrium (no further changes) or dynamic equilibrium (a sustained pattern of changes) typically requires several simulation steps. The mutual influence among elements during this time corresponds to the flow of thought during self-reflection.

Figure 2.1 shows a typical course of simulation. In the starting configuration, the positive and negative elements are arranged randomly, corresponding to a self that is lacking in structure (i.e., no evaluative differentiation). To capture the positivity bias in self-evaluation (e.g., Taylor & Brown, 1988; Tesser, 1988), 60% of the elements are positive and 40% are negative. The initial 60%–40% distribution corresponds to weighted average values for overall self-evaluation that vary around a mean of $+0.2$ (where 0 represents neutral self-evaluation). At the beginning of the simulation, there are pronounced dynamics, with many elements changing their state to come into alignment with neighboring elements. Over the course of simulation, the number of changes decreases until an equilibrium state is finally reached (the ending configuration in Figure 2.1). Note the emergence of clusters, with randomly distributed positive and negative elements forming well-defined domains. The development of differentiation reflects the local nature of influence among elements. If an element is surrounded primarily by elements of the same valence, its valence does not change. But if the element happens to be surrounded by elements with a different valence, it is likely to change its state to conform to these elements, although if it is highly central it may resist this influence. As a result of this process, elements of similar valence tend to cluster and produce coherent areas of similar valence.

In addition to the emergence of differentiation, the number of positive elements increases during the course of simulation. In an undifferentiated (disordered) system, the proportion of positive and negative elements in any region corresponds roughly to the proportion of positive and negative elements in the system as a whole. Any given element, then, is more likely to be surrounded by positive than by negative elements and thus is likely to experience a pull in the positive direction. Note, however, that the negative elements that do manage to survive tend to be highly central and hence resistant to further change. Stated differently, the mean weight of negative elements increases as less central negative elements are eliminated. This result is consistent with considerable research showing that although positive information is more prevalent than negative information in cognitive structures, negative information tends to be given greater weight (e.g., Cacioppo, Gardner, & Berntson, 1997; Coovert & Reeder, 1990; Kanouse & Hanson, 1971; Peeters & Czapinski, 1990; Pratto & John, 1991; Skowronski & Carlston, 1989; Taylor, 1991).

Beyond promoting the emergence of structure, the self-organizational tendencies displayed in these simulations also provide for stability and resistance to change in self-understanding. This is because most elements in a differentiated system are surrounded by elements of the same valence, so that only elements on the borders of substructures are exposed to conflicting influence. Evaluative differentiation, then, serves to stabilize the self system, making it less open to change when exposed to outside pressures or contradictory information (e.g., social feedback). By stabilizing the self system, the emergence of evaluation differentiation lends continuity to self-understanding, enabling people to maintain a consistent perspective on themselves despite the vicissitudes of everyday experiences and social interactions.

STRUCTURE AND DYNAMISM IN SELF-EVALUATION

The flow of thought is self-sustaining, never coming to rest for want of external influence or new information. In this sense, the mental system can be said to display *intrinsic dynamics* (Vallacher, Nowak, & Kaufman, 1994) in the same way that other complex systems in nature display internally generated dynamics in the absence of external forces (e.g., Haken, 1982; Prigogine & Stengers, 1984). The flow of thought is also noted for its idiosyncrasy and diversity, with a wide array of images, episodic memories, momentary concerns, and self-perceived traits tumbling over one another in a manner that calls to mind James's (1890/1950) stream-of-consciousness metaphor (e.g., Pope & Singer, 1978; Singer & Bonanno, 1990). But just as a real-world stream conforms to a particular path, following the contours of the landscape in which it is embedded, the stream of thought is ultimately constrained by the particular organization of cognitive elements currently on call for activation. In the following section, we develop this linkage between structure and dynamism in the context of the self system.

The Interplay of Structure and Dynamics

Because of the press for evaluative coherence, the various thoughts and images that arise in the course of self-reflection do not simply mirror the current organization of self-structure, they also interact to promote reconfigurations of self-structure. For the most part, the mutual influences among thoughts in the stream of thought serve to enhance the coherence of the self system. The sudden prepotence of a negative element while one is thinking about one's positive features, for example, is likely to set in motion various mechanisms designed to reverse the valence of the element. Thus, being reminded of an action with unflattering moral implications might lead the person who thinks of him- or herself as a moral agent to re-identify the action as morally benign or even positive with respect to other evaluative criteria.

The potential for achieving and maintaining evaluative coherence in self-structure clearly depends on the operation of integrative mechanisms. There is reason to think, however, that these mechanisms vary in strength in accord with meaningful and specifiable factors. Self-awareness theory (Duval & Wicklund, 1972) is particularly relevant in this regard. According to this theory, a person in a self-aware state attempts to maintain consistency with respect to whatever aspect of the self is currently salient for him or her. Incoming information that is incongruent with the salient self-domain becomes a source of discomfort, leading to compensatory thought and behavior to restore consistency to the system. For instance, a person might reject incongruent social feedback after considering it in light of well-structured (and hence well-protected) clusters of relevant thoughts and feelings. Such concerns are said to be lacking when a person is not in a state of self-focused attention. Instead, the non-self-aware person is said to be responsive to rewards, costs, and other factors in the immediate context, with little regard for the implications of his or her thoughts and actions for self-concept congruence. Under this mental set, self-relevant information at odds with one's self-image in a particular domain may gain entry to the self system and provide a frame of reference for subsequent thought and behavior. When self-focused attention is subsequently reinstated, however, the incongruent information is likely to promote feelings of self-concept incoherence and attempts to restore consistency.

Variability in the press for integration is also consistent with theory and research on cognitive busyness (cf. Gilbert, 1993), if one assumes that mental resources are required to engage in integrative processes. Presumably, any factor that drains cognitive resources (e.g., a parallel task, distraction, stress) can both inhibit the comparison of elements with respect to mutual consistency and weaken the mutual influences among elements that would establish coherence. In line with this possibility, research has shown that when people are put under cognitive load, they demonstrate an enhanced tendency to incorporate information that is inconsistent with their prevailing self-concept (e.g., Swann, Hixon, Stein-Seroussi, & Gilbert, 1990). So, although people with low self-esteem, for example, tend to reject positive information because of its inconsistency with a particular self-image, they tend to readily embrace such information in situations that induce cognitive busyness (e.g., Paulhus & Levitt, 1987). Presumably, the drain on mental resources weakens the press for integration that would otherwise protect them against the incongruent (but flattering) self-relevant information.[2]

Even when sufficient cognitive resources are available for integration, the interaction of elements in the course of self-reflection can serve to undermine rather than enhance the coherence of self-evaluation. This is likely if an element of inconsistent self-relevant information—brought to mind in the course of social interaction, perhaps, or through the priming of an episodic memory—is too central to self-definition to be ignored and is identified at too high a level for it to be reframed in other, more benign terms. Being reminded of a serious moral failing in one's past, for example, can introduce incoherence into an otherwise positive region of one's self-structure. Subsequent self-reflection is likely to be characterized by sustained volatility in self-evaluation as the conflicting elements relevant to one's self-image of morality are juxtaposed over time but fail to achieve integration. Conceivably, in fact, a highly salient discrepant element may begin to reverse the valence of less central consistent elements, thereby further increasing the evaluative inconsistency in this region of the self-structure.

---

[2]It is interesting to consider this scenario in light of research documenting people's inability to screen irrational beliefs (Gilbert, 1993) or suppress unwanted thoughts and memories (e.g., Pennebaker, 1988; Wegner, 1989) when under cognitive load. When integrative mechanisms are diluted by parallel tasks (e.g., cognitive busyness manipulations) or overwhelmed by the sheer intensity of incoming information (see Nowak et al., 2000), elements that would normally be defended against or redefined in benign terms can enter the mental system and prove difficult to dislodge or ignore. This perspective on judgment and thought suppression is necessarily speculative at this point, of course, but would seem to warrant systematic investigation.

Ironically, then, the press for evaluative integration can subvert its own purpose and create regions of ambivalence in people's self-concept.[3]

Energy Landscapes of the Stream of Self-Reflection

As a result of self-organization processes, different regions of the self system are likely to have varying degrees of evaluative coherence. Perhaps a person has an entirely positive view of him- or herself as a worker but a somewhat mixed assessment of him- or herself as an athlete. Such variation in evaluative coherence constrains the course of internally generated self-reflective thought. Self-reflection tends over time to concentrate in those regions of self-structure that have the most evaluative coherence. Such regions promote consistent self-evaluation and thus provide a stable equilibrium for the stream of self-reflection. When people reflect on elements that have low evaluative coherence (i.e., those with mixed valence), they are likely to experience rapid shifts in self-evaluation as they consider the various elements in that region. When people recall elements that are highly similar in content (e.g., all pertain to athlete) but different in valence, they are also likely to recall similarly valenced elements from different regions. A person's ability to serve a tennis ball during a match, for example, may bring to mind a recent success in preparing a manuscript rather than a recent botched serve during practice (cf. Bower, 1981, 1990; Isen, 1987). Each such shift in self-evaluation is likely to override the dynamics dictated by content, causing people to switch their attention to a relatively coherent region of the self-structure that is evaluatively consistent with the momentary self-evaluation.

The link between self-structure and the stream of self-reflection can be illustrated with a graphic metaphor, whereby the relationship between a region of self-structure and its evaluative coherence can be expressed as a specific value of energy (the higher the coherence, the lower the energy). Visualize these energy values as balls rolling through a landscape of hills and valleys. Each valley represents a local minimum in the energy function corresponding to a stable equilibrium, with the depth of the valley depicting the stability provided by the equilibrium. In a region of self-structure marked by a high degree of evaluative consistency, the energy value is close to 0, signifiying that all the cognitive elements in this region share a common

---

[3]At some point, this scenario might promote a reversal in self-evaluation with respect to the region as a whole. Depending on the importance of the region to self-understanding, a person may tolerate considerable inconsistency before finally succumbing to the weight of contradictory evidence and switching to the opposing (but more coherent) valence. Thus, a positive view of oneself with respect to, say, athletic competence, may cause a person to resist change in the face of performance setbacks and unflattering social comparisons, until the positive image collapses and is replaced by a negative view of one's competence. Prior to this catastrophic change, the person may display considerable defensiveness regarding his or her unstable self-assessment, even to the point of reacting with violence to negative social feedback that might be ignored by someone with an evaluatively coherent view of him- or herself in this area (cf. Baumeister, Smart, & Bowden, 1996).

valence. Even if the particular thoughts and images that arise in the course of self-reflection have disparate content, their shared valence ensures that self-evaluation will remain stable over time. In a region marked by weaker evaluative consistency, the energy is correspondingly greater in magnitude, with self-reflection exhibiting some variability in self-evaluation over time. This variability reflects the existence of evaluatively inconsistent elements in this region that become activated in the stream of self-reflection. Figures 2.2, 2.3, 2.4, and 2.5 illustrate this metaphor.

In these figures, different regions of a self-structure are plotted on the x-axis, with relatively negative regions located to the left and relatively positive regions located to the right. The y-axis plots the energy value (depicted as a ball) associated with each region. Shifts in attention to different subsets of elements are indicated by arrows. The ball tends to roll down the hills and settle in the valleys. The system's temporal trajectory thus consists of the descent from any region to the nearest local minimum (equilibrium).[4] In this sense, the equilibrium provided by an energy minimum can be considered a *fixed-point attractor* (cf. Nowak & Lewenstein, 1994; Schuster, 1984), because the trajectory of self-reflective thought tends to converge on this state over time. Each figure portrays an evaluatively differentiated self system, with energy minima associated with both negative and positive self-evaluation. This means that both positive and negative self-evaluation represent equilibria for self-reflective thought. Within each region, in other words, energy is at a minimum and the volatility of self-evaluation diminishes. The figures differ with respect to the relative energy of the positive and negative equilibria, however, and these differences have implications for the trajectory of self-reflection, the relative stability of self-evaluation, and the resistance of the system to external influences (e.g., evaluatively inconsistent social feedback).

Figure 2.2 portrays a differentiated system with a positivity bias. The deeper valley for positive self-evaluation signifies that there is greater internal coherence within the positive regions of the self-structure than within the negative regions. Thus, when positive features of the self are activated, the system is likely to stabilize on a positive self-evaluation because each positive self-relevant thought calls to mind other positive self-relevant thoughts, and so on, in a self-reinforcing manner. In effect, the system is maintained in a deep valley from which escape is relatively difficult. When negative regions of the self-structure are activated, however, the system is likely to show some degree of volatility in self-evaluation because a negative self-relevant thought may call to mind a conflicting self-assessment (i.e., a positive self-relevant thought). Once activated in this fashion, a positive set of thoughts is likely to push the system toward the positive equilibrium,

---

[4]A similar approach has proven useful in characterizing the dynamics in attractor neural networks (see Nowak, Vallacher, & Burnstein, 1998).

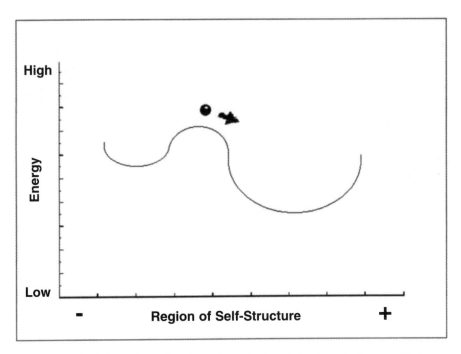

Figure 2.2. Depiction of a self system characterized by self-evaluative equilibria with positivity bias. The ball plots an energy value expressing the relationship between the region of self-structure and its evaluative coherence. The arrow depicts the direction of shifts in attention to a subset of elements in a region of self-structure.

where it then achieves stability. In terms of the landscape metaphor, negative self-evaluation is associated with a relatively shallow valley, from which escape is correspondingly easy.

This scenario is interesting to consider in light of research demonstrating a pronounced positivity bias in self-concept (e.g., Showers & Kling, 1996; Taylor & Brown, 1988; Tesser & Campbell, 1983). Although the trajectory of self-reflective thought for most people is more likely to converge on positive than on negative regions of the self-structure, the potential for negative self-evaluation exists and may become manifest if contradictory information (e.g., reminders of negative acts in the past, negative feedback from a credible source) is sufficiently strong. It is also conceivable that some people experience the mirror image of the positivity bias—namely, have a self-structure in which the negative regions have greater internal coherence and hence greater stability. This scenario is depicted in Figure 2.3. In this case, the trajectory of self-reflection is more likely to converge on a negative rather than positive state of self-evaluation.

Together, these figures capture the variable of self-esteem: The bias toward positivity in Figure 2.2 corresponds to high self-esteem, whereas the negativity bias in Figure 2.3 corresponds to lower levels of self-esteem.

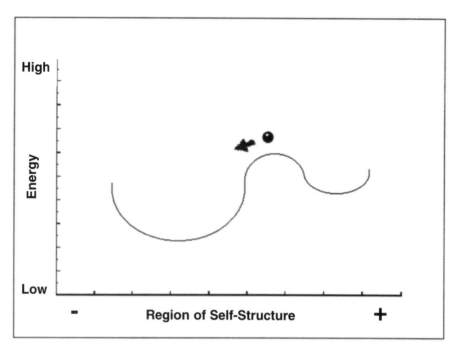

Figure 2.3. Self-evaluative equilibria with a negativity bias. The ball plots an energy value expressing the relationship between the region of self-structure and its evaluative coherence. The arrow depicts the direction of shifts in attention to a subset of elements in a region of self-structure.

Although an attractor for the opposing valence exists in each case, over time the system is likely to converge on the equilibrium associated with the lowest energy (most coherence). By extension, the asymmetry in equilibrium coherence is reflected in each system's response to external influence. When evaluatively inconsistent information (e.g., social feedback or self-perceived success vs. failure) enters a region with low energy, it is likely to be undermined or changed by the combined influence of other elements in that region. If a person has an evaluatively consistent view of him- or herself as a good parent, for example, the reminder that he or she forgot about a parent–teacher conference may have only a temporary effect on self-image in this domain. As the person thinks about the event in the context of myriad sources of evidence painting a more flattering picture, the isolated incident diminishes in its relative impact and may even be reinterpreted in positive terms (e.g., a sign of how hard one works to maintain a quality life for one's children). The same reasoning holds, of course, for a self-structure with a negativity bias. Inconsistent (i.e., positive) information about the self may have only a short-lived impact as the mutual influences among elements in the negative substructure reinforce one another and thereby diminish the impact of the new information. By this account, it takes a greater amount of evaluatively inconsistent information to disrupt self-evaluation with respect to a stable as opposed to an unstable equilibrium. Metaphorically, it is harder to push the ball out of the deep valleys corresponding to low-energy regions than out of the shallow valleys corresponding to high-energy regions.

Figure 2.4 portrays a differentiated self-structure in which the positive and negative regions provide the same (relatively high) degree of stability for self-evaluation. In this case, the negative elements of self-understanding cluster to the same degree as do the positive elements. This means that once self-relevant information in an evaluative substructure is activated, self-evaluation is likely to stabilize with respect to the corresponding valence. In effect, the system is bi-stable, showing that the flow of either negative or positive self-relevant thoughts is sustained over a period of time. By the same token, though, the very equality of these conflicting equilibria make the system dependent on influences (e.g., new information, social feedback, memory priming) that push the energy down one hillside rather than the other. This reflects the scenario described earlier in which self-reflection is stabilized by external influences that bias self-reflection toward one self-evaluative state and away from the other. In the absence of such influences, the system is drawn equally to both equilibria, so that self-reflection is marked by ambivalence, uncertainty, and sustained volatility in self-evaluation.

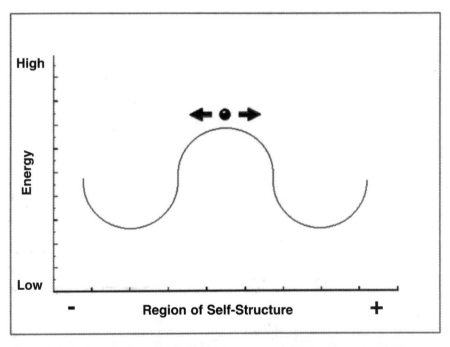

Figure 2.4. Self-evaluative equilibria with low energy. The ball plots an energy value expressing the relationship between the region of self-structure and its evaluative coherence. The arrow depicts the direction of shifts in attention to a subset of elements in a region of self-structure.

Finally, Figure 2.5 portrays a system in which positive and negative self-evaluation each provide only shallow equilibria (a relatively high degree of energy). In this system, there are evaluatively inconsistent elements within each region, so that the activation of elements in each is likely to produce changes over time in self-evaluation. Because the local interactions in each valley do not provide sufficient mutual support to stabilize the system, self-evaluation remains volatile, even when external influences reinforce the majority valence in that region. Incoming information may push the system to one of the equilibria, but the inconsistent influences of neighboring elements in that region quickly dislodge the system and restore its volatility. Whereas the self system represented in Figure 2.4 is marked by conflicting self-assessments and sensitivity to new information and external influences, the self system in Figure 2.5 is characterized by confusion and instability, despite the receipt of new information and feedback from external sources.

Self-Concept and Dynamism in Self-Reflection

The energy landscapes for self-reflection are interesting to consider in light of extensive theory and research regarding individual variation in self-concept. The most popular and well-documented dimension, of course, is

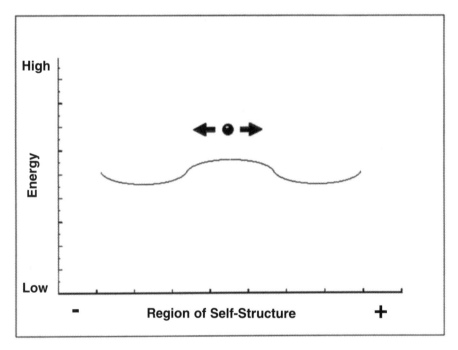

Figure 2.5. Self-evaluative equilibria with high energy. The ball plots an energy value expressing the relationship between the region of self-structure and its evaluative coherence. The arrow depicts the direction of shifts in attention to a subset of elements in a region of self-structure.

self-esteem (cf. Baumeister, 1998; Rosenberg, 1965; Wylie, 1974). To the extent that people have a stable level of global self-esteem, this variable represents a fixed-point attractor in the stream of reflection. People with high self-esteem tend over time to converge on positive thoughts about themselves, whereas those with low self-esteem tend to converge on negative thoughts. Support for this possibility is provided by research on thought-induced attitude polarization (Tesser, 1978). Simply thinking about a target person tended to produce a more extreme evaluation of him or her, provided the target was important to the judge (e.g., Liberman & Chaiken, 1991; Tesser & Leone, 1977). Judgments of oneself, of course, clearly meet the criterion of importance. This suggests that after a brief period of time characterized by volatility in self-evaluation, people with high self-esteem should become progressively more positive in their self-reflective thought and stabilize on a highly positive equilibrium, whereas people with low self-esteem should become progressively more negative over time, eventually stabilizing in a negative self-evaluative state.

The emphasis in recent research on self-concept has broadened from self-esteem per se to incorporate issues of clarity and certainty in people's self-understanding (e.g., Baumgardner, 1990; Campbell et al., 1996; Kernis, 1993; Pelham, 1991; Swann & Ely, 1984; Vallacher, 1980; Vallacher & Wegner, 1989). Not surprisingly, self-concept uncertainty is said to reflect conflict and instability in self-understanding. The nature of this conflict and instability is not entirely clear, however. From the dynamical systems perspective, conflict and instability in the self system reflect the coexistence of conflicting but equally salient fixed-point attractors for self-evaluation, both vying for prepotence in the stream of self-reflective thought. It is not known, however, whether these respective regions of self-structure each provide low-energy valleys for self-evaluation (as in Figure 2.4) or whether they each represent unstable equilibria characterized by poor internal consistency with respect to evaluation (as in Figure 2.5).

It is possible to distinguish between these two possibilities by tracking the temporal trajectory of self-evaluation during self-reflection. In both cases, self-concept uncertainty reflects the coexistence of conflicting fixed-point attractors—one converging on a positive self-evaluative state, the other converging on a negative state. The difference between the two cases centers on the ability of these states to anchor subsequent self-evaluation. If the positive and negative regions of self-structure both provide relatively stable equilibria for self-evaluation, an uncertain person should be highly vulnerable to outside influences that favor one equilibrium over the other. Such influences in effect stabilize the system on one of its attractors, short-circuiting the tendency to move back and forth between the conflicting equilibria. In line with this possibility, there is evidence that people who are uncertain about their standing on self-concept dimensions tend to be especially sensitive to social feedback regarding these dimensions and begin to see themselves in line with such feedback over time (e.g., Swann & Ely, 1984). Self-uncertainty is also associated with a tendency to identify one's behavior in relatively low-level (mechanistic, detailed) terms (Vallacher & Wegner, 1989), which suggests that uncertain people are prime candidates for emergent self-understanding in line with social feedback and other sources of high-level action identification (e.g., Wegner et al., 1986).

If an uncertain self-concept represents the coexistence of unstable equilibria for self-evaluation, self-reflective thought should be characterized by erratic changes in self-evaluation occurring on a relatively short time scale. Social feedback and other outside influences are likely to have at best a temporary effect in stabilizing the system on a single self-evaluative state. The uncertain person might be inclined to embrace such feedback, but the relatively random nature of subsequent self-reflection is likely to promote rapid movement toward the opposing equilibrium. Because this equilibrium, in turn, also contains some evaluatively inconsistent elements, the flow of self-reflective thought is likely to reverse again, moving back to the earlier equilibrium state, and so on. Over time, then, self-evaluation is unlikely to converge on a stable state, but rather should display sustained volatility, with vacillation between positive and negative self-assessments.

The empirical validity of this depiction of structure and dynamics in the self system depends on the ability to measure the temporal course of self-evaluation in the stream of thought. To that end, Vallacher, Nowak, Froehlich, and Rockloff (1998) adapted a mouse paradigm used in previous research on the intrinsic dynamics of social judgment (Vallacher & Nowak, 1994b, 1997; Vallacher et al., 1994). Vallacher et al.'s (1998) approach centered on a computer mouse used to control a cursor on a computer screen. Two symbols are presented on the screen: a small circle positioned in the middle of the screen that represents the target of judgment and an arrow showing the position of the cursor. In line with the suggestion that evaluation is an implicit approach–avoid response (Hovland, Janis, & Kelley, 1953), research participants are instructed to position the cursor with respect to the circle to express their current feelings about the target. The less the distance, the more positive the feeling toward the target. By extension, movement toward or away from the target represents changes in the participants' feelings about the target.

In Vallacher et al.'s (1998) modified procedure, participants were instructed to describe themselves by speaking into a microphone (connected to a tape recorder) positioned next to a computer. They were encouraged to describe as fully and completely as possible their personality traits, goals, plans, relationships, or whatever else came to mind. On completion of the tape, participants listened to it and used the mouse to indicate on a moment-to-moment basis how positive versus negative their recorded self-descriptive comments were. They were instructed to position the cursor close to the circle if the momentary self-description conveyed positive feelings about themselves and to position the cursor distant from the circle if the self-description conveyed negative feelings. By tracking the position of the cursor several times a second, it was possible to chart a trajectory of self-evaluation for each participant's stream-of-thought narrative and to derive dynamic properties from the trajectory (e.g., rate of change in self-evaluation, convergence to a stable state).

Prior to creating the self-description narrative, two-thirds of the participants were asked to think about several past actions that reflected either positively or negatively on themselves and to type a brief (one-sentence) description of each action on the computer keyboard. The remaining participants were not asked to think of past actions. At earlier mass testing situations, participants had completed a set of self-report instruments, from which measures of self-esteem, self-concept certainty, and self-concept stability were derived.[5] This allowed for comparison of the dynamic properties of self-evaluative thought as a function of individual variation in self-concept and the priming of different evaluative states (positive vs. negative) for self-reflection. Analyses focused on overall self-evaluation, as represented by distance from the circle, and several aspects of change in self-evaluation during the self-reflection period (e.g., the rate, regularity, and amplitude of change). To test for convergence on stable equilibria, Vallacher et al. examined how the dynamic properties changed from the early to the late portions of the self-description narratives.

The most basic prediction was that self-evaluation (distance) would vary as a function of priming and individual differences in self-esteem. Positive priming was expected to promote more positive self-evaluation (less distance) than was negative priming; the absence of priming was expected to promote intermediate self-evaluation. Self-esteem was expected to be inversely related to self-evaluation; the higher the self-esteem, the less the overall distance from the target circle. This effect was expected to increase over time, with participants' self-reflective comments becoming more valenced in line with their prevailing self-evaluative equilibria. This prediction follows from research demonstrating thought-induced attitude polarization

---

[5]Self-esteem and self-stability were assessed with an instrument developed by Rosenberg (1965). There are 14 items on this measure, each of which provides a Likert-type response format. Ten items assess respondents' level of self-regard ($\alpha = .87$) and 4 items assess the degree to which respondents' self-regard changes over time ($\alpha = .68$). Responses to each set of items were averaged to yield measures of self-esteem and self-stability, respectively. To measure self-certainty, we asked participants to indicate how certain versus uncertain they were of their standing with respect to 20 common personality traits (e.g., sincerity, independence, sociability). A 7-point scale, anchored by *not at all certain* and *very certain* was provided for each rating. Participants' ratings formed a highly reliable scale ($\alpha = .78$) and thus were averaged to yield a measure of self-certainty. In line with previous research (e.g., Baumgardner, 1990; Campbell et al., 1996; Vallacher, 1978), self-esteem and self-certainty were reliably correlated ($r = .50$), and both measures were reliably correlated with self-stability ($r = .40$ for self-esteem, .47 for self-certainty).

for subjectively important targets that are seen in largely univalent terms (cf. Liberman & Chaiken, 1991; Tesser & Leone, 1977).

The predictions regarding self-concept certainty and stability, meanwhile, centered on change in self-evaluation. In general, uncertainty and instability were expected to be associated with evaluative volatility in self-reflection. There are two possibilities, however, regarding the nature of this volatility—one reflecting a system organized with respect to conflicting (i.e., positive and negative) and relatively coherent self-evaluative equilibria, and the other reflecting a relatively disordered system with less well-defined equilibria for self-evaluation. If uncertainty or instability reflect a system with conflicting but relatively stable self-evaluative equilibria, dynamism should be observed primarily in the no-priming condition. In effect, the conflicting equilibria have equal advantage as they vie for prepotence in participants' stream of self-reflection. The valenced priming conditions, however, should bias participants' self-reflection toward one of the potential equilibria in their self-structures. In effect, priming makes one equilibrium prepotent at the expense of the other, enabling the self system to stabilize on a single self-evaluative state. Conversely, if uncertainty or instability reflect a self-structure with conflicting but weak self-evaluative equilibria, changes in self-evaluation should be observed even in the valenced priming conditions. The evaluative disorder in participants' self system makes it likely that elements of conflicting valence will arise in the stream of thought, disrupting whatever provisional equilibrium is provided by the priming manipulation. Hence, there should be heightened volatility on the part of uncertain or unstable participants in all conditions, with relatively erratic changes in self-evaluation regardless of the priming manipulation.

To assess these hypotheses and alternative scenarios, Vallacher et al. divided the sample into the upper and lower 40% on each self-concept measure (self-esteem, self-certainty, and self-stability) and examined the dynamic properties of each resultant variable in the context of the priming conditions. Despite the shared variance among the self-concept measures, each displayed a unique pattern of results. The findings for self-esteem were straightforward (see Figure 2.6). Participants with low self-esteem displayed more negative self-evaluation (i.e., greater distance from the circle) than did participants with high self-esteem. Paralleling this effect, negative priming promoted more negative self-evaluation than did the absence of priming, which in turn promoted more negative self-evaluation than did positive priming. Results also revealed polarization in self-evaluation, but only in the no-priming condition (see Figure 2.7). Thus, the difference in self-evaluation between participants with low and high self-esteem became greater from the early to the late portions of their stream-of-thought narratives, primarily because of increased negativity on the part of those with low self-esteem. The tendency for participants with high self-esteem to become more positive over time was not statistically reliable, perhaps because of a ceiling effect

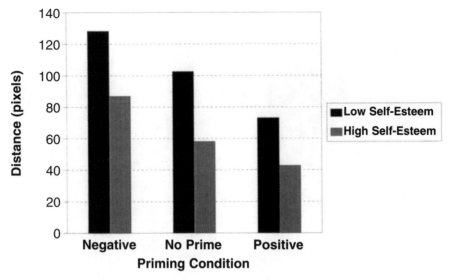

Figure 2.6. Self-evaluation by self-esteem and priming.

(i.e., the initial proximity to the circle limited the room available for change).[6]

Results of a different kind were observed for self-certainty and self-stability. When the effects of self-esteem were controlled for (in analyses of covariance), these variables were not associated with the overall valence of self-evaluation (average distance from the target circle), but they were associated with the dynamic measures. Self-stability, first of all, was reliably associated with rate of change in self-evaluation (i.e., speed of mouse movement). Participants with an unstable self-concept changed their self-evaluative stance more frequently than did those with a more stable self-concept, and this difference was observed in each of the priming conditions. And whereas participants with high self-stability demonstrated a reduced rate of change in self-evaluation over time, their unstable counterparts tended to maintain the same (high) rate of change from the beginning to the end of their self-narratives (see Figure 2.8). Participants with an unstable self-concept, then, demonstrated sustained dynamism in their self-reflection rather than convergence on a single self-evaluative equilibrium.

Self-certainty was also associated with rate of change in self-evaluation, with uncertain participants displaying greater evaluative volatility in their self-narratives. But whereas unstable participants displayed self-evaluative dynamism regardless of how they were primed, uncertain participants demonstrated heightened change in self-evaluation only in the no-priming

---

[6]Interestingly, despite the impact of the prime on participants' self-evaluation, the past acts they mentioned in response to this induction were never referred to in their subsequent self-narratives.

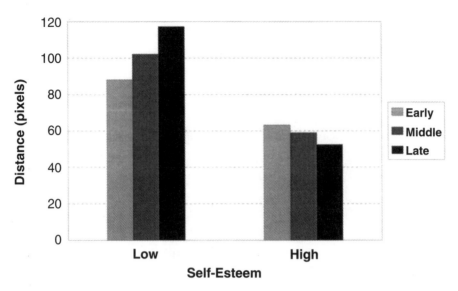

Figure 2.7. Polarization of self-evaluation by self-esteem. *Note:* Data from participants in No-Priming condition.

condition (see Figure 2.9). In a similar vein, uncertain participants displayed
diminishing volatility in self-evaluation over time when induced to think
about themselves in either positive or negative terms but increasing self-
evaluative volatility over time in the absence of priming (see Figure 2.10).
So, although uncertain participants vacillated between positive and negative
self-evaluative states when left to their own devices, their stream of self-
reflective thought tended to converge on a relatively stable equilibrium
when they were induced to think about themselves from either a positive or
negative self-evaluative perspective.

This pattern of results suggests that individual variation in self-esteem,
self-stability, and self-certainty can be understood in terms of distinct energy
landscapes. High and low self-esteem correspond to relatively stable positive
and negative self-evaluative equilibria, respectively. The fact that both the
samples with high and low self-esteem were affected by the priming manipulation, meanwhile, suggests that the opposing equilibria were available for
participants. Thus, the positive and negative primes not only influenced
participants' self-evaluation, they also disrupted the tendency toward
thought-induced polarization that was observed in the absence of priming.
Nonetheless, within each priming condition, participants with either high
or low self-esteem differed in their self-evaluation throughout their respective narratives, indicating that they had relatively stable equilibria for evaluating themselves.

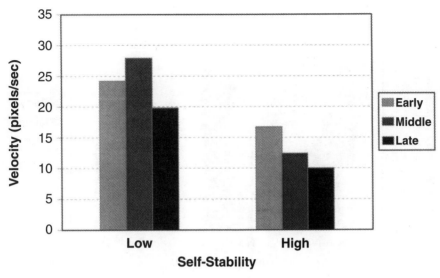

Figure 2.8. Dynamism in self-evaluation by self-stability and time.

Both instability and uncertainty in self-concept, however, are associated with volatility in self-evaluation. These phenomenal states can be distinguished, however, in terms of the stability afforded by positive and negative regions of self-structure. Participants with an unstable sense of self did not show convergence on a stable self-evaluative stance, even when induced to think about themselves in an evaluatively coherent fashion. Presumably, the positive and negative regions in their self-structure each contained conflicting

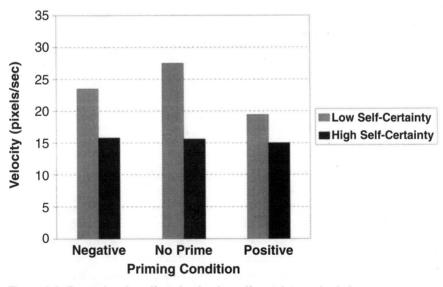

Figure 2.9. Dynamism in self-evaluation by self-certainty and priming.

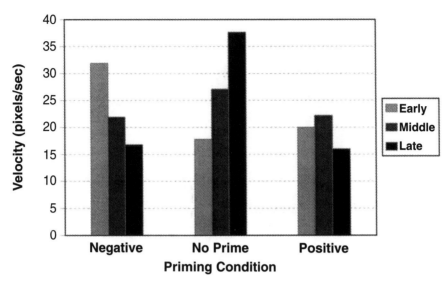

Figure 2.10. Change in dynamism by priming for low self-certainty. *Note:* Data from participants with low self-certainty.

elements, so that the priming of one region promoted thoughts that were evaluatively consistent with the other region. Participants who lacked certainty in their self-concept, however, tended to embrace the self-evaluation provided in the priming manipulation. This suggests that uncertainty is associated with conflicting equilibria for self-evaluation, each consisting of evaluatively consistent self-relevant information. This organizational structure enables uncertain people to achieve stability in their self-evaluation, but only when they are provided with external prompts that favor one of their latent equilibria over the other. In the absence of such prompts, uncertain people demonstrate sustained conflict and instability in their self-assessment as they reflect on themselves.

CONCLUSION

The self is clearly a special object of cognitive representation. It is arguably the largest structure in the cognitive system, encompassing all the experiences and personally relevant information in one's life (e.g., Greenwald & Pratkanis, 1984; Kihlstrom & Cantor, 1984; Markus, 1983). The elements constituting the self, moreover, are unique in that they represent thoughts and feelings derived in part from real and imagined relationships with specific and generalized others (e.g., Cooley, 1902; Felson, 1989; Festinger, 1954; Goffman, 1959; Mead, 1934; Rogers, 1961). In recognition of the special nature of self-understanding, psychologists have identified a variety of processes that are unique to the self. These include phenomena such as self-esteem maintenance (Tesser & Campbell, 1983), identity maintenance (Brewer & Kramer, 1985), self-affirmation (Steele, 1988), self-verification (Swann, 1990), self-deception (Gur & Sackheim, 1979), self-conscious emotions such as guilt and shame (Tangney & Fischer, 1995), and self-regulation (e.g., Carver & Scheier, 1999; Duval & Wicklund, 1972; Higgins, 1996).

Its unique features notwithstanding, the self can be viewed in formal terms as a complex system composed of many interdependent elements that achieve self-organization. Indeed, none of the defining processes of the self would be possible without the operation of integrative mechanisms promoting evaluative coherence among otherwise diverse elements of self-relevant information. Before one can maintain a level of self-esteem, recognize social feedback as inconsistent, or experience self-concept discrepancy and its corresponding self-conscious emotion, one must have a relatively coherent perspective on the vast number of features relevant to self-understanding. As observers, knowing only the proportion of positive and negative self-relevant thoughts in a person's self system would provide little insight into his or her degree of self-certainty, nor would such knowledge help in predicting the person's response to social feedback or performance setbacks.

Given the ups and downs of everyday life, perfect coherence in self-understanding is virtually impossible to maintain—assuming that it can be achieved in the first place. Even someone with the highest level of self-regard in a given domain is no doubt plagued from time to time by self-generated doubts or unflattering feedback from someone whose opinions matter. The variable nature of evaluative coherence is manifest both within and between people. For a given person, one region of self-structure may have greater evaluative coherence than other regions and, accordingly, provide for greater stability in self-evaluation. Some individuals, meanwhile, have particularly shallow equilibria for self-evaluation, so that their stream of self-reflection displays considerable volatility despite the ongoing operation of self-organization processes. People who express instability or uncertainty regarding their self-concept are especially at risk for displaying constantly shifting self-evaluations when they are asked to reflect on themselves.

Conceptualizing the self as a self-organizing system enables investigators to use new research strategies to supplement the traditional methods of psychological science (cf. Nowak & Vallacher, 1998a; Vallacher & Nowak, 1994a). Because the work on nonlinear dynamical systems is explicitly concerned with identifying the relation between structure and dynamics, the tools developed within this paradigm are ideally suited for investigating the structural and dynamic properties of the self. Computer simulations are especially notable in this regard (see Nowak & Lewenstein, 1996; Nowak & Vallacher, 1998b; Read & Miller, 1998; Smith, 1996). This approach enables one to investigate a large number of interacting elements and to track the behavior generated by these interactions over many trials. The very nature of computer simulations is ideal for studying the effects of multiple iterations of a process, making this approach particularly well-suited to investigate the dynamic consequences of a theory. Computers are also the most potent tool for visualization of structure and dynamics. One can literally see temporal patterns of change and the emergence of structure as a system evolves through repeated iterations of an underlying process.

Computer simulations, however, cannot substitute for experimental data. When developing a theory about people, at some point it is reasonable to actually involve people in the process. With respect to the structural and dynamical properties of the self, we found it useful simply to track the temporal trajectories of people's stream of thought as they reflect on themselves. The resultant data corroborated the simulation results and thus provided verification of our theoretical perspective. For the most part, the data collected within this approach were analyzed in only very intuitive ways (e.g., distance, speed, and changes in these properties over time). The work on nonlinear dynamical systems, however, has generated powerful analytical and statistical tools, each of which provides unique information about patterns of temporal variation and the structure of the underlying system producing such patterns (see Nowak & Lewenstein, 1994; Nowak & Vallacher, 1998a). We suspect that these tools will someday become indispensable elements in the analysis of self-concept dynamics—and of social psychological processes generally. Such tools will provide an important complement to the use of computer simulations and the traditional methods of social psychology. Working in concert, this multifaceted approach to theory construction and hypothesis testing holds as-yet-untapped potential for revealing both what is unique about a given phenomenon and what is invariant across complex systems generally.

REFERENCES

Abelson, R. P., Aronson, E., McGuire, W. J., Newcomb, T. M., Rosenberg, M. J., & Tannenbaum, P. H. (Eds.). (1968). *Theories of cognitive consistency: A sourcebook*. Chicago: Rand McNally.

Baumeister, R. F. (1998). The self. In D. T. Gilbert, S. T. Fiske, & G. Lindzey (Eds.), *The handbook of social psychology* (Vol. 1, pp. 680–740). Boston: McGraw-Hill.

Baumeister, R. F., Smart, L., & Bowden, J. M. (1996). Relation of threatened egotism to violence and aggression: The dark side of self-esteem. *Psychological Review, 103*, 5–33.

Baumgardner, A. H. (1990). To know oneself is to like oneself: Self-certainty and self-affect. *Journal of Personality and Social Psychology, 58*, 1062–1072.

Bower, G. H. (1981). Mood and memory. *American Psychologist, 36*, 129–148.

Bower, G. H. (1990). Mood-congruity of social judgments. In J. Forgas (Ed.), *Emotion and social judgments* (pp. 31–54). Oxford: Pergamon Press.

Brewer, M. B., & Kramer, R. M. (1985). The psychology of intergroup attitudes and behavior. *Annual Review of Psychology, 36,* 219–243.

Cacioppo, J. T., Gardner, W. L., & Berntson, G. G. (1997). Beyond bipolar conceptualizations and measures: The case of attitudes and evaluative space. *Personality and Social Psychology Review, 1,* 3–25.

Campbell, J. D., Trapnell, P. D., Heine, S. J., Katz, I. M., Lavallee, L. F., & Lehman, D. R. (1996). Self-concept clarity: Measurement, personality correlates, and cultural boundaries. *Journal of Personality and Social Psychology, 70,* 141–156.

Carver, C. S., & Scheier, M. F. (1981). *Attention and self-regulation: A control-theory approach to human behavior.* New York: Springer-Verlag.

Carver, C. S., & Scheier, M. F. (1999). Themes and issues in the self-regulation of behavior. In R. S. Wyer, Jr. (Ed.), *Advances in social cognition* (Vol. 12, pp. 1–105). Mahwah, NJ: Erlbaum.

Cooley, C. H. (1902). *Human nature and the social order.* New York: Scribner.

Coovert, M. D., & Reeder, G. D. (1990). Negativity effect in impression formation: The role of unit formation and schematic expectation. *Journal of Personality and Social Psychology, 26,* 49–62.

Duval, S., & Wicklund, R. A. (1972). *A theory of objective self-awareness.* New York: Academic Press.

Eiser, J. R. (1990). *Social judgment.* Pacific Grove, CA: Brooks/Cole.

Felson, R. B. (1989). Parents and the reflected appraisal process: A longitudinal analysis. *Journal of Personality and Social Psychology, 56,* 965–971.

Festinger, L. (1954). A theory of social comparison processes. *Human Relations, 7,* 117–140.

Fiske, S. T., & Taylor, S. E. (1991). *Social cognition* (2nd ed.). New York: McGraw-Hill.

Gilbert, D. T. (1993). The ascent of man: Mental representation and the control of belief. In D. M. Wegner & J. W. Pennebaker (Eds.), *Handbook of mental control* (pp. 57–87). Englewood Cliffs, NJ: Prentice-Hall.

Goffman, E. (1959). *The presentation of self in everyday life.* Garden City, NY: Doubleday/Anchor Books.

Greenwald, A. G., & Pratkanis, A. R. (1984). The self. In R. S. Wyer & T. K. Srull (Eds.), *Handbook of social cognition* (pp. 129–178). Hillsdale, NJ: Erlbaum.

Gur, R. C., & Sackheim, H. A. (1979). Self-deception: A concept in search of a phenomenon. *Journal of Personality and Social Psychology, 37,* 147–169.

Haken, H. (Ed.). (1982). *Order and chaos in physics, chemistry, and biology.* Berlin: Springer.

Heider, F. (1944). Social perception and phenomenal causality. *Psychological Review, 51,* 358–374.

Heider, F. (1958). *The psychology of interpersonal relations.* New York: Wiley.

Higgins, E. T. (1987). Self-discrepancy: A theory relating self and affect. *Psychological Review, 94,* 319–340.

Higgins, E. T. (1996). Ideals, oughts, and regulatory focus: Affect and motivation from distinct pains and pleasures. In P. M. Gollwitzer & J. A. Bargh (Eds.), *The psychology of action: Linking cognition and motivation to behavior* (pp. 91–114). New York: Guilford Press.

Higgins, E. T., Van Hook, E., & Dorfman, D. (1988). Do self-attributes form a cognitive structure? *Social Cognition, 6,* 177–206.

Hovland, C., Janis, I., & Kelley, H. H. (1953). *Communication and persuasion.* New Haven, CT: Yale University Press.

Isen, A. (1987). Positive affect, cognitive processes, and social behavior. In L. Berkowitz (Ed.), *Advances in experimental social psychology* (Vol. 20, pp. 203–253). San Diego: Academic Press.

James, W. (1950). *The principles of psychology.* New York: Dover. (Original work published 1890)

Jones, E. E., & Gerard, H. B. (1967). *Foundations of social psychology.* New York: Wiley.

Kanouse, D. E., & Hanson, L. R. (1971). *Negativity in evaluations.* Morristown, NJ: General Learning Press.

Kernis, M. H. (1993). The roles of stability and level of self-esteem in psychological functioning. In R. F. Baumeister (Eds.), *Self-esteem: The puzzle of low self-regard* (pp. 167–182). New York: Plenum Press.

Kihlstrom, J. F., & Cantor, N. (1984). Mental representations of the self. In L. Berkowitz (Ed.), *Advances in experimental social psychology* (Vol. 17, pp. 2–48). New York: Academic Press.

Lewenstein, M., Nowak, A., & Latané, B. (1992). Statistical mechanics of social impact. *Physics Review A, 45,* 763–776.

Liberman, A., & Chaiken, S. (1991). Value conflict and thought-induced attitude change. *Journal of Experimental Social Psychology, 27,* 203–216.

Linville, P. W. (1985). Self-complexity and affective extremity: Don't put all your eggs in one cognitive basket. *Social Cognition, 3,* 94–120.

Markus, H. (1980). The self in thought and memory. In D. M. Wegner & R. R. Vallacher (Eds.), *The self in social psychology* (pp. 102–130). New York: Oxford University Press.

Markus, H. (1983). Self-knowledge: An expanded view. *Journal of Personality, 51,* 543–565.

Markus, H., & Nurius, P. (1986). Possible selves. *American Psychologist, 41,* 954–969.

Mead, G. H. (1934). *Mind, self, and society.* Chicago: University of Chicago Press.

Nowak, A., & Lewenstein, M. (1994). Dynamical systems: A tool for social psychology? In R. R. Vallacher & A. Nowak (Eds.), *Dynamical systems in social psychology* (pp. 17–53). San Diego: Academic Press.

Nowak, A., & Lewenstein, M. (1996). Modeling social change with cellular automata. In R. Hegselman, K. Troitzch, & U. Muller (Eds.), *Modeling and simulation in the social sciences from the philosophy of science point of view* (pp. 249–285). Dordrecht, The Netherlands: Kluwer Academic.

Nowak, A., Lewenstein, A., & Szamrej, J. (1993). Social transitions occur through bubbles. *Scientific American* (Polish version), *12*, 16–25.

Nowak, A., Szamrej, J., & Latané, B. (1990). From private attitude to public opinion: A dynamic theory of social impact. *Psychological Review, 97*, 362–376.

Nowak, A., & Vallacher, R. R. (1998a). *Dynamical social psychology*. New York: Guilford Press.

Nowak, A., & Vallacher, R. R. (1998b). Toward computational social psychology: Cellular automata and neural network models of interpersonal dynamics. In S. J. Read & L. C. Miller (Eds.), *Connectionist models of social reasoning and social behavior* (pp. 277–311). Mahwah, NJ: Erlbaum.

Nowak, A., Vallacher, R. R., & Burnstein, E. (1998). Computational social psychology: A neural network approach to interpersonal dynamics. In W. Liebrand, A. Nowak, & R. Hegselman (Eds.), *Computer modeling and the study of dynamic social processes* (pp. 97–125). New York: Sage Publications.

Nowak, A., Vallacher, R. R., Tesser, A., & Borkowski, W. (2000). Society of self: The emergence of collective properties in self-structure. *Psychological Review, 107*.

Paulhus, D. L., & Levitt, K. (1987). Desirable responding triggered by affect: Automatic egotism? *Journal of Personality and Social Psychology, 52*, 245–259.

Peeters, G., & Czapinski, J. (1990). Positive–negative asymmetry in evaluations: The distinction between affective and informational negativity effects. In W. Stroebe & M. Hewstone (Eds.), *European review of social psychology* (Vol. 1, pp. 33–60). London: Wiley.

Pelham, B. W. (1991). On confidence and consequences: The certainty and importance of self-knowledge. *Journal of Personality and Social Psychology, 60*, 518–530.

Pennebaker, J. W. (1988). *Opening up*. New York: Morrow.

Pope, K. S., & Singer, J. L. (Eds.). (1978). *The stream of consciousness: Scientific investigations into the flow of human experience*. New York: Plenum Press.

Pratto, F., & John, O. P. (1991). Automatic vigilance: The attention grabbing power of negative information. *Journal of Personality and Social Psychology, 61*, 380–391.

Prigogine, I., & Stengers, I. (1984). *Order out of chaos*. New York: Bantam.

Read, S. J., & Miller, L. C. (Eds.). (1998). *Connectionist models of social reasoning and social behavior*. Mahwah, NJ: Erlbaum.

Rogers, C. R. (1961). *On becoming a person*. Boston: Houghton Mifflin.

Rosenberg, M. (1965). *Society and the adolescent self-image*. Princeton, NJ: Princeton University Press.

Schuster, H. G. (1984). *Deterministic chaos*. Vienna, Austria: Physik Verlag.

Showers, C. J. (1992). Compartmentalization of positive and negative self-knowledge: Keeping bad apples out of the bunch. *Journal of Personality and Social Psychology, 62*, 1036–1049.

Showers, C. J., & Kling, K. C. (1996). Organization of self-knowledge: Implications for recovery from sad mood. *Journal of Personality and Social Psychology, 70*, 578–590.

Singer, J. L., & Bonanno, G. A. (1990). Personality and private experience: Individual variations in consciousness and in attention to subjective phenomena. In L. A. Pervin (Ed.), *Handbook of personality: Theory and research* (pp. 419–444). New York: Guilford Press.

Skowronski, J. J., & Carlston, D. E. (1989). Negativity and extremity biases in impression formation: A review of explanations. *Psychological Bulletin, 105*, 131–142.

Smith, E. R. (1996). What do connectionism and social psychology have to offer each other? *Journal of Personality and Social Psychology, 70*, 893–912.

Steele, C. M. (1988). The psychology of self-affirmation: Sustaining the integrity of the self. In L. Berkowitz (Ed.), *Advances in experimental social psychology* (Vol. 21, pp. 261–302). New York: Academic Press.

Swann, W. B., Jr. (1990). To be adored or to be known? The interplay of self-enhancement and self-verification. In E. T. Higgins & R. M. Sorrentino (Eds.), *Handbook of motivation and cognition: Foundations of social behavior* (Vol. 2, pp. 408–448). New York: Guilford Press.

Swann, W. B., & Ely, R. J. (1984). A battle of wills: Self-verification versus behavioral confirmation. *Journal of Personality and Social Psychology, 46*, 1287–1302.

Swann, W. B., Hixon, J. G., Stein-Seroussi, A., & Gilbert, D. (1990). The fleeting gleam of praise: Cognitive processes underlying behavioral reactions to self-relevant feedback. *Journal of Personality and Social Psychology, 59*, 17–26.

Tangney, J. P., & Fischer, K. W. (Eds.). (1995). *Self-conscious emotions.* New York: Guilford Press.

Taylor, S. E. (1991). Asymmetrical effects of positive and negative events: The mobilization-minimization hypothesis. *Psychological Bulletin, 110*, 67–85.

Taylor, S. E., & Brown, J. D. (1988). Illusion and well-being: A social psychological perspective on mental health. *Psychological Bulletin, 103*, 193–210.

Tesser, A. (1978). Self-generated attitude change. In L. Berkowitz (Ed.), *Advances in experimental social psychology* (Vol. 11, pp. 85–117). New York: Academic Press.

Tesser, A. (1988). Toward a self-evaluation maintenance model of social behavior. In L. Berkowitz (Ed.), *Advances in experimental social psychology* (Vol. 21, pp. 181–227). New York: Academic Press.

Tesser, A., & Campbell, J. (1983). Self-definition and self-evaluation maintenance. In J. Suls & A. G. Greenwald (Eds.), *Psychological perspectives on the self* (Vol. 2, pp. 1–31). Hillsdale, NJ: Erlbaum.

Tesser, A., & Leone, C. (1977). Cognitive schemas and thought as determinants of attitude change. *Journal of Experimental Social Psychology, 13*, 340–356.

Tesser, A., Martin, L., & Cornell, D. (1996). On the substitutability of self-protective mechanisms. In P. M. Gollwitzer & J. A. Bargh (Eds.), *The psychology of action: Linking motivation and cognition to behavior* (pp. 48–68). New York: Guilford Press.

Vallacher, R. R. (1978). Objective self-awareness and the perception of others. *Personality and Social Psychology Bulletin, 4*, 63–67.

Vallacher, R. R. (1980). An introduction to self theory. In D. M. Wegner & R. R. Vallacher (Eds.), *The self in social psychology* (pp. 3–30). New York: Oxford University Press.

Vallacher, R. R., & Nowak, A. (Eds.). (1994a). *Dynamical systems in social psychology*. San Diego: Academic Press.

Vallacher, R. R., & Nowak, A. (1994b). The stream of social judgment. In R. R. Vallacher & A. Nowak (Eds.), *Dynamical systems in social psychology* (pp. 251–277). San Diego: Academic Press.

Vallacher, R. R., & Nowak, A. (1997). The emergence of dynamical social psychology. *Psychological Inquiry, 4*, 73–99.

Vallacher, R. R., Nowak, A., Froehlich, M., & Rockloff, M. (1998). [Reflections in the stream of consciousness: The intrinsic dynamics of self-evaluation]. Unpublished raw data.

Vallacher, R. R., Nowak, A., & Kaufman, J. (1994). Intrinsic dynamics of social judgment. *Journal of Personality and Social Psychology, 66*, 20–34.

Vallacher, R. R., & Wegner, D. M. (1989). Levels of personal agency: Individual variation in action identification. *Journal of Personality and Social Psychology, 57*, 660–671.

Wegner, D. M. (1989). *White bears and other unwanted thoughts*. New York: Viking Press.

Wegner, D. M., & Vallacher, R. R. (1977). *Implicit psychology: An introduction to social cognition*. New York: Oxford University Press.

Wegner, D. M., Vallacher, R. R., Kiersted, G., & Dizadji, D. (1986). Action identification in the emergence of social behavior. *Social Cognition, 4*, 18–38.

Weisbuch, G. (1992). *Complex system dynamics*. Redwood City, CA: Addison-Wesley.

Wylie, R. (1974). *The self concept*. Lincoln: University of Nebraska Press.

3

STRUCTURAL FEATURES OF THE SELF-CONCEPT AND ADJUSTMENT

JENNIFER D. CAMPBELL, SUNAINA ASSANAND,
AND ADAM DI PAULA

Psychologists' view of the self-concept has undergone a dramatic transformation over the past two decades (Markus & Wurf, 1987). Early researchers treated the self-concept as a unitary, monolithic entity and typically focused their research efforts on a single aspect: self-esteem (Wylie, 1979). In contrast, contemporary theorists rely on a multifaceted, dynamic construal in which the self-concept is defined as a cognitive schema—that is, as an organized knowledge structure that contains beliefs about one's attributes as well as episodic and semantic memories about the self and that controls the processing of self-relevant information (e.g., Greenwald & Pratkanis, 1984; Kihlstrom & Cantor, 1984). This conceptualization allows for a distinction between the contents of the self-concept and its structural features.

The contents of the self-concept generally refer to an individual's beliefs about the self. These include beliefs about one's attributes (e.g., personality traits, abilities, physical features, values, goals, and roles), how an individual answers the question "Who/what am I?". The beliefs also include an evaluation of those attributes as indicated by the positivity or social desirability of the attributes and self-esteem—a global evaluation of the self. The structure of the self-concept refers to how the contents are organized. For example, Linville (1985) used the term self-complexity to reference the number of independent dimensions underlying the organization. Structural properties of the self-concept are theoretically independent of the contents; for example, any specific set of self-beliefs could show a complex or simple organization.

The impact of self-beliefs such as self-esteem (contents) on psychological functioning is well documented. Distinguishing between content and structure, however, permits an increasing appreciation of the fact that the organization of those beliefs may play an important role as well. Consider, for example, two individuals who both sustain an athletic injury. The impact of that injury will depend not only on the presence or absence of an athletic self-conception, but also on the structural properties of that self-conception. Is it a central or defining aspect of the self? Is it closely linked to other self-conceptions? If so, we might anticipate that the injury will have more deleterious effects on psychological well-being.

Our general aim in this chapter is to explore the structure of the self-concept and its relation to psychological adjustment. First, we describe a number of constructs that have been used to assess different aspects of self-structure, and we briefly review the literature relating these constructs to psychological adjustment. Second, we report the results of four studies in which we assessed the relations among several measures of self-structure, as well as their relations with a common set of adjustment indices. Third, we highlight a number of conceptual and methodological issues that make it difficult to accurately portray the interrelations among structural aspects of the self-concept and their relations with adjustment. Finally, we propose some alternative methods of data collection and analysis that may allow for a more precise assessment of the role of self-structure in psychological adjustment.

DIFFERENTIATION AND INTEGRATION

Two primary types of structural features are differentiation and integration. Differentiation generally refers to the degree of pluralism in the structure, the number of different facets or dimensions an individual spontaneously uses in thinking about the self. For example, social roles represent one potential source of differentiation. Although individuals may occupy numerous social roles, only those that they internalize in the self-concept are developed into differentiated role identities. Integration refers to the degree of unity in the structure. For example, one individual may have developed role identities that are highly variable or even discrepant across different roles, whereas another individual may have developed role identities that are highly consistent across roles. Differentiation and integration are not completely independent of one another in that a person who views the self as an amorphous whole (no differentiation at all) is obviously high in integration. On the other hand, a person whose self-schema is multifaceted can have discrepant (low integration) or unified (high integration) self-views.

How are differentiation and integration theoretically related to adjustment? One camp (e.g., Gergen, 1972; Goffman, 1959; Snyder, 1974) has argued that people with highly differentiated self-views have specialized identities that enable them to respond flexibly and adaptively to changing circumstances or role requirements, whereas those low in differentiation are rigid, inflexible, and unable to accommodate to the shifting requirements of social life. Another camp (e.g., Lecky, 1945; Rogers, 1959) has argued that having a coherent, integrated self is the hallmark of mental health; the individual with a fragmented or divided sense of self is "plagued by self-doubts and despairs for he has no internal reference which can affirm his continuity and self-integrity" (Block, 1961, p. 392). This apparently simple contrast in views, however, is muddied by the fact that high self-differentiation is often conceptually and empirically equated with low integration. That is, those who advocate the beneficial effects of a unified self use the term *self-concept differentiation* to refer to a lack of integration across self-aspects (e.g., roles). And even those who favor the beneficial effects of "specialized identities" typically use the term to reference variability (flexibility) in one's characteristics across self-aspects (low integration) as opposed to the number of different self-aspects an individual uses in thinking about the self. Another complication in relating self-structure to adjustment lies in the fact that some researchers posit and test direct associations between self-structure and adjustment, whereas others posit and test interactive relations such as a stress-diathesis model (self-structure buffers or interacts with stress in affecting adjustment).

A CLASSIC PERSPECTIVE ON STRUCTURE

Before describing the contemporary measures of self-structure and their relations to adjustment, it is helpful to provide a common conceptual map for viewing measures of self-structure. We do this by summarizing the classical properties of cognitive structure described by Zajonc (1960). Zajonc described four properties of cognitive structure, two of these assess differentiation and two assess integration in the structure. A concrete example (Zajonc, 1960, Study 1) best illustrates these properties. Participants read a letter written by a target individual and were asked to imagine what sort of person the target was. They then wrote on index cards the different characteristics that they believed the target possessed. The number of cards or characteristics that a participant generated constituted the structural property that Zajonc called *differentiation*, the number of attributes the participant was capable of identifying and discriminating in the target. Subsequently, participants were asked to sort their cards into groups that they felt belonged together and then to see if they could further break their groups into subgroups. When participants felt that the subgroups they had generated could not be divided further, they labeled all of the groups and subgroups. The property Zajonc called *complexity* was derived by determining, for each attribute, the number of groups and subgroups to which it belonged and summing across attributes. Therefore, differentiation was assessed by the sheer number of attributes in the schema and the complexity of the organization of those attributes into groups and subgroups.

In terms of integration, Zajonc defined a structural property called *unity*, which reflected the extent to which the attributes depended on each other. Participants laid out their cards in alphabetical order and, for each attribute, listed all of the other attributes that would change if that attribute was changed, absent, or untrue of the target. The unity measure was the total number of such contingencies among the attributes normalized by the number of attributes. Zajonc's second integration measure was a property he called *organization*, which reflected the extent to which a guiding force or principle dominated the whole. Using the contingency matrix just described, he calculated, for each attribute, the extent to which it determined other attributes and then took the determinance of the strongest attribute and divided it by the unity measure.

SOME CONTEMPORARY MEASURES OF STRUCTURE

Contemporary theorists of the self have independently defined and measured various structural features of the self-concept. Examples include self-concept complexity (Linville, 1985), self-concept compartmentalization (Showers, 1992a), self-concept differentiation (Donahue, Robins, Roberts, & John, 1993), self-concept clarity (Campbell et al., 1996), and self-discrepancies (Higgins, Klein, & Strauman, 1985). Each construct has provided some insight into the relation between self-concept structure and psychological adjustment, but relatively little attention has been paid to the relations among these constructs. We (Campbell, 1997; Campbell, Assanand, & DiPaula, 1999) recently reported the results of four studies in which we examined the relations among two measures that assess the degree of differentiation in self-structure and four measures that assess the degree of integration in self-structure. These measures are described briefly in the following sections.

Differentiation

Self-Concept Complexity

The first measure of differentiation included in the studies was Linville's (1985) measure of self-concept complexity. This measure requires participants to sort a set of experimenter-provided traits into groups that describe "an aspect of you or your life." Participants can form as many groups as are meaningful to them, and traits can be placed in more than one group. From the trait sort, the statistic H (Attneave, 1959; Scott, Osgood, & Peterson, 1979) is calculated as an index of self-concept complexity. H reflects the number of self-aspect groups that a participant has generated and the degree of redundancy between these self-aspects. A high H value indicates that the participant generated many self-aspects groups that were nonredundant in terms of the specific traits that characterized each group. This measure is conceptually akin to Zajonc's property of complexity but differs in that it uses a set of experimenter-provided traits rather than participant-generated attributes. Linville hypothesized that a high degree of self-complexity buffers the harmful effects of stress by preventing negative events that occur in one self-aspect from "spilling over" and adversely affecting other self-aspects (a stress-buffering hypothesis). Several studies have provided support for this hypothesis (e.g., Dixon & Baumeister, 1991; Linville, 1985, 1987; Niedenthal, Setterlund, & Wherry, 1992).

Compartmentalization

The second measure of differentiation was Showers's (1992a) measure of compartmentalization. Compartmentalization describes the degree to which positive and negative traits are sorted into separate self-aspect groups. It is measured by having participants perform the Linville sorting task described previously. From this sort, the statistic phi or Cramer's V (Cramer, 1974) is calculated as an index of the extent to which the number of positive and negative traits in each group deviates from what would be expected based on the overall ratio of positive to negative traits used in the participant's sort. Compartmentalization has no parallel in Zajonc's structural properties.[1] It describes an additional aspect of structure—the extent to which the dimensions or self-aspect groups in the structure are differentiated with respect to valence.

---

[1]Compartmentalization does not cleanly fall into the category of either differentiation or integration. Although we labeled it as a measure of differentiation, it does not tap (nor is it dependent on) the number of different dimensions that people use in thinking about themselves. Unlike the other measures of self-structure considered here, it focuses on a *mixture* of self-schema content (positive vs. negative self-attributes) and structure (the extent to which the dimensions used in thinking about the self separate one's positive and negative attributes).

Showers hypothesized that compartmentalization interacts with the differential importance (Pelham & Swann, 1989) of positive and negative self-aspects in affecting adjustment. She asked participants to rate each self-aspect group with respect to positivity and negativity and personal importance and correlated the positivity and importance ratings across self-aspects. She argued that, for those with high correlations (those whose positive self-aspects are generally more important than their negative self-aspects), compartmentalization should be associated with positive moods and high self-esteem, because activation of the positive self-aspects floods the individual with purely positive information about the self rather than a combination of positive and negative information. In contrast, for those with low differential importance correlations (those whose negative self-aspects are generally more important than their positive self-aspects), compartmentalization should be associated with negative moods and low self-esteem, because activation of the negative self-aspects floods the individual with purely negative information about the self rather than a combination of positive and negative information. Empirical support for Showers's hypothesis is summarized in Showers and Kling (1996a).

Integration

Average Correlation Among Roles

We included four measures that tap integration or unity in the self-structure. The first measure was patterned after one described by Donahue et al. (1993). They provided participants with a set of 60 traits and asked them to rate how descriptive each trait was of them on a set of five experimenter-provided social roles (e.g., student, romantic partner). Each participant's ratings were correlated across the five roles, and the proportion of unshared variance among the roles provided an inverse measure of integration (which they unfortunately labeled *self-concept differentiation*). In our studies, we used the average correlation among the roles as a measure of integration so that higher values would reflect higher levels of integration. This measure is conceptually comparable to Zajonc's measure of unity, but it differs in that the experimenter, rather than the participant, provides both the attributes and the categories or self-aspects (social roles) under consideration. Donahue et al. (1993) have shown that lower levels of integration are associated with poorer emotional adjustment (e.g., depression) as well as poorer social adjustment (e.g., rejection of social norms, low socialization).

Average Correlation Among Self-Aspects

The second measure of integration assessed in our studies was similar to Donahue et al.'s (1993) measure but was based on the self-aspect groups that our participants generated in the Linville sorting task. Participants labeled each of their self-aspect groups and, for each self-aspect label, rated how descriptive each of the experimenter-provided traits was of them. The average correlation among the self-aspect groups constituted our second measure of integration. This measure is also conceptually similar to Zajonc's property of unity but, unlike the average correlation among roles, it uses participant-generated self-aspects and is not restricted to social roles. The labels participants used often included social roles (e.g., myself as a student), but they also included moods (e.g., me when I'm happy), self-evaluations (e.g., things I don't like about myself), and circumstances (e.g., me when I'm alone).

Self-Concept Clarity

The third measure of integration tapped Campbell's (1990) construct of self-concept clarity—the extent to which self-beliefs are clearly and confidently defined, internally consistent, and temporally stable. Campbell (1990) measured clarity by examining the extremity, confidence, internal consistency, and temporal stability of participants' self-descriptions. However, Campbell et al. (1996) demonstrated good convergence between these indirect indices of clarity and a self-report scale that we used to measure clarity in our studies. Clarity, like compartmentalization, has no direct parallel in Zajonc's structural properties. It describes the extent to which the contents of the self-concept are well articulated. Low clarity has been found to be associated with low self-esteem, emotional maladjustment (e.g., depression, neuroticism, negative affectivity; Campbell, 1990; Campbell et al., 1996), and the utilization of more passive coping styles (Smith, Wethington, & Zhan, 1996).

Self-Discrepancies

The final measures of integration were based on Higgins's self-discrepancy theory (Higgins, 1989). Participants generated lists of traits that described their actual self from their own perspective and from the perspective of their parent and a best friend. From these lists, we calculated Self–Parent and Self–Friend discrepancies using Higgins's idiographic method. First, we compared the relevant lists that participants generated and determined which traits matched and mismatched. Second, we subtracted the total number of matches from the total number of mismatches to produce a self-discrepancy score. Higher scores reflected higher levels of self-discrepancies among participants (inverse measures of integration). Self-discrepancies also have no parallel in Zajonc's properties and differ from the other measures in that they do not capture a generic feature of the structure. They tap a more circumscribed, but nonetheless potentially important, aspect of structure—discrepancies between how people view themselves and how they believe they are viewed by significant others.

INTERRELATIONS AMONG MEASURES OF SELF-STRUCTURE AND ASSOCIATIONS WITH ADJUSTMENT

The four studies that we conducted varied with respect to the specific measures collected, the total number of traits provided, and the ratio of positive to negative traits. Table 3.1 summarizes this information for each study. Study 2 was a repeated-measures design—the measures were collected twice (at a one-week interval) from the same sample. In the following section, we summarize the results of the studies. We first examine the relations among the self-structure measures and then present the relations between these measures and a common set of adjustment indices.

Interrelations Among Measures of Self-Structure

The two measures of differentiation, Linville's complexity (H) and Showers's compartmentalization (phi), were not associated with one another. Across the four studies, the correlations between them ranged from $-.17$ to $.07$, with an average correlation of $-.06$. This outcome is perhaps not surprising given that compartmentalization is not a measure of differentiation per se but is a hybrid of structure and contents (the extent to which self-aspect groups separate negative from positive contents). There is no theoretical reason to expect a relation between the number of independent categories or dimensions in the structure and the degree to which the categories generated partition positive and negative features of the self.

The measures of integration were more strongly associated with one another. Study 1 contained only one measure of integration, and Studies 2a, 2b, and 3 contained only two measures of integration—the average correlation among self-aspects and self-concept clarity. The correlations between these two measures were consistently positive and statistically significant in Study 2a ($r = .28$, $p < .05$) and Study 3 ($r = .34$, $p < .01$). In Study 4 we assessed the relations among all five measures of integration—the average correlation among roles, the average correlation among self-aspects, self-

TABLE 3.1
Measures of Self-Structure Traits in Four Studies of Self-Concept Structure

Study	Measure of self-structure	No. of participants	No. of positive traits	No. of negative traits
1	H, phi, r self-aspects	66	18	9
2a	H, phi, r self-aspects, SCC	71	22	11
2b	H, phi, r self-aspects, SCC	71	11	22
3	H, phi, r self-aspects, SCC	62	22	8
4	H, phi, r roles, r self-aspects, SCC, self-discrepancies	64	20	15

Note. H = complexity; phi = compartmentalization; r self-aspects = average correlation between self-aspects; SCC = self-concept clarity; r roles = average correlation between roles.

concept clarity, self-parent discrepancies, and self-friend discrepancies. All of the measures were associated with one another in the expected direction (the discrepancy measures, being inverse indices of integration, exhibited negative correlations with the other measures). The magnitude of correlations ranged from .07 to .45, with an average of .27, suggesting some conceptual overlap in these various aspects of integration despite the fact that they differ substantially in terms of their specific focus and methodology.

In general, the various measures of differentiation and integration were not associated with one another. Self-complexity was uncorrelated with the average correlation among self-aspects (average $r = -.04$, Studies 1–4), self-concept clarity (average $r = -.03$, Studies 2–4), the average correlation among roles ($r = .02$, Study 4), and the two self-discrepancy measures (average $r = .17$). The correlations between compartmentalization and the integration measures showed a similar pattern with the exception that compartmentalization was correlated with the average correlation among self-aspects (average $r = -.38$). The two measures were derived from the same trait sort for each participant, and the correlation simply reflects the fact that participants who formed self-aspect groups that separated their positive and negative traits tended to view themselves less similarly across those particular groups.

The general lack of association between Linville's self-complexity (an unambiguous measure of differentiation) and the integration measures suggest that theoretical orientations equating low integration with high differentiation are misleading, because their terminology and measures completely confound high differentiation with low integration. Whereas high scores on measures of integration could indeed reflect low differentiation (the self is simply viewed as an amorphous whole), they may also reflect a diverse, multifaceted structure whose many features have been integrated into a unified whole. The earlier literature on integrative complexity (e.g., Schroeder, Driver, & Streufert, 1967) is instructive here in that it suggests that differentiation and integration should be viewed hierarchically. Higher levels of integrative complexity are achieved by first distinguishing between different aspects of the stimulus (i.e., differentiating) and then reconciling or integrating these differentiated aspects via superordinate concepts. In other words, integration is not possible without differentiation. Those whose follow this orientation deliberately confound differentiation and integration, but in a direction that is opposite to those who equate low integration with high differentiation. Our data suggest, relying on Zajonc's classic definitions, that in the self-schema they are relatively independent of one another.

Associations Between Measures of Self-Structure and Adjustment

To assess the relations between the measures of self-structure and a common set of adjustment indices, we included measures of adjustment in each of the four studies. Because Study 4 was the only study that included all of the self-structure measures and all of the adjustment measures (self-esteem, neuroticism, trait negative affectivity), we show the correlations for that study in Table 3.2. In the other studies that contained comparable self-structure and adjustment measures, the correlations were highly similar to those in Table 3.2. In general, the adjustment measures were uncorrelated with complexity (H) and compartmentalization (phi); across the four studies, the average correlation between these measures and adjustment was −.03. In contrast, the measures of adjustment were consistently correlated with the measures of integration such that integration was positively associated with self-esteem and negatively associated with neuroticism and negative affectivity. Although the measures of adjustment were most highly correlated with self-concept clarity, the greater magnitude of these correlations probably reflects the influence of shared method variance (self-report scales). Across the four studies, the average correlation between the measures of adjustment and the measures of integration was .31, indicating that integration is a relatively consistent concomitant of better adjustment.

There are several possible explanations for the lack of association between the measures of differentiation and adjustment. One obvious explanation is that, theoretically, one should not necessarily expect differentiation to have a main or direct effect on adjustment. Showers (1992a) argued that compartmentalization *interacts* with differential importance in affecting adjustment; our studies did not include measures of the differential importance of the self-aspects. Linville (1985) postulated that complexity *moderates* affective extremity in response to self-relevant events by decreasing the magnitude of positive affect in response to positive events and decreasing the magnitude of negative affect in response to negative events. Thus, complexity should have beneficial effects on adjustment only via a stress-buffering role; when negative events occur, having many independent self-aspects

TABLE 3.2
Correlations Between Adjustment and Self-Structure (Study 4)

Measure	Self-esteem	Neuroticism	Negative affectivity
H	−.16	−.08	−.12
phi	−.10	−.02	.01
r self-aspects	.22	−.28*	−.26*
SCC	.63**	−.61**	−.52**
r roles	.43**	−.52**	−.32**
self–parent	−.38**	.20	.09
self–friend	−.49**	.31*	.36**

Note. H = complexity; phi = compartmentalization; r self-aspects = average correlation between self-aspects; SCC = self-concept clarity; r roles = average correlation between roles; self–parent = discrepancy between self and perceived parent ratings; self–friend = discrepancy between self and perceived friend ratings.
*p < .05, **p < .01.

should prevent the impact of a negative outcome in one aspect from spilling over into other self-aspects and adversely affecting the whole. Our studies also did not include measures of stress and, thus, we were unable to test a stress-buffering role for complexity.

Another possible explanation is that the effect of differentiation on adjustment may depend critically on the valence of the contents of the self-concept. As was just noted, Showers (1992a) argued that compartmentalization has a positive effect on adjustment only for those individuals whose positive self-aspects are more important than their negative self-aspects. Indeed, when negative self-aspects are more important, Showers (1992a, 1992b) has shown that integrating positive and negative traits within self-aspect groups is related to better adjustment. Regarding complexity, Woolfolk, Novalany, Gara, Allen, and Polino (1995) computed complexity scores separately for the positive (positive complexity) and the negative (negative complexity) traits in participants' sorts. They found that the measure of positive complexity was highly sensitive to methodological factors (e.g., the number of positive traits provided to participants in the sorting task) and was generally not associated with adjustment. In contrast, the measure of negative complexity was relatively stable across different stimuli and tasks and was consistently related to low self-esteem, distress, and psychopathology.

Morgan and Janoff-Bulman (1994) also found a direct relation between higher levels of negative complexity and maladjustment and no direct relation between positive complexity and adjustment. They did, however, report a strong association between positive complexity and adjustment following a traumatic event (i.e., a stress-buffering outcome). They concluded that, among those who had suffered a traumatic event, psychological adjustment was best predicted by the presence of many independent positive self-aspects (positive self-complexity) but that, among those who had not experienced a traumatic event, psychological adjustment was best predicted by the absence of many independent negative self-aspects (negative self-complexity).

Although space precludes a full review here, studies of the relation between differentiation and adjustment have produced mixed results. One study showed a direct positive relation between overall complexity and adjustment (Campbell, Chew, & Scratchley, 1991), other studies have shown a direct negative relation between overall complexity and adjustment (e.g., Jordan & Cole, 1996; Woolfolk et al., 1995, Study 1), and still other studies have shown no direct relation between overall complexity and adjustment (e.g., Morgan & Janoff-Bulman, 1994). As was noted earlier, some studies have also shown a direct negative relation between negative complexity and adjustment but no direct relation between positive complexity and adjustment (Morgan & Janoff-Bulman, 1994; Woolfolk et al., 1995). In addition, some have reported a stress-buffering effect for overall complexity (Dixon & Baumeister, 1991; Jordan & Cole, 1996; Linville, 1985, 1987; Smith &

Cohen, 1993), whereas others have reported a stress-buffering effect for positive complexity but not for overall complexity or negative complexity (Morgan & Janoff-Bulman, 1994; Woolfolk et al., 1995, Studies 5 and 6). The research on compartmentalization has also yielded some contradictory findings, with some studies showing a direct positive relation with adjustment (Hart, Field, Garfinkle, & Singer, 1997; Showers, 1992a, Studies 1 and 2) and other studies showing only an interaction with differential importance (Showers, 1992a, Study 3; Showers & Kling, 1996b).

The literature on integrative complexity discussed earlier suggests that people who are higher in integrative complexity (a combination of high differentiation and high integration) should be better adjusted than are those who are lower in integrative complexity. In Study 4, we assessed whether these participants were better adjusted than other participants by examining various combinations of high–low differentiation and high–low integration as independent variables in 2×2 analyses of variance on the measures of adjustment. Although the means were consistently in the appropriate direction (the highest adjustment means resided in the high–high cell), the interaction never approached significance (the statistical analysis yielded only main effects for integration). Significant interactions also failed to emerge in regression analyses that used the full range of self-structure scores.

Summary

The results of our four studies show moderate but consistent relations between the different measures of integration and moderate but consistent relations between the measures of integration and adjustment. The measures of differentiation, in contrast, were not related to one another, were not related to the measures of integration, and were not related to adjustment.

Our results, together with the inconsistencies that have emerged from prior research on differentiation, have raised a number of conceptual and methodological issues regarding the assessment of self-structure and its relation to adjustment. In the next section, we discuss some of these issues and make some tentative suggestions that would allow for a more accurate comparison of the various components of self-structure and their impact on adjustment.

ASSESSMENT OF SELF-STRUCTURE

Most of the methods that we have described rely on participants sorting or rating a list of experimenter-provided traits. Recall that in Zajonc's (1960) classic paper on the properties of structure, he first had participants list the attributes that they used to identify objects or events in the cognitive domain. His first structural property (the one that he called differentiation) was the total number of attributes that participants listed. His remaining three structural properties were then assessed with the idiographic attribute lists that the participants had generated. Although generating an exhaustive list of attributes is probably not feasible in a domain as rich as the self, it would nonetheless seem important in assessing the structure of a particular individual's self-concept to use the idiographic contents of that person's self-concept.

Providing participants with a list of traits has a number of drawbacks. First, it renders comparisons between studies ambiguous because differences in the results may derive from the number or content of the traits provided. For example, Woolfolk et al. (1995, Study 1) manipulated list content by providing participants with trait lists in which the ratio of positive to negative traits was 1:2, 1:1, or 2:1 and then asked them to perform the Linville sorting task. They found that complexity (the H statistic) was highly dependent on the percentage of positive traits in the list; as the percentage of positive traits increased, so did complexity. In the second of our four studies, we had the same participants perform the sorting task twice—once with a list of traits in which the ratio of positive to negative traits was 2:1 and once with a list of traits in which the ratio of positive to negative traits was 1:2 (order was counterbalanced). Like Woolfolk et al. (1995), we found that complexity scores were significantly higher when more positive traits were included in the list.

Of greater importance is the fact that experimenter-provided trait lists may not include attributes that are critical (accessible or important) to the way that participants think about themselves. One consequence of omitting critical traits is that potentially important self-aspect groups or dimensions may not emerge when there are no traits relevant to this self-aspect in the trait list. For example, the trait list used by Linville (1985, 1987) and others does not contain any traits pertaining to physical appearance or prowess, an omission that would preclude a participant from forming a self-aspect group having to do with athletic ability, fitness, or physical appearance.

One resolution for this problem is based on a technique used by Hart, Field, Garfinkle, & Singer (1997). They had participants list traits in response to a set of 14 standard probes: 6 probes were "self" probes (e.g., actual, past, future, ideal, ought, and undesired self), and 8 probes were "other" (mother, father, five well-known persons, and a known but disliked person). After removing duplicates, they noted that their participants provided between 50 and 120 unique traits. Then, to ensure that each participant made the same number of judgments, the number of traits was reduced to a maximum of 50 by first selecting traits that appeared in more than one list (assuming that more frequently listed traits were more salient) and then randomly sampling from the master list until an idiographic list of 50 traits had been constructed. The use of traits generated in response to "other" probes can be justified by the fact that attributes important to the self are typically used in descriptions of others (Lemon & Warren, 1976; Shrauger & Patterson, 1976), but an alternative to using "other" probes is to expand the list of "self" probes to include different roles and activities (e.g., "your favorite recreational activities").

Armed with an idiographic list of attributes, one could have participants undertake the Linville sorting task to derive a measure of self-complexity or dimensionality. However, because the list of 50 traits is considerably longer than the lists used in prior studies (maximum of 33 traits), this may be impractical. Our second suggestion is this: Instead of deriving self-aspect groups or categories from participants' trait sorts, participants could be asked to generate personally relevant self-aspect groups in response to probes. Although this suggestion appears to be a major departure from Linville's trait-sorting procedure, Dixon and Baumeister (1991) have noted that, in practice, when participants perform the trait-sorting task, they first generate their self-aspect groups and then fill in each self-aspect group with relevant traits from the list of provided traits. Indeed, one could argue that generating self-aspect groups without a list of traits (even an idiographic list) is preferable in that it provides a more spontaneous measure of what participants consider to be important aspects of themselves and their lives. In two studies, Woolfolk et al. (1995, Studies 4 and 6) derived measures of self-complexity by providing participants with one or two concrete examples of a self-aspect or role (e.g., student role) and then asking them to generate an exhaustive list of self-aspects. The results of these studies were consistent with the results of other studies that they conducted using Linville's trait-sorting procedure.

To ensure comparability across studies, it would again seem preferable for researchers to use a standard set of probes or examples. Participants could be told that, in generating their self-aspect groups, they should consider the roles that they occupy (e.g., student, son or daughter, friend, romantic partner), the activities in which they engage (e.g., sports, hobbies), and the groups to which they belong, but not to be constrained by these suggestions, and to write down anything that they consider to be an aspect of themselves and their lives.

Now armed with idiographic lists of attributes and self-aspect groups, one could ask participants to assign the attributes to the appropriate groups (allowing for duplicate attributes and not requiring that all attributes be used). This would yield data identical to those obtained with Linville's sorting task; thus, one could calculate the H statistic as a measure of dimensionality. However, because this procedure (and the original Linville task) yields only binary information about which attributes belong to which self-aspect groups (present or not present), it may be preferable to have participants rate all of their attributes on all of their self-aspect groups, a method similar to one that Donahue et al. (1993) described earlier to assess integration (except that their participants rated 60 experimenter-provided attributes on 5 experimenter-provided roles). In addition to allowing participants to indicate which attributes belong to which self-aspect groups, this method would allow participants to indicate the degree to which each attribute belongs to each self-aspect group. Donahue et al. (1993) used an 8-point rating scale anchored by 1 = *not at all descriptive of me* and 8 = *highly descriptive of me*. Although preferable to binary information, this rating scale does not allow participants to describe attributes as being opposite or antithetical to how they view themselves in that category. To capture this information, it may be better to use a 9-point scale anchored by 1 = *extremely uncharacteristic of me* to 9 = *extremely characteristic of me*, with the midpoint indicating that the attribute is irrelevant or intermediate on the category. From the resultant attribute $\times$ category rating matrix, one could calculate both the average correlation among self-aspect groups (the measure of integration or unity) and the statistic D, which is a measure of dimensionality (complexity) that is equivalent, for interval scales, to Attneave's H (Scott et al., 1979; see Woolfolk et al., 1995, for an example). Thus, the measures of self-differentiation and self-integration for each participant are derived from the identical database, allowing for a more accurate assessment of their differences and commonalities in predicting adjustment.

With this method, some of the other measures of self-structure could also be derived. Regarding compartmentalization, one would first have participants rate the positivity of each attribute to classify the attributes as either a positive or negative feature of the self. The attribute $\times$ category rating matrix could then be decomposed into lists of attributes present in each self-aspect category by simply including in each category list those attributes rated a 6 or greater (on the 9-point scale). The resultant data are then identical in form to those yielded by the Linville trait-sorting task, allowing the calculation of the phi statistic used by Showers (1992a). The differential importance of positive and negative self-aspects could also be calculated as Showers did (1992a) by collecting additional information about the perceived positivity and importance of each self-aspect group. Higgins's self-discrepancies or discrepancies between how one views the self and how one believes he or she is viewed by significant others could be derived by having participants rate their idiographic list of attributes on the appropriate labels or self-aspect categories (e.g., rate the attributes according to how you view yourself, how you believe your mother views you, how you ought to be). The average correlation between the categories or labels constitute inverse (proximity) measures of such discrepancies (see Hart et al., 1997, for an example).

Relatively little attention has been paid to the property of cognitive structure of Zajonc's (1960) "organization." Organization refers to the extent to which a particular self-aspect or category dominates the whole—thus, we refer to it as *dominance*, although the term *centrality* would be equally appropriate. There are theoretical and empirical reasons to believe that having a highly dominant self-aspect may increase vulnerability to domain-relevant negative events. If a negative event occurs in some domain, the extent to which the negative affect associated with the event "spills over" to affect the whole may depend more on the dominance of the domain than on the number of other independent self-aspects present in the structure (i.e., complexity). Brewer (1993) measured the dominance of the athletic role (via a self-report scale) and found that participants with higher levels of athletic role dominance experienced more depression following an athletic injury. Similarly, Smith and Cohen (1993) measured the proportion of total self-complexity that involved a "romantic relationship self-aspect" and found that the greater the proportion, the greater the distress experienced following the breakup of a relationship.

A number of methods that can be used to assess the dominance of any particular self-aspect in relation to the whole. One would be to decompose the rating matrix into trait sort data (see our earlier comments regarding the computation of compartmentalization) and use the formula given by Smith and Cohen (1993; see also Cohen, Pane, & Smith, 1997) to determine dominance. Although space precludes a detailed description here, the formula is basically a ratio of the impact of the self-aspect (the number of attributes in the self-aspect category and the overlap of those attributes with other self-aspects) divided by total complexity. A second method would be to present participants with a circle or pie and their list of self-aspect groups and ask them to divide the pie into wedges, where the size of each wedge represents the importance of each self-aspect group in the way that they think about themselves. The size of each wedge (as assessed by the number of degrees it occupies of the circle) would constitute a measure of the dominance of each self-aspect group.

SOME ISSUES REGARDING THE RELATION BETWEEN STRUCTURE AND ADJUSTMENT

Some researchers have examined zero-order correlations between measures of self-structure and adjustment, whereas others have taken measures of (or manipulated) stress and examined the interactive effects of self-structure and stress on adjustment. If measures of stress are taken, it is possible to assess in the same study both the direct and indirect (stress-buffering) effects of self-structure on adjustment via hierarchical regression analyses. When collecting measures of stress is not feasible, it is especially important for researchers to explicitly acknowledge that a stress-buffering effect was not tested, given that stress-buffering is the theoretical mechanism associated with some of the structural properties (e.g., complexity).

A second issue has to do with controlling for the contents of the self-concept when assessing the effect that structure has on adjustment. Showers's research (e.g., 1992a) is exemplary in this regard because she typically conducts hierarchical regressions in which the overall positivity of the contents is entered before testing for the impact of compartmentalization. She does this by providing participants with trait lists that contain a mixture of designated positive and negative traits and indexing positivity by the proportion of negative traits used, but with participant-provided traits it would be necessary to ask participants to also rate the perceived positivity of their attributes. Our own studies did not include this control because many of our traits were near the midpoint of standard social desirability ratings and we did not collect participant ratings. Nonetheless, to establish a strong case for the role of self-structure in affecting adjustment, it would be important to demonstrate that structural features have explanatory power even after controlling for the well-established effects of content (especially the overall positivity of the contents).

Finally, we have discussed the various structural aspects of the self-concept as if they were stable or invariant features of the self. This assumption has been largely untested, and a recent article by Showers, Abramson, and Hogan (1998) provides some evidence that structural features may indeed change over time and that they do so in a manner that helps to counteract stress and negative mood. More specifically, their data suggest that changes in the content of the self-concept simply reflect changes in the content of life events and mood, whereas changes in the structure of the self-concept may reflect attempts to minimize the impact of stress. In support of this latter point, they found that complexity and compartmentalization increased over time among those participants who showed better adjustment to stress.

CONCLUSION

Contemporary theory and research on the self has highlighted the importance of examining the structural features of the self-concept. These features have generally fallen into one of two categories—those that reflect the extent to which aspects of the self are differentiated and those that reflect the extent to which aspects of the self are integrated. The purpose of this chapter was to examine how measures of these features relate to each other and how they relate to psychological adjustment.

The measures of integration yielded a relatively simple picture. These measures were moderately correlated with one another and with adjustment in our studies, and the prior research literature has been consistent in demonstrating positive associations between integration and adjustment. Stress-buffering effects of integration have not been directly tested, but it would seem plausible that the beneficial effects of having a unified sense of self may be especially important under stressful conditions.

The measures of differentiation were not generally correlated with integration or with adjustment. Although prior studies of the relation between differentiation and adjustment have yielded inconsistent findings, these studies, in conjunction with our own, broadly suggest that differentiation may not have a main or direct effect on adjustment. Rather, its effects on adjustment appear to be more complicated in that the effect is either indirect via a stress-buffering effect (e.g., Linville's research on the stress-buffering role of complexity) or may depend on whether one is examining the differentiation of positive or negative self-attributes (e.g., positive versus negative complexity).

To allow for a more accurate comparison of structural features and their impact on adjustment, we made several recommendations for future research. First, and most important, idiographic attributes and self-aspects should be assessed to ensure that personally relevant features of the self are measured. If participants rate these attributes for the extent to which they belong to each self-aspect group, the measures of differentiation and integration may be derived from the same database, enhancing their comparability. Second, the impact that dominance of the self-aspects has on adjustment should be investigated. Third, efforts should be made to examine (a) both the direct and indirect effects of structural features on adjustment, (b) the extent to which structural features affect adjustment after controlling for the overall positivity of the contents of the self-concept, and (c) whether structural features change over time. Implementing these recommendations in future research should enhance our understanding of the relations among structural features of the self-concept and their impact on psychological functioning.

REFERENCES

Attneave, F. (1959). *Applications of information theory to psychology.* New York: Hort-Dryden.

Block, J. (1961). Ego-identity, role variability, and adjustment. *Journal of Consulting and Clinical Psychology, 25,* 392–397.

Brewer, B. W. (1993). Self-identity and specific vulnerability to depressed mood. *Journal of Personality, 61,* 343–364.

Campbell, J. D. (1990). Self-esteem and clarity of the self-concept. *Journal of Personality and Social Psychology, 59,* 538–549.

Campbell, J. D. (1997, October). *Structural aspects of the self-concept.* Paper presented at the Preconference of the Society for Experimental Social Psychology: Self, Toronto, Canada.

Campbell, J. D., Chew, B., & Scratchley, L. S. (1991). Cognitive and emotional reactions to daily events: The effects of self-esteem and self-complexity. *Journal of Personality, 59,* 473–505.

Campbell, J. D., Trapnell, P. D., Heine, S. J., Katz, I. M., Lavallee, L. F., & Lehman, D. R. (1996). Self-concept clarity: Measurement, personality correlates, and cultural boundaries. *Journal of Personality and Social Psychology, 70,* 141–156.

Campbell, J. D., Assanand, S., & DiPaula, A. (1999). *Is it better to be differentiated or integrated?: An analysis of the relation between self-concept structure and psychological adjustment.* Unpublished manuscript, University of British Columbia.

Cohen, L. H., Pane, N., & Smith, H. S. (1997). Complexity of the interpersonal self and affective reactions to interpersonal stressors in life and in the laboratory. *Cognitive Therapy and Research, 21,* 387–407.

Cramer, H. (1974). *Mathematical methods of statistics.* Princeton, NJ: Princeton University Press.

Dixon, T. M., & Baumeister, R. F. (1991). Escaping the self: The moderating effect of self-complexity. *Personality and Social Psychology Bulletin, 17,* 363–368.

Donahue, E. M., Robins, R. W., Roberts, B. W., & John, O. P. (1993). The divided self: Concurrent and longitudinal effects of psychological adjustment and social roles on self-concept differentiation. *Journal of Personality and Social Psychology, 64,* 834–846.

Gergen, K. J. (1972, May). The healthy, happy human wears many masks. *Psychology Today,* pp. 31–35, 64–66.

Goffman, E. (1959). *The presentation of self in everyday life.* Garden City, NY: Doubleday.

Greenwald, A. G., & Pratkanis, A. R. (1984). The self. In R. S. Wyer & T. K. Srull (Eds.), *Handbook of social cognition* (Vol. 3, pp. 129–178). Hillsdale, NJ: Erlbaum.

Hart, D., Field, N. P., Garfinkle, J. R., & Singer, J. L. (1997). Representations of self and other: A semantic space model. *Journal of Personality, 65,* 77–105.

Higgins, E. T., Klein, R., & Strauman, T. (1985). Self-concept discrepancy theory: A psychological model for distinguishing among different aspects of depression and anxiety. *Social Cognition, 3,* 51–76.

Higgins, E. T. (1989). Self-discrepancy theory: What patterns of self-beliefs cause people to suffer? In L. Berkowitz (Ed.), *Advances in experimental social psychology* (Vol. 22, pp. 93–136). New York: Academic Press.

Jordan, A., & Cole, D. A. (1996). Relation of depressive symptoms to the structure of self-knowledge in childhood. *Journal of Abnormal Psychology, 105,* 530–540.

Kihlstrom, J. F., & Cantor, N. (1984). Mental representations of the self. In L. Berkowitz (Ed.), *Advances in experimental social psychology* (Vol. 17, pp. 1–47). Hillsdale, NJ: Erlbaum.

Lecky, P. (1945). *Self-consistency: A theory of personality.* New York: Anchor Books.

Lemon, N., & Warren, N. (1976). Salience, centrality, and self-relevance of traits in construing others. *British Journal of Social and Clinical Psychology, 13,* 119–124.

Linville, P. W. (1985). Self-complexity and affective extremity: Don't put all of your eggs in one cognitive basket. *Social Cognition, 3,* 94–120.

Linville, P. W. (1987). Self-complexity as a cognitive buffer against stress-related illness and depression. *Journal of Personality and Social Psychology, 52,* 663–676.

Markus, H. R., & Wurf, E. (1987). The dynamic self-concept: A social psychological perspective. *Annual Review of Psychology, 38,* 299–337.

Morgan, H. J., & Janoff-Bulman, R. (1994). Positive and negative self-complexity: Patterns of adjustment following traumatic versus nontraumatic life experiences. *Journal of Social and Clinical Psychology, 13*, 63–85.

Niedenthal, P. M., Setterlund, M. B., & Wherry, M. B. (1992). Possible self-complexity and affective reactions to goal-relevant evaluation. *Journal of Personality and Social Psychology, 63*, 5–16.

Pelham, B. W., & Swann, W. B., Jr. (1989). From self-conceptions to self-worth: On the sources and structure of global self-esteem. *Journal of Personality and Social Psychology, 57*, 672–680.

Rogers, C. R. (1959). A theory of therapy, personality, and interpersonal relationships, as developed in the client-centered framework. In S. Koch (Ed.), *Psychology: A study of a science* (Vol. 3, pp. 1–59). New York: McGraw-Hill.

Schroeder, H. M., Driver, M. J., & Streufert, S. (1967). *Human information processing.* New York: Holt, Rinehart & Winston.

Scott, W. A., Osgood, D. W., & Peterson, C. (1979). *Cognitive structure: Theory and measurement of individual differences.* Washington, DC: Winston.

Showers, C. (1992a). Compartmentalization of positive and negative self-knowledge: Keeping bad apples out of the bunch. *Journal of Personality and Social Psychology, 62*, 1036–1049.

Showers, C. (1992b). Evaluatively integrative thinking about characteristics of the self. *Personality and Social Psychology Bulletin, 18*, 719–729.

Showers, C. J., Abramson, L. Y., & Hogan, M. E. (1998). The dynamic self: How the content and structure of the self-concept change with mood. *Journal of Personality and Social Psychology, 75*, 478–493.

Showers, C. J., & Kling, K. C. (1996a). The organization of self-knowledge: Implications for mood regulation. In L. L. Martin & A. Tesser (Eds.), *Striving and feeling: Interactions among goals, affect, & self-regulation* (pp. 151–173). Hillsdale, NJ: Erlbaum.

Showers, C. J., & Kling, K. C. (1996b). Organization of self-knowledge: Implications for recovery of sad mood. *Journal of Personality and Social Psychology, 70*, 578–590.

Shrauger, S. J., & Patterson, M. B. (1976). Self-evaluation and the selection of dimensions for evaluating others. *Journal of Personality, 42*, 569–585.

Smith, H. S., & Cohen, L. H. (1993). Self-complexity and reactions to a relationship breakup. *Journal of Social and Clinical Psychology, 12*, 367–384.

Smith, M., Wethington, E., & Zhan, G. (1996). Self-concept clarity and preferred coping styles. *Journal of Personality, 64*, 407–434.

Snyder, M. (1974). Self-monitoring of expressive behavior. *Journal of Personality and Social Psychology, 30*, 526–537.

Woolfolk, R. L., Novalany, J., Gara, M. A., Allen, L. A., & Polino, M. (1995). Self-complexity, self-evaluation, and depression: An examination of form and content within the self-schema. *Journal of Personality and Social Psychology, 68*, 1108–1120.

Wylie, R. (1979). *The self-concept* (Vol. 2). Lincoln: University of Nebraska Press.

Zajonc, R. B. (1960). The process of cognitive tuning in communication. *Journal of Abnormal and Social Psychology, 61*, 159–167.

II

Self-Motives

4

ON THE EVOLUTIONARY FUNCTIONS OF THE SYMBOLIC SELF: THE EMERGENCE OF SELF-EVALUATION MOTIVES

CONSTANTINE SEDIKIDES
JOHN J. SKOWRONSKI

The human self-concept has captured the fascination and imagination of intellectuals from many walks of life—writers and poets, religious and political figures, philosophers and scientists. These intellectuals have described the self-concept as enigmatic and mysterious; the key to understanding the essence of human nature; the basis of motivation, emotion, and behavior; and the royal road to personal misery and societal woes.

Some of our previous theorizing has focused on the possible evolutionary bases of the *symbolic self*, the type of self-concept that is possessed by humans (Sedikides & Skowronski, 1997; Skowronski & Sedikides, 1999). It is

We thank several anonymous reviewers for their constructive comments on earlier versions of this manuscript. Correspondence concerning this chapter should be addressed to Constantine Sedikides at the Department of Psychology, University of Southampton, Highfield Campus, Southampton, SO17 1BJ, England, UK, or at C.Sedikides@soton.ac.uk.

our contention that the symbolic self is a uniquely human attribute that is distinct from two other types of self-conceptions that occur in the natural world. The *subjective self* refers to an organism's capacity to differentiate crudely between the organism (the self) and the physical or social environment. This type of self-awareness is widespread: All living species are able to make this self-versus-environment distinction, which need involve only simple, implicit, and automatic mechanisms. These mechanisms allow organisms to respond to environmental stimulation and to engage in self-regulation.

In comparison, relatively sophisticated cognitive capabilities are essential to a second type of self-concept, the *objectified self*. An organism with objective self-awareness has the capacity to "become the object of its own attention" (Gallup, 1992, p. 117), to be "aware of its own state of mind" (Cheyney & Seyfarth, 1992, p. 240), and to "know it knows; to remember it remembers" (Lewis, 1992, p. 124). This type of self-awareness is present only in a few species, such as chimpanzees, orangutans, and bonobos (Hyatt & Hopkins, 1994; Suarez & Gallup, 1981). However, even the relatively sophisticated cognitive abilities that underlie this form of the self-concept are not comparable to the cognitive abilities of human adults. Indeed, the objectified self is similar to the type of self-concept that human toddlers have in the age range of 15–24 months (Gallup & Suarez, 1986).

The symbolic self possessed by human adults subsumes the other two types of self-concepts and requires far greater sophistication in cognitive capabilities than is required by the objectified self. More specifically, in our view, there are three aspects to the symbolic self. The representational aspect of the symbolic self refers to the representation of one's personality and characteristics (Higgins, 1996; Kihlstrom & Cantor, 1984; Kihlstrom & Klein, 1994) in the memory system. Mental representations that are relevant to the symbolic self contain many different kinds of information. These representations contain abstract, language-based representations of an individual's demographic, physical, trait, or behavioral attributes (Markus, 1983). Self-relevant mental structures also contain temporally organized semantic, episodic, and perceptual representations of an individual's personal history (Thompson, Skowronski, Larsen, & Betz, 1996). Furthermore, self-relevant mental representations contain knowledge about goals, values, and feelings (Emmons, 1989); imagined, desired, or feared information in future or hypothetical contexts (Higgins, 1987; Kato & Markus, 1993); information about possessions, social roles, and social relations; and beliefs about how others might perceive one's personality and characteristics (Belk, 1988; Shrauger & Schoeneman, 1979).

The second aspect of the symbolic self refers to its executive functions (Baumeister, chapter 1, this volume; Breckler & Greenwald, 1986; Cantor, Markus, Niedenthal, & Nurius, 1986). The symbolic self is involved in and helps to guide information-seeking, goal-setting, and goal-directed behavior. As Baumeister (1998, p. 712) noted, "Without this active function, the self would merely be a passive spectator, aware of itself and related to others, but unable to do anything except perceive and interpret the flow of events and to experience emotions." Instead, the symbolic self helps an individual to experience agency: the desire to choose, to control, to have an impact on situations (although this desire may not always be present—see Skowronski & Carlston, 1982). This choice-making aspect of the symbolic self is often guided by perceived self-interest. Hence, this aspect of the symbolic self is implicated when potentially negative feedback is avoided, rationalized, derogated, or discredited (Taylor & Brown, 1988). Similarly, it is partly because of this aspect of the symbolic self that favorable outcomes lead to uplifting psychological states (e.g., experiencing high self-esteem or pride), whereas unfavorable outcomes lead to deflating psychological states (e.g., experiencing shame, guilt, or embarrassment). In summary, the executive aspect of the symbolic self is involved in making choices, coping with feedback, and experiencing the emotional consequences of outcomes.

The third aspect of the symbolic self is its reflexive potential. In simple terms, this aspect refers to the capacity of the organism to be conscious of itself (Baumeister, 1998). However, this reflexive potential is often manifested in the interchange between the executive and representational aspects of the self. This interchange has its roots in the notorious malleability of the self-concept. Many psychologists explain this malleability by hypothesizing that the self is not a single, stable entity. Instead, there may be a set of diverse self-representations that are stored in memory, and these diverse selves may not be well integrated. Hence, the self that one is experiencing at any given moment (the phenomenal self-concept) may simply be a reflection of the self-representation that is temporarily activated in working memory.

What determines the representation that is activated? We conjecture that different aspects of the symbolic self may be activated in accordance with the goals of the individual. That is, the elements of situations and the goals set by the executive system in those situations may contribute to the activation of a given self-representation, and thus they can cause perceptions of the self to vary across the situations (Markus & Kunda, 1986; McGuire, McGuire, & Winton, 1979).

Furthermore, the guidance provided by this temporarily activated self-knowledge is dynamic in that it can affect the processing of self-relevant information and the subsequent storage of this information (Showers, 1992; Vallacher & Nowak, chapter 2, this volume). Because different aspects of the self may be active at different times, the guidance provided by these aspects of the self can allow individuals to develop and store bodies of self-relevant information that are inconsistent with each other (Fazio, Effrein, & Falender, 1981). Such flexibility may operate in the service of self-regulation. Others have already observed that the self has an extensive capacity for its own regulation, that is, for minimizing, maximizing, or overriding previous cognitive, affective, motivational, and behavioral processes (Carver & Scheier, 1990; Higgins, 1996).

To summarize, then, current thinking about the symbolic self suggests that it is a dynamic system containing multiple components. One key component of this system is storage: the essential library of an individual's past and present and the repository for an individual's goals and aspirations for the future. The second key component is regulatory: The symbolic self is a crucial originator, mediator, or moderator of an individual's thinking, feeling, and behaving. The third key component is flexibility: Both the situation and individual goals and aspirations can cause the phenomenal self to shift across time and situations by activating or deactivating components of stored self-knowledge.

The voluminous research that has arisen around the construct of the self in psychology attests to the importance of these aspects. However, one question that has remained relatively unexplored concerns the origins of the symbolic self. Why do humans have a symbolic self? Where did it come from? How did it evolve? Discerning the answers to such questions may further the understanding of some of the current characteristics of the symbolic self and may help us to fathom the functions that the symbolic self has in human life.

THE SYMBOLIC SELF AS AN ADAPTATION: EVOLUTIONARY PRESSURES AND FUNCTIONS

In our previous theoretical work, we addressed the possibility that the symbolic self is a biologically selected adaptation that evolved in response to the pressures of natural selection (Sedikides & Skowronski, 1997; Skowronski & Sedikides, 1999). In that work we argued that the symbolic self is a capacity that was selected and distributed in the human population because of its high adaptive value. In thinking about our ideas, it is important to note that we presuppose that the emergence of this capacity is relatively unique to the hominid evolutionary past. Many of the evolutionary pressures that we discuss in this chapter (the capacity to hunt, a social habit) would seem to apply equally to other species, such as lions. So why don't lions have a symbolic self? The answer is that evolution does not magically conjure traits from nothing—a trait must be present before natural selection exerts its effects. We are making the huge assumption that somewhere along the way a happy accident occurred: A mutation or a favorable mating produced hominid individuals with the capacity for a symbolic self, a capacity that has (so far as we know) as yet not emerged in the feline population.

Given the existence of a favorable, selectable trait in a population, to make an evolutionary argument one needs to identify the situational pressures that are responsible for the selection of the trait, and one must be able to understand how the selected trait helps overcome those pressures. Our analyses of alternative sources of evidence, including evidence from physical anthropology, the possible evolutionary timelines implied by that evidence, and evidence of the self in nonhuman species, led us to speculate that the evolution of the symbolic self was tied to two factors. The first of these factors was the emergence of symbolic reasoning capabilities, which were spurred, in part, by the unique problems that confronted individuals who were sometimes poorly equipped for the task of food procurement. The second of these factors was the socially oriented structure of early human life. It is our opinion that the development of cognition and high intellect set the cognitive foundation for the development of the symbolic self. However, in our view, this high level of cognition is not sufficient for the development of the symbolic self; the social habit of humans was also a critical determining factor. In the next sections, we review briefly each factor and discuss its synergistic relation (for more detail and empirical support, see Sedikides & Skowronski, 1997).

Ecological Pressures and the Cognitive Foundations of the Self

One of the main story lines of human evolution follows the emergence of cognition and intellect. Current thinking among many students of human evolution suggests that the evolution of human thinking abilities was driven in part by difficulties in finding and procuring food. Survival and procreation rely on adequate procurement of food. If the food procurement environment is difficult, one can overcome the difficulty either by becoming more intellectually adept overall or by improving a specific cognitive ability related to food procurement.

The record of natural history and comparative biology makes a strong case that such a relation is plausible. For example, problems in foraging and finding food are linked with increased encephalization: The irregular (in time and space) distribution of food supplies is associated with larger brain-to-body ratios among frugivore primates (Milton, 1988). In addition, an animal's food procurement lifestyle is related to its intellective abilities: Omnivorous extractive foragers have the largest brain-to-body ratios among primates (Gibson, 1986). In short, then, one likely lesson from natural history is that either the entire intellect or aspects of the intellect are subject to selection pressures, and one of the important selection pressures is food procurement.

Some scholars in the area of evolution have argued that the intellectual abilities of human ancestral species were prime targets for the influence of natural selection, especially given their rather modest physical abilities. As Fox (1980) put it: "Very little about . . . our . . . forebears could have inspired confidence . . . not the stature, the speed, the strength, the ferocity. . . . And the answer to this ultimate success can only lie in the very helplessness of the original creature" (p. 175). Fox probably overstated the case. It may be more appropriate to hypothesize that the evolutionary ancestors of modern humans may sometimes have found themselves underequipped to deal with their environment—an opportune scenario for evolutionary change.

This ill fit could have been caused by a couple of factors. One is migration. One of the remarkable observations about humans is that they are widespread in distribution, occupying environments that range from icy cold to blistering hot. It is not difficult to imagine that survival is difficult and that an increased intellective capacity may be an advantage in these extreme environments. However, although the issue is still under debate, the evidence currently suggests that this wide distribution may have emerged relatively late in hominid evolutionary history. A second possibility is that the evolution of increased cognitive capacity was the consequence of environmental changes that prompted a shift in lifestyle. Although the exact status of the human lineage is under constant revision, some current thinking suggests that our human ancestors came from an arboreal background (e.g., *Australopithecus ramadus*) and only gradually made the transition to land-based bipedalism. One might guess that the arboreal origins of the early ancestral line were rather incompatible with life on the ground, especially given that this shift in environment may have also been related to a shift in lifestyle from a diet that relied mainly on plant material to one that included meat. In addition, recurring climactic changes (which may have prompted bipedalism in the first place) could have made food procurement even more difficult by spreading out food sources in time and space.

If evolution operates on the mind, then environmental pressures associated with food procurement could have worked to enhance several specific mental faculties. Locating and recognizing food sources requires enhanced categorization and memory processes. Searching for food requires enhanced spatial memory and cognitive mapping. Handling, processing, and storing food requires enhanced cognitive representation abilities and the capacity to anticipate future events. In addition, the challenges associated with hunting large and mobile animals could have further added to the evolutionary selection of mental abilities. Pursuit in hunting requires accurate perception of fast-moving targets, mental orientation and rotation, split-second recognition, rapid taxonomic memory, and the ability to act on quick or reflexive ("gut feeling") responses. More important, these activities may have prompted the evolutionary emergence of symbolic reasoning. Approaching game closely and being competent in stalking require sophisticated planning and decision-making abilities. The ability to plan an optimal route of attack involves being able to remember or to imagine how prey might react to an attack. This ability to imagine and plan involves symbolic reasoning: the capacity to think about things by manipulating images or concepts. Similar skills are involved in tool construction and use. For example, excellence in flint-knapping requires a good deal of planning and imagination while working the stone. Similarly, developing optimal shapes for the flints presupposes knowledge about the effectiveness of different shapes and how they can be used in hunting.

Social Pressures and the Evolution of the Symbolic Self

In addition to the possibility that problems in food procurement led to increases in cognitive ability, such increases may also have come from the social nature of human ancestors. The anthropological evidence suggests that human ancestors were social organisms living in extended family units or small groups (Isaac, 1981). From an evolutionary perspective, membership in such groups has its plusses and minuses. Among the benefits are improved predation (e.g., hunting efficiency, food sharing), reduction of predation risk, and cooperative defense of essential resources (e.g., food sources and mates) against rival groups.

Interestingly, one of the side benefits of group living is that it may be related to enhanced thinking prowess. In primate species, there is a strong positive relation between group size and brain size: Species that have a terrestrial lifestyle and that live in large groups have bigger brains than do other species (Dunbar, 1992, 1993). This relation appears to hold, even when one accounts for lifestyle differences, such as diet. A moment's thought will lead to the realization of why this relation may exist. Relationships with a single individual can be quite complex, and the more individuals there are with whom to interact, the greater the complexity will become. A good dollop of intelligence (or of social intelligence, if one is inclined to think in modular terms) helps to more effectively navigate the complexities of group life and can result in better reproductive fitness.

Let us elaborate on this point. One of the possible consequences of group living, especially in individuals with enhanced cognitive and memory capacities (which, as we have already argued, were emerging in human ancestor species) is the evolution of a complex social organization with numerous rules, roles, and patterns of relationships. This complexity can evolve for several reasons. One source of role differentiation comes from the different tasks that individuals in the group can perform. For example, in ancestral human species, labor was probably divided along gender lines (Tanner, 1983; Tooby & DeVore, 1987). Men hunted for big game and protected the group against rival groups; women carried out the tasks of gathering food, preparing food, and caring for children.

However, other types of within-group differentiations can emerge. For example, group members can differ in social status, and these differences can contribute to the evolutionary pressures that may have caused the symbolic self to develop. It is important to note that in the cognitively flexible humans this status may not have taken the form of a simple dominance hierarchy of the type observed in many animal species—that would not put much pressure on the evolution of the symbolic self. Instead, more pressure would occur if humans maintained a relatively loose and flexible social structure in which status differentiation was somewhat flexible and dependent on circumstances. In such structures, one does not always know where one stands in the group. Instead, one must engage in numerous cognitive tasks to determine one's social standing. One must pay attention to the situation and remember how one interacted with a given subgroup at any point in time. In such groups, interaction and coordination pose a tremendously complex cognitive problem, and part of the solution to this problem might have been the eventual development of a symbolic self that could better keep up with rapidly changing situations, subgroups, and interactions.

The various elements of interactions that occur in these groups can increase this complexity. When in a group, one can experience various kinds of cooperative dyadic interactions (e.g., feeding, grooming, fighting), dyadic relationships (e.g., kinship, friendship), and intragroup interactions. Within-group cooperation presupposes role differentiation (i.e., well-defined roles maximize interactive goal attainment), coordination of individual effort, conformity with the majority of group members, group loyalty, and fear of social exclusion. All of these, again, can challenge an individual's intellective capacities. Furthermore, within-group cooperation can lead to coalition formation. The decision to enter or exit a coalition compels an elaborate and ever-changing cost–benefit analysis.

Intragroup interactions can also be characterized by competition, most notably intrasexual competition for suitable mates. This form of competition can place additional cognitive demands on the individual, such as remembering and recognizing relationships with other adults in the group (e.g., social rank), monitoring the rank of potential competitors, being capable of deceiving higher-ranked competitors, monitoring the sexual receptivity and fitness of potential mates, exhibiting physical and social prowess to attract potential mates, cheating, and detecting cheating. In addition, women need to safeguard against men's attempts at forced copulation. Finally, intergroup competition (e.g., maintaining a level of vigilance, defending offspring and territory, initiating hostilities at an opportune time) can also place demands on the cognitive system.

The natural history evidence suggests that the social pressures that are accompanied by a group lifestyle could have stimulated the development of the brain in human ancestral species. As was noted earlier in this chapter, group size in terrestrial primates is related to brain size. Furthermore, examination of casts of fossilized brains suggests that Broca's area was distinctly formed as early as *Homo habilis*. Thus, with the passage of time, communication skills were apparently becoming increasingly critical in the evolving hominids, a conclusion that is supported by the presence of other physiological changes in the fossil record. For example, an expanded and lowered pharynx, which is a physiological necessity for complex articulate speech, appears to have evolved by late *Homo erectus*.

Hence, we conclude that the social nature of the human ancestors probably contributed to the evolution of the brain, in both its enlargement and its differentiation. As we noted earlier in the chapter, similar effects were probably produced as a consequence of the ecological pressures experienced by human ancestor species. We propose that these ecological and social pressures worked synergistically toward the evolution of individuals who could engage in symbolic reasoning and who were habitually social.

In our view, the development of symbolic reasoning capabilities, the development of sophisticated communication capabilities, and the social context in which humans existed were the preconditions that set the stage for the evolution of the symbolic self. We note that we are not alone in this opinion. Other theorists, following similar lines of reasoning, have reached similar conclusions (Caporael, 1997; Caporael & Brewer, 1991; Maryanski & Turner, 1992; Wilson & Sober, 1994). The unique aspect of our own theoretical position is our emphasis on both social and nonsocial factors in the evolution of the symbolic self.

The adaptive utility of a symbolic self becomes evident if one considers the social and intellectual context experienced by human ancestor species members. We propose that the ability to construct a symbolic self led to enhanced functioning of the individual within the group and even enhanced the functioning of the group as a whole. For example, by becoming a communication referent, the symbolic self could have facilitated verbal and nonverbal exchanges among group members in various aspects of task performance (e.g., duty assignment during hunting expeditions, splitting of prey among group members, interchanging child-rearing tasks). Furthermore, the ability to construct and use a symbolic self could have allowed an individual to adopt the perspective of others in thinking about the self. This allows an individual to anticipate and influence how others might respond to one's own behavior, and it could contribute to an increased facility to handle the social dilemmas that invariably emerge when interacting with others. The use of a symbolic self could have facilitated decision making (e.g., joining maximal resource utility bands), goal setting (e.g., setting goals that matched the individual's capabilities), and behavior (e.g., withdrawing or aggressing depending on history of previous encounters with the antagonistic opponent). In short, we believe that the capacity to form and use a symbolic self added malleability, flexibility, and purpose to the individual's cognitive armamentarium and, by doing this, enhanced the adaptive fit between individuals and their environment.

The evolution of the capacity for a symbolic self may have had other effects as well. For example, the symbolic self can affect the nature of the communications that one has with others. To communicate with others, to enact social roles, and to influence others, an individual needs to possess knowledge of how to manipulate the presentation of self to others. Thus, these social processes can lead to the emergence of the public self: the self as presented to other group members. The public self, in turn, can contribute to the continued evolution of private self-knowledge through the process of reflected appraisal (i.e., seeing the self as important group members see the self) and through the incorporation of multiple group membership identities into the self concept. Our use of the plural in reference to group identity is important, for we assume that individuals need to have some flexibility in how group membership affects the self-concept. Such flexibility would be a seeming aid in groups in which roles are not rigidly fixed and in which alliances among subgroup's members are constantly shifting. Finally, the capacity to construct a symbolic self can ultimately have emotional consequences, because individual self-esteem can come to depend on the interpersonal evaluations provided by other group members.

SELF-EVALUATION MOTIVES AND THEIR ADAPTIVE VALUE

A logical next step in the argument that we have developed focuses on the acquisition of self-relevant information. If the construction and maintenance of a symbolic self is adaptive, then individuals will be especially sensitive to information that has implications for the symbolic self. Several lines of research attest to the power that self-relevant information has on human information processing (for a review, see Baumeister, 1998). Humans have a nonconscious processing sensitivity for self-relevant stimuli, are speedier in the processing of self-descriptive than self-irrelevant information, and better remember self-relevant than other relevant information. Furthermore, humans have better memory for material that has been self-referentially encoded than for material that has been encoded with reference to other people, and they remember self-generated material better than they do material generated by someone else. Moreover, the symbolic self exerts a strong effect on the processing of information about others. Humans selectively perceive and judge others on self-relevant dimensions: When these dimensions are central to the self, humans process the information deeply and draw a large number of (usually extreme) inferences about others (e.g., Sedikides & Skowronski, 1993). The self is also implicated in the choice of people with whom to affiliate. It is understandable, then, why Greenwald (1980) referred to the self as "the totalitarian ego."

However, in all of these cases, the perceiver is treated as a passive entity, as a mere information recipient. It should be obvious that humans are not simply information recipients, but they are also information seekers. Early hominid survival probably depended, in part, on the kinds of information sought and acquired from the environment, the way in which this information was interpreted, and the way in which it was translated into judgment and behavior. We hypothesize that this information-seeking tendency was applied to the symbolic self.

What kind of information did our ancestors want and need to know about themselves? We speculate that several classes of information must be acquired to maintain the adaptiveness of the symbolic self. We further speculate that the symbolic self motivates the selective pursuit of some types of information over others and causes information searchers to filter out (or to facilitate the processing of) certain kinds of self-relevant information. Different motives may have evolved (or may have been adapted) to prompt the acquisition of these kinds of information.

Our analysis of the self-motivated information-seeking process relies on three classes of self-evaluation motives: *valuation motives, learning motives,* and *homeostatic motives.* The two valuation motives are self-protection and self-enhancement (Brown & Dutton, 1995; Kunda, 1990; Tesser, 1988). The self-protection motive works to filter out, negate, or discredit information that is unfavorable to the self. The self-enhancement motive works to filter in, accept, and magnify information that is favorable to the self. The two learning motives are self-assessment (Sedikides & Skowronski, 1995; Strube & Roemmele, 1985; Trope, 1983, 1986) and self-improvement (Taylor, Neter, & Wayment, 1995; Taylor, Wayment, & Carrillo, 1996). The self-assessment motive refers to the pursuit of accurate self-knowledge, be it favorable or unfavorable to the self. The self-improvement motive refers to the pursuit of knowledge that can be used to improve the self, regardless of the negative short-term potential of this knowledge. The sole representative of the homeostatic motive category is self-verification (Lecky, 1945; Swann, 1983, 1990). The self-verification motive refers to the pursuit or endorsement of information that is consistent with the self. Verification can apply to either negative or positive aspects of the self. Obviously, when the characteristics at issue are positive, it is difficult to determine whether the motive underlying information-seeking is verification or enhancement. It is this confound that explains why much of the empirical work addressing the self-verification motive has focused on verification of negative characteristics (e.g., Swann, Wenzlaff, Krull, & Pelham, 1992).

The three classes of self-evaluation motives are widely held in the human population and are currently adaptive (Sedikides & Strube, 1995, 1997). The naturalistic fallacy notwithstanding, we propose that the current adaptiveness of the motives constitutes a legitimate basis for exploring the possibility that the motives evolved in response to environmental pressures. More specifically, we consider the three classes of self-evaluation motives as secondary adaptations. We hypothesize that the role of these motives was to promote the adaptive value of the symbolic self and, in the long run, to better an individual's standing in the group, thus maximizing the chances for the individual's survival.

Furthermore, we assume that the motives were modular and domain specific. That is, the motives served specific adaptive purposes in response to specific environmental problems (Buss, 1996). We propose that the motives evolved in response to individual-level and group-level adaptive problems and that the motives served cognitive, affective, and behavioral functions. At the same time, we assume interactive relations among the motives, and we will discuss a theoretical model that explicates these interactive relations.

Exactly when these motives began to serve the symbolic self is difficult to determine. Given that we have previously speculated that the symbolic self began to emerge in *Homo erectus*, it seems reasonable to hypothesize that the self-evaluation motives also began to emerge in that species. As we noted in Sedikides and Skowronski (1997), the *Homo erectus* species shows evidence of a large and differentiated brain and a speech production anatomy that could potentially concoct relatively elaborate vocalizations. However, neither of these was comparable to the more evolved anatomy of *Homo sapiens*. Furthermore, concrete evidence for symbolic thought (e.g., art, ornamentation) in the fossil record does not appear until after the emergence of *Homo sapiens*, with the possible exception of stone tools. Hence, perhaps it would be best to consider *Homo erectus* as the earliest possible species in which the symbolic self, and its associated motives, emerged.

Of course, there is no reason to believe that the symbolic self and its associated motives emerged fully formed. Instead, it is probably the case that the motives emerged gradually with the evolution of *Homo sapiens* and *Homo sapiens sapiens*. Given the importance of affect to human existence, it is reasonable to speculate that the valuation motives evolved first, followed by the learning and homeostatic motives. Furthermore, the motives may have initially emerged at the preconscious level and only later became a target of conscious awareness as the reflexive capacity of the symbolic self evolved. In fact, it is possible that our present treatise is mostly relevant to *Homo sapiens sapiens* rather than its predecessors. These are caveats of which we are aware, but we will not address them in the present chapter. Instead, we will proceed with our quixotic quest into the evolutionary utility of the self-evaluation motives.

Valuation Motives

There are numerous adaptive benefits that could have accrued from the presence of the valuation motives. Valuation motives can interact with the executive aspect of the self to affect choice-making activities. For example, valuation motives can lead individuals to avoid tasks with a high risk of failure (and hence, a threat to the symbolic self) and to select tasks on which success is likely (hence, bolstering the symbolic self). Of course, mere success may not have been the only criterion for task selection—it may also have been the case that maximum benefit for the symbolic self could have been obtained by selecting tasks that included an optimum combination of challenge and success probability. Protection or augmentation of the self could have been further achieved by the interaction of these valuation motives with the representational and reflexive aspects of the symbolic self: forgetting failures and remembering successes, making self-serving inferences and attributions, holding beliefs about the relative superiority of the self compared to other group members, engaging in downward social comparisons, and presenting the self advantageously to others. These strategies probably served affective functions, most directly the maintenance or enhancement of the individual's self-esteem. More specifically, the self-protection motive probably operated to maintain self-esteem, whereas the self-enhancement motive probably operated to heighten self-esteem.

Some measure of self-esteem seems to facilitate adaptive functioning: A relatively high level of self-esteem is associated with active engagement in everyday activities, planning, an optimistic attitude, improved coping, better psychological health (e.g., lower depression, anxiety, and loneliness), and better physical health (Ryff & Singer, 1998; Taylor & Brown, 1988). From an evolutionary perspective, one might surmise that some measure of self-esteem was necessary for an individual to initiate attempts at reproductive activity. It is also reasonable to guess that an individual who had some measure of self-esteem had heightened appeal as a mate, thus improving the individual's chances of reproductive success. A happy, active, confident partner is an attractive partner.

However, this enhanced reproductive success may have occurred, in part, because it aided the individual in interactions with other group members. That is, the relatively high self-esteem promoted by the valuation motives may have facilitated both dyadic interactions and group-level interactions. A relatively high level of self-esteem can work to make an individual a more effective group member. For example, others in a group may view an individual with high self-esteem as a safe bet for the accomplishment of important group-wide tasks. He or she could be trusted to assume posts of increased responsibility within the group hierarchy. Hence, a reasonably high level of individual self-esteem may have maximized opportunities for advancement in the group hierarchy and minimized the possibility of social exclusion. Both of these outcomes could have improved an individual's chances for reproductive success in several ways. First, high group status was probably associated with successful mating. Second, the offspring of high-status individuals were probably less likely to be neglected by the group as a result of social exclusion.

Some theorists have argued that natural selection operates not only at the individual level, but also at the group level (Wilson, 1998; Wilson & Sober, 1994). If this idea is credible, (and we note that it is, currently, controversial), it may also contribute to the present argument. For example, one can also make a reasonable argument that, in the long run, the group itself benefited from the action of the valuation motives to produce relatively high self-esteem in group members. This high self-esteem could have promoted a high group activity level, a sense of group purpose and direction, and an aura of group optimism and morale, as well as the illusion of group cohesiveness under decisive leadership. Also, such high self-esteem could have made the group more effective in intra- and interspecies competitive encounters. High individual self-esteem in group members allows the group to engage effectively in both careful, protective planning (e.g., maintaining a climate of vigilance to thwart the possibility of hostile actions from others groups) and bold endeavors (e.g., daring hunting and gathering expeditions in the face of imminent danger from antagonistic groups), as needed.

Learning Motives

We have argued that the learning motives of self-assessment and self-improvement serve to clarify and enrich the symbolic self. These could have been adaptive to human ancestor species members in several ways. The self-assessment motive could have contributed to the clarification of the representational aspect of the symbolic self via the executive aspect of the self. That is, individuals could have been motivated to pursue, choose, and construct tasks that were high rather than low in diagnosticity with respect to an underlying capacity. Because such high-diagnosticity tasks have the potential to provide a definitive test of whether the organism possesses an underlying capacity (a conclusion that is added to an individual's self-representational structure), they allow efficiency in later choices and time allocations.

For example, individuals may have deliberately selected tasks within particular domains (e.g., hunting, gathering, or child-rearing duties) that presented a challenge, that tested their abilities to perform within the domain. One result of such tests could have been increased veridicality of self-conceptions. This result has adaptive consequences. Individuals can use veridical self-knowledge in task planning to place themselves in environments whose demands match their abilities well, thus optimizing individual (and perhaps group) success. Hence, if an individual discovers that he or she has a good knack for discovering and gathering food, it would seem to be beneficial to both him- or herself and to the group to exploit this ability to its fullest.

Alternatively, if the results of high-diagnosticity tasks reveal that there is a deficiency in an area, then two courses of action are plausible. The first is the allocation of an individual's time to alternative pursuits. For example, an individual who is deficient at child-watching might be shifted to food gathering. In the second course of action, the self-improvement motive may be activated. Activation of this motive could prompt the individual to find ways to improve, such as engaging in practice, information gathering, and technological innovation. To the extent that these attempts at improvement were successful, they could have promoted individual and group fitness. For example, by becoming a better hunter, not only the individual, but also the whole group, may benefit. By aiding both themselves and the group, self-assessing and self-improving individuals could have enhanced their own reproductive fitness relative to a nonassessing and nonimproving counterpart.

The learning motives and their effects on the symbolic self could have increased the adaptiveness of the group, as well. For example, the learning motives were probably beneficial to group life. The self-assessment motive can promote the smooth functioning of the group, as its members gain a genuine knowledge of their hierarchical standing and of others' expectations of them. Furthermore, individuals can use veridical self-knowledge (e.g., accurate knowledge of their abilities) to place themselves in suitable and appropriate positions in the social hierarchy, thus minimizing disadvantageous conflict with conspecifics. For example, an individual with high social intelligence may effectively occupy the leader or counselor position in the group. Moreover, the self-improvement motive can increase the group's chances for survival by promoting trying. That is, the self-improvement motive can prompt the group to be persistent in its efforts to master challenges (e.g., increase the status of the group compared to groups of conspecifics) and create new ones (e.g., expand to new territory).

Finally, we propose that the learning motives may have served critical cognitive and affective functions for group members. For one thing, the self-assessment motive may have acted to reduce an individual's uncertainty about aspects of the self and aspects of the social or physical environment. In addition, the self-improvement motive could have worked to elevate an individual's sense of progress. This two-step benefit (i.e., a sense of self-certainty and progress-making) facilitates positive feelings of personal adjustment.

Homeostatic Motives

We have argued that the homeostatic motive of self-verification serves to stabilize the representational aspect of the self. The self-verification motive contributes to the stabilization of the self by numerous executive strategies that work toward the confirmation of existing self-views. These executive strategies include direction of attention to self-confirming information, bias in rehearsal and recall, solicitation of self-confirming feedback, biased interpretation of ambiguous feedback, biased causal inferences, and the prompting of self-confirming behavior.

We hypothesize that our hominid ancestors selected tasks (e.g., hunting, gathering, child-rearing) that were likely to confirm their preexisting competence beliefs. Furthermore, we think that the confirmation of self-attributes provided by these tasks rendered the social milieu more predictable and served the affective function of increasing feelings of control over the environment. This, in turn, cultivated a sense of personal efficacy.

Such a sense of efficacy can be highly adaptive. Using such feelings of efficacy, an individual can make wise decisions about energy expenditure and can set goals that are congruent with the content of the symbolic self. This sense of efficacy can also be used to shift behavior so that it comes to be consistent with those goals. This pattern maximizes outcome success and, in the long run, reproductive fitness.

In addition, self-verification could have brought about favorable consequences for group life. Knowing his or her limitations, an individual may have sought and received confirming feedback from group members regarding social standing, roles expected from her or him, and the relative success with which these roles were carried out. This confirming feedback could have helped the individual to avoid the waste of energy that might accompany pursuit of a goal that is incompatible with group goals. Furthermore, this confirming feedback had may have had affective consequences: It could have produced feelings of satisfaction and allowed the individual to avoid negative emotions (e.g., shame, guilt, and embarrassment). Moreover, the confirming feedback may have contributed to a stable internal structure of group governance and to the solidification of acquired resources (e.g., territory).

THE PROCESS OF SELF-EVALUATION: AN INTEGRATIVE VIEW

It would appear from our discussion so far that the self-evaluation motives and their corresponding functions would, more often than not, be in a state of friction. Would an individual be more likely to self-enhance or to self-assess? Would an individual opt to self-improve or to self-verify? Would an individual opt for self-esteem elevation or for uncertainty reduction? Would an individual opt for a sense of progress and growth or for a sense of control and predictability?

We propose that the self-evaluation motives did not operate independently in the prehistoric environment. Instead, the motives were dynamically interrelated and served complementary purposes. Furthermore, we propose that friction among the motives was the exception rather than the rule.

More concretely, we postulate that the self-evaluation process was carried out chiefly through the valuation motives (Sedikides & Strube, 1997). To elaborate on this point, we distinguish between two types of self-enhancement, candid and tactical. *Candid self-enhancement* refers to flagrant attempts on the part of the individual to increase the positivity of the self-concept or to decrease its negativity. This type of self-enhancement is achieved either through brute self-aggrandization (e.g., ostentatious display of one's physical prowess) or through denial of clear wrongdoing (e.g., being caught subverting the dominance ranks). *Tactical self-enhancement* refers to indirect attempts to increase the positivity of the self or decrease its negativity. This type of self-enhancement is carried out through the learning and

homeostatic motives. Its mannerisms are subtle, mindful of the balance between immediate and delayed rewards, and sensitive to social context.

We propose that the affective functions served by the self-evaluation
motives followed a similar pattern. We have argued that self-enhancement
increased self-esteem, that self-verification gave way to feelings of control,
that self-assessment reduced uncertainty, and that self-improvement instilled a sense of progress. However, we do not view control, certainty, and
a sense of progress as functions that the organism would necessarily seek for
their own sake. Rather, these functions were critical to individuals because
they were linked to the more basic desire for self-enhancement.

In addition, we argue that the self-evaluation process consisted of two
components: information and action. The information component referred
to the generation, refinement, and testing of hypotheses concerning the
quality of the person–environment fit (e.g., "Am I strong enough to over-
throw the higher-ranking group member?" "Can I hunt effectively with the
weapons that I have?" "How can I use better child-rearing methods?"). This
information reflects the extent to which the attributes or abilities of the individual match the demands of a given situation. The data that result from
the information component can be used to carry out candid and, more often,
tactical self-enhancement through action (e.g., coalition-building for bringing about change in the dominance hierarchy, striving to improve existing
weapons or child-rearing practices). Thus, the action component pertains
primarily to opportunistic responses to existing conditions or to the strategic creation of new conditions that could yield beneficial outcomes or by-
pass harmful ones.

Information and action are interdependent. In the prehistoric environment, to the extent that information about person–environment fit was
veridical, likely to lead to improvement, and verifying of self-views, resulting actions were likely to be successful. Success was more likely because the
individual was in a position to deliberately guide the creation of performance settings or to effectively manage the reaction to them; thus, the outcome was more self-enhancing than a less informed action. Likewise, the
success of action probably provided crucial feedback about the validity of
the action, the rate of improvement in behavior, and the verifying value of
the information on which it was based.

When self-enhancement was carried out effectively through the information and action components (i.e., when the person–environment fit was
successful), self-esteem, control, certainty, and a sense of progress would have
been heightened for the individual. When this happened, the individual
would have experienced the emotion of happiness. That is, we propose that
the emotion of happiness would be produced when the organism fit environmental requirements and was also challenged adequately. Additionally, happiness can signal to the organism the effective operation of feedback loops
among motives. For example, consider the case in which self-assessment

leads to the reduction of uncertainty, which itself sets the stage for self-improvement. In turn, self-improvement, the outcome of successful learning, instills a sense of progress that increases perceptions of control. This fuels organismic activity, giving way to the elevation of self-esteem. The resulting emotion is happiness. In summary, we speculate that one of the functions that happiness came to serve was as the overflow emotion, a check that the motives and their functions were in symbiotic relation with each other.

In our view, then, self-esteem consequences were probably the most immediate outcomes of the self-enhancement process and provided the essential gauge regarding the utility of the individual's actions for the group (e.g., Did the group approve of the organism? Should the organism persist along the same path or redirect action instead? See Leary, Tambor, Terdal, & Downs, 1995). However, under some circumstances, striving for immediate self-esteem gains may have often been a less-than-optimal adaptive response. Although we believe that the typical state of affairs was for the self-evaluation motives underlying the information and action components to work together, it is also the case that these could have occasionally been working at cross-purposes. What happened when these motives were in conflict? In these cases, which motive was likely to "win?"

It makes sense that the continued activation of a particular motive depended, in part, on the type of existing information available. For example, when the individual was highly certain about the possession of an attribute, then gathering additional diagnostic information would not be efficient. Thus, in this situation, the self-assessment motive would not be activated or would not be powerful. Instead, the self-verification motive would emerge as the more powerful of the two motives, and behavior designed to confirm the attribute in question clearly would be the more likely response. This self-verification would help the individual to resist unwarranted changes in self-knowledge, thus maintaining the integrity of the self-concept. Conversely, in the absence of certainty about a given attribute, neither the self-assessment nor the self-improvement motive would be more powerful. Instead, both of these motives can prompt the individual to master the contingencies necessary for informed and fruitful transactions with the social environment. However, even under these circumstances, the long-term demands for veridical, improving, and positively verifying information might dictate that unflattering information about the self (i.e., nonenhancing or verifying of negative attributes—e.g., "I can't do this") be uncovered or disclosed in the short run. As is often said, the first step to rectifying a problem is the admission that a problem exists, and that initial admission is often emotionally costly.

More generally, we hypothesize that the activation of a particular motive relative to others depends on the trade-off between the worth of the veridical (i.e., high diagnosticity) information and its emotional costs (Strube, 1990). For example, what if negative information about a person's capabilities pertained to an important domain (e.g., being terrible at crucial gathering or hunting tasks)? In this case, admitting to the veridicality of the information could bring about unbearable affective consequences (e.g., depression to the effect of malfunctioning). Conversely, neglecting the information via dismissal, denial, or even self-deception could allow the individual to function effectively in daily tasks (e.g., by focusing attention on and sharpening alternate skills) but could also cause other irreparable damage (e.g., eventual social exclusion). In this case, a pragmatic cost–benefit analysis may have been required before an individual opted to be influenced by either the self-protection motive or the self-assessment and self-improvement motives.

Another consideration is the possibility that the organism's response was contingent on the modifiability of the attribute under consideration (Dunning, 1995). That is, an individual might be predisposed to accept high diagnosticity feedback regarding skills that are thought to be modifiable through practice, and his or her self-improvement motive would clearly be applicable in this circumstance. However, the individual might have opted to pursue self-protection when attributes were thought to be unmodifiable. The relative worth of information, as perceived by the organism, might also have been contingent on the organism's affective state. For example, if the individual's self-esteem had suffered a recent blow, the individual may be particularly attuned to the immediate needs for self-protection and thus would avoid high diagnosticity, but negative, information.

The utility of the various motives in responding to challenges in the person–environment fit can also depend on the availability of cognitive resources (Paulhus, 1993; Swann, Hixon, Stein-Seroussi, & Gilbert, 1990). For example, sometimes the external challenge to one of our ancestors (e.g., a public provocation by other group members) may have required an expedient response. In such cases, a deliberate analysis of the situation may have had deleterious consequences for the individual, as the others threatened immediate action. Instead, candid self-enhancement (e.g., display of physical prowess, vocal denial of the charges, verbal attack of the offensive opponent) would take precedence. At other times, as when the external challenge was amenable to a delayed response (planning to replace an ineffective leader), tactical self-enhancement (e.g., emphasizing one's ability to self-assess and self-improve) may have been a more appropriate motivation.

It is likely that other features of the social context were also crucial determinants of candid versus tactical self-enhancement. For example, tactical self-enhancement would be the more sensible alternative when one was accountable for her or his behavior to other group members or when one's behavior was easily verifiable by others (Felson, 1993). Tactical self-enhancement would also be the more adaptive response when one presented the self to closely affiliated others. Interpersonal closeness might have inhibited candid self-enhancement because, given their familiarity with the individual's record, close others limit the individual's opportunities to engage in self-aggrandization (Sedikides, Campbell, Reeder, & Elliot,

1998; Tice, Butler, Muraven, & Stillwell, 1995). Alternatively, the individual may not be self-serving in interactions with close others because of kin selection pressures. This form of cooperation refers to altruistic behavior toward kin that results in their having a selective advantage (Hamilton, 1964).

In the cases described so far, we have treated the results of the antagonistic competition among self-evaluative motives very simply: One motive remains active while the others are suppressed. Of course, this suppression need not be permanent. Instead, an individual may prioritize motives and choose to pursue one course of action immediately while planning to satisfy the other motive at a later date. For example, we have argued that the symbolic self was embedded in a social context and was defined with reference to that context. Accordingly, pursuit of the candid self-enhancement motives cannot proceed without restraint: An individual needs to also be concerned about the feedback that is received from others. Although an individual might act selfishly from time to time, in a social context, consistently selfish behavior is likely to bring social approbation, leading to negative affect. Hence, an individual might delay the implementation of selfish motives until more appropriate circumstances are available (e.g., one can execute a selfish behavior without being seen).

Other situations may have similarly involved a conflict between candid self-enhancement objectives and long-term tactical self-enhancement objectives. For example, because it denotes acceptance of another individual's superiority, willingly giving up control to a more powerful group member may seem maladaptive. However, control relinquishment may have been an effective (i.e., conflict-free) strategy for satisfying long-term objectives (e.g., gaining acceptance; see Rothbaum, Weisz, & Snyder, 1982). Likewise, expressing pessimism for one's impending performance may have appeared self-defeating, but this strategy safeguarded the individual against the debilitating effects of anxiety and thus maximized the achievement of long-term self-enhancing objectives (e.g., task success; see Norem & Cantor, 1986).

SELF-EVALUATION MOTIVES GONE AWRY

We have argued that self-evaluation motives served critical functions and contributed substantially to our human ancestors' ability to adapt to their environment. Undoubtedly, though, there were instances of malfunctioning in motive operation. This observation is not threatening to our evolutionary argument. As is illustrated by the example of sickle-cell anemia, adaptations that increase overall species fitness in a particular environment can have negative consequences for specific individuals or can be maladaptive under different environmental circumstances.

Nonetheless, it is useful to consider some of the ways in which the motives that serve the symbolic self go awry. Of course, one way in which these motives can go awry is when they become too powerful and overly dominate the thoughts, actions, and emotions of individuals. For example, excessive pursuit of self-enhancement could ultimately be nonadaptive, as it could lead the organism to take unnecessary risks (Baumeister, Heatherton, & Tice, 1993). Excessive pursuit of self-protection (e.g., denial) could temporarily maintain psychological health, but it could also render the individual incapable of meeting long-term challenges by causing individuals to avoid potentially useful feedback. Additionally, excessive pursuit of both self-enhancement and self-protection would probably alienate the individual from other group members, because they would make negative inferences about the individual. Among these inferences would be that the individual was conceited, uncooperative, and hostile (Baumeister, Smart, & Boden, 1996) and, hence, unfit for group life. Because group life seemed to be an adaptive trait for human ancestral species members, exclusion from the group would have reduced the reproductive fitness of the excluded individual.

Likewise, the excessive action of the learning and homeostatic motives could have disastrous repercussions for the individual and also for the group. An excessive emphasis on self-assessment could obstruct, if not paralyze, individual and group action. An excessive emphasis on self-improvement could pose strenuous demands on the individual and create an unduly competitive group environment. In the same vein, an excessive emphasis on self-verification would undermine the dynamism of the individual and would reinforce apathy at both the individual and group level. An overemphasis on self-improvement might be similarly counterproductive, causing individuals to waste time attempting to improve skills that are already near enough to optimum levels that continued improvement would not significantly increase the survival and reproduction chances of the individual or group.

Of course, insufficient exercise of the motives could also have had deleterious consequences. An individual engaging in suboptimal self-enhancement or self-protection could place the self at risk for psychopathology. In addition, the individual could be seen as a meek and dysfunctional group member, one that lacks potential; a demotion in group ranks would be a likely outcome of the development of such perceptions. Similar social disapprobation, and consequent lowered reproductive fitness, is a likely result of deficiencies in the operation of the other self-evaluation motives. Insufficient pursuit of self-assessment or self-improvement could cause an individual to be viewed as an unproductive group member, lowering his or her social rank. Insufficient pursuit of self-verification could result in apparently inconsistent behaviors. This would cause the individual to be perceived as inconsistent, unreliable, and untrustworthy. Obviously (current American politicians notwithstanding), these individuals would tend to be low in social rank in the group.

In summary, we speculate that nonoptimal action of the self-evaluation motives, either excessive action or insufficient action, probably proved costly to human ancestor species members. We further speculate that this nonoptimal activity contributed to a weak, uncertain, and confused symbolic self; inhibited good person–environment fit; and hampered the harmony of group life. Interactive relations among the motives exacerbated these costs: Malfunction of any given motive had the potential to block the feedback loops among the motives. Disarray of the self-system would be the result.

CONCLUSION

In previous work (Sedikides & Skowronski, 1997; Skowronski & Sedikides, 1999), we argued for the symbolic self as an evolutionary adaptation. In the present chapter, we have further advanced our thinking by advocating the thesis that three classes of self-evaluation motives—valence, learning, and homeostatic—were secondary adaptations that evolved to facilitate the smooth functioning of the symbolic self.

We argue that the self-evaluation motives served specialized cognitive and affective functions and that these motives evolved in response to specific environmental challenges. We conceptualize the motives as innate learning modules (Pinker, 1997). At the same time, we are obligated to express skepticism for this view, because we are as yet unable to provide credible neuroanatomical evidence for this proposition.

Despite the domain specificity of the self-evaluation motives, we also argue for their dynamic interplay. This idea is consistent with the speculations of some anthropologists who argue that the mind of our evolutionary ancestors (starting with *Homo erectus*) was characterized by the constant flow of knowledge among the various modules making up the mind. Cognitive fluidity was the norm rather than the exception (Mithen, 1996). Through its reflexive and executive capacity, the symbolic self could have constantly regulated the emergence, suppression, or synergistic action of the motives.

We hope that our speculative exposition into the evolutionary origins and functions of the self-evaluation motives will eventually be supplemented by empirical evidence. Research validating the notion that the motives are secondary adaptations will need to clarify the operations of the motives (e.g., What are the conditions that trigger the activation of each motive? What are the rules that govern motive interplay?) and to document the specific evolutionary problems that were solved by the evolution of the motives.

REFERENCES

Baumeister, R. F. (1998). The self. In D. T. Gilbert, S. T. Fiske, & G. Lindzey (Eds.), *The handbook of social psychology* (Vol. 1, pp. 680–740). New York: Oxford University Press.

Baumeister, R. F., Heatherton, T. F., & Tice, D. M. (1993). When ego threats lead to self-regulation failure: Negative consequences of high self-esteem. *Journal of Personality and Social Psychology, 64,* 141–156.

Baumeister, R. F., Smart, L., & Boden, J. M. (1996). Relation of threatened egotism to violence and aggression: The dark side of high self-esteem. *Psychological Review, 103,* 5–33.

Belk, R. W. (1988). Possessions and the extended self. *Journal of Consumer Research, 15,* 139–168.

Breckler, S. J., & Greenwald, A. G. (1986). Motivational facets of the self. In R. M. Sorrentino & E. T. Higgins (Eds.), *Handbook of motivation and cognition: Foundations of social behavior* (Vol. 1, pp. 145–164). New York: Guilford Press.

Brown, J. D., & Dutton, K. A. (1995). Truth and consequences: The costs and benefits of accurate self-knowledge. *Personality and Social Psychology Bulletin, 21,* 1288–1296.

Buss, D. M. (1996). The evolutionary psychology of human social strategies. In E. T. Higgins & A. W. Kruglanski (Eds.), *Social psychology: Handbook of basic principles* (pp. 3–38). New York: Guilford Press.

Cantor, N., Markus, H., Niedenthal, P., & Nurius, P. (1986). On motivation and the self-concept. In R. M. Sorrentino & E. T. Higgins (Eds.), *Motivation and cognition: Foundations of social behavior* (pp. 96–127). New York: Guilford Press.

Caporael, L. R. (1997). The evolution of truly social cognition: The core configurations model. *Personality and Social Psychology Review, 1,* 276–298.

Caporael, L. R., & Brewer, M. B. (1991). Reviving evolutionary psychology: Biology meets society. *Journal of Social Issues, 47,* 187–195.

Carver, C. S., & Scheier, M. F. (1990). Principles of self-regulation: Action and emotion. In E. T. Higgins & R. M. Sorrentino (Eds.), *Handbook of motivation and cognition: Foundations of social behavior* (Vol. 2, pp. 3–52). New York: Guilford Press.

Cheyney, D. L., & Seyfarth, R. M. (1992). Precis of how monkeys see the world. *Behavioral and Brain Sciences, 15,* 135–182.

Dunbar, R. I. M. (1992). Neocortex size as a constraint on group size in humans. *Journal of Human Evolution, 20,* 469–493.

Dunbar, R. I. M. (1993). Coevolution of neocortical size, group size, and language in humans. *Behavioral and Brain Sciences, 16,* 681–735.

Dunning, D. (1995). Trait importance and modifiability as factors influencing self-assessment and self-enhancement motives. *Personality and Social Psychology Bulletin, 21,* 1297–1306.

Emmons, R. A. (1989). The personal striving approach to personality. In L. A. Pervin (Ed.), *Goal concepts in personality and social psychology* (pp. 87–126). Hillsdale, NJ: Erlbaum.

Fazio, R. H., Effrein, E. A., & Falender, V. J. (1981). Self-perceptions following social interactions. *Journal of Personality and Social Psychology, 41*, 232–242.

Felson, R. B. (1993). The (somewhat) social self: How others affect self-appraisals. In J. Suls (Ed.), *Psychological perspectives on the self* (Vol. 4, pp. 1–26). Hillsdale, NJ: Erlbaum.

Fox, R. (1980). *The red lamp of incest.* New York: Dutton.

Gallup, G. G., Jr. (1992). Levels, limits and precursors to self-recognition: Does ontogeny recapitulate phylogeny? *Psychological Inquiry, 3*, 117–118.

Gallup, G. G., Jr., & Suarez, S. D. (1986). Self-awareness and the emergence of mind in humans and other primates. In J. Suls & A. G. Greenwald (Eds.), *Psychological perspectives on the self* (Vol. 3, pp. 3–26). Hillsdale, NJ: Erlbaum.

Gibson, K. R. (1986). Cognition, brain size, and the extraction of embedded food resources. In J. G. Else & P. C. Lee (Eds.), *Primate ontogeny, cognition and social behavior* (pp. 93–103). Cambridge, England: Cambridge University Press.

Greenwald, A. G. (1980). The totalitarian ego: Fabrication and revision of personal history. *American Psychologist, 35*, 603–618.

Hamilton, W. D. (1964). The genetic evolution of social behavior, Part I and II. *Journal of Theoretical Biology, 7*, 1–52.

Higgins, E. T. (1987). Self-discrepancy: A theory relating self and affect. *Psychological Review, 94*, 319–340.

Higgins, E. T. (1996). The "self-digest": Self-knowledge serving self-regulatory functions. *Journal of Personality and Social Psychology, 71*, 1062–1083.

Hyatt, C. W., & Hopkins, W. D. (1994). Self-awareness in bonobos and chimpanzees: A comparative perspective. In S. T. Parker, R. W. Mitchell, & M. L. Boccia (Eds.), *Self-awareness in animals and humans: Developmental perspectives* (pp. 248–253). New York: Cambridge University Press.

Isaac, G. (1981). Stone age visiting cards: Approaches to the study of early land-use patterns. In I. Hodder, G. Isaac, & N. Hammond (Eds.), *Patterns of the past* (pp. 131–155). Cambridge, England: Cambridge University Press.

Kato, K., & Markus, H. R. (1993). The role of possible selves in memory. *Psychologia: An International Journal of Psychology in the Orient, 36*, 73–83.

Kihlstrom, J. F., & Cantor, N. (1984). Mental representations of the self. In L. Berkowitz (Ed.), *Advances in experimental social psychology* (Vol. 17, pp. 1–47). New York: Academic Press.

Kihlstrom, J. F., & Klein, S. B. (1994). The self as a knowledge structure. In R. S. Wyer, Jr., & T. K. Srull (Eds.), *Handbook of social cognition* (Vol. 1, pp. 153–208). Hillsdale, NJ: Erlbaum.

Kunda, Z. (1990). The case for motivated reasoning. *Psychological Bulletin, 108*, 480–498.

Leary, M. R., & Tambor, E. S., Terdal, S. K., & Downs, D. L. (1995). Self-esteem as an interpersonal monitor: The sociometer hypothesis. *Journal of Personality and Social Psychology, 68*, 518–530.

Lecky, P. (1945). *Self-consistency: A theory of personality.* New York: Island Press.

Lewis, M. (1992). Will the real self or selves stand up? *Psychological Inquiry, 3,* 123–124.

Markus, H. (1983). Self-knowledge: An expanded view. *Journal of Personality, 51,* 543–565.

Markus, H. R., & Kunda, Z. (1986). Stability and malleability of the self-concept. *Journal of Personality and Social Psychology, 51,* 858–866.

Maryanski, A., & Turner, J. H. (1992). *The social cage: Human nature and the evolution of society.* Stanford, CA: Stanford University Press.

McGuire, W. J., McGuire, C. V., & Winton, W. (1979). Effects of household sex composition on the salience of one's gender in the spontaneous self-concept. *Journal of Experimental Social Psychology, 15,* 77–90.

Milton, K. (1988). Foraging behavior and the evolution of primate intelligence. In R. Byrne & A. Whiten (Eds.), *Machiavellian intelligence: Social expertise and the evolution of intellect in monkeys, apes and humans* (pp. 285–305). Oxford, England: Oxford University Press.

Mithen, S. (1996). *The prehistory of the mind: The cognitive origins of art, religion, and science.* London: Thames & Hudson.

Norem, J. K., & Cantor, N. (1986). Anticipatory and post hoc cushioning strategies: Optimism and defensive pessimism in "risky" situations. *Cognitive Therapy and Research, 10,* 347–362.

Paulhus, D. L. (1993). Bypassing the will: The automatization of affirmations. In D. M. Wegner & J. M. Pennebaker (Eds.), *Handbook of mental control* (pp. 573–587). Englewood Cliffs, NJ: Prentice-Hall.

Pinker, S. (1997). *How the mind works.* New York: Norton.

Rothbaum, F., Weisz, J. R., & Snyder, S. S. (1982). Changing the world and changing the self: A two-process model of perceived control. *Journal of Personality and Social Psychology, 42,* 5–37.

Ryff, C. D., & Singer, B. (1998). The contours of positive human health. *Psychological Inquiry, 9,* 1–28.

Sedikides, C., Campbell, W. K., Reeder, G., & Elliot, A. J. (1998). The self-serving bias in relational context. *Journal of Personality and Social Psychology, 74,* 378–386.

Sedikides, C., & Skowronski, J. J. (1993). The self in impression formation: Trait centrality and social perception. *Journal of Experimental Social Psychology, 29,* 347–357.

Sedikides, C., & Skowronski, J. J. (1995). On the sources of self-knowledge: The perceived primacy of self-reflection. *Journal of Social & Clinical Psychology, 14,* 244–270.

Sedikides, C., & Skowronski, J. J. (1997). The symbolic self in evolutionary context. *Personality and Social Psychology Review, 1,* 80–102.

Sedikides, C., & Strube, M. J. (1995). The multiply motivated self. *Personality and Social Psychology Bulletin, 21,* 1330–1335.

Sedikides, C., & Strube, M. J. (1997). Self-evaluation: To thine own self be good, to thine own self be sure, to thine own self be true, and to thine own self be better. In M. P. Zanna (Ed.), *Advances in experimental social psychology* (Vol. 29, 209–269. New York: Academic Press.

Showers, C. (1992). Compartmentalization of positive and negative self-knowledge: Keeping bad apples out of the bunch. *Journal of Personality and Social Psychology, 62,* 1036–1049.

Shrauger, J. S., & Schoeneman, T. J. (1979). Symbolic interactionist view of the self-concept: Through the looking glass darkly. *Psychological Bulletin, 86,* 549–573.

Skowronski, J. J., & Carlston, D. E. (1982). Effects of previously experienced outcomes on the desire for choice. *Journal of Personality and Social Psychology, 43,* 689–701.

Skowronski, J. J., & Sedikides, C. (1999). Evolution of the symbolic self. In D. H. Rosen & M. C. Luebbert (Eds.), *Evolution of the psyche* (pp. 78–94). Westport, CT: Greenwood Publishing.

Strube, M. J. (1990). In search of self: Balancing the good and the true. *Personality and Social Psychology Bulletin, 16,* 699–704.

Strube, M. J., & Roemmele, L. A. (1985). Self-enhancement, self-assessment, and self-evaluative task choice. *Journal of Personality and Social Psychology, 49,* 981–993.

Suarez, S. D., & Gallup, G. G., Jr. (1981). Self-recognition in chimpanzees and orangutans, but not gorillas. *Journal of Human Evolution, 10,* 175–188.

Swann, W. B. (1983). Self-verification: Bringing social reality into harmony with the self. In J. Suls & A. G. Greenwald (Eds.), *Psychological perspectives on the self* (Vol. 2, pp. 33–66). Hillsdale, NJ: Erlbaum.

Swann, W. B. (1990). To be adored or to be known? The interplay of self-enhancement and self-verification. In E. T. Higgins & R. M. Sorrentino (Eds.), *Handbook of motivation and cognition: Foundations of social behavior* (Vol. 2, pp. 408–448). New York: Guilford Press.

Swann, W. B., Jr., Hixon, J. G., Stein-Seroussi, A., & Gilbert, D. T. (1990). The fleeting gleam of praise: Cognitive processes underlying behavioral reactions to self-relevant feedback. *Journal of Personality and Social Psychology, 59,* 17–26.

Swann, W. B., Wenzlaff, R. M., Krull, D. S., & Pelham, B. W. (1992). Allure of negative feedback: Self-verification strivings among depressed persons. *Journal of Abnormal Psychology, 101,* 293–306.

Tanner, N. M. (1983). Hunters, gatherers, and sex roles in space and time. *American Anthropologist, 85,* 335–341.

Taylor, S. E., & Brown, J. D. (1988). Illusion and well-being: A social psychological perspective on mental health. *Psychological Bulletin, 103,* 193–210.

Taylor, S. E., Neter, E., & Wayment, H. A. (1995). Self-evaluation process. *Personality & Social Psychology Bulletin, 21,* 1278–1287.

Taylor, S. E., Wayment, H. A., & Carrillo, M. (1996). Social comparison, self-regulation, and motivation. In R. M. Sorrentino & E. T. Higgins (Eds.), *Handbook of motivation and cognition* (Vol. 3, pp. 3–27). New York: Guilford Press.

Tesser, A. (1988). Toward a self-evaluation maintenance model of social behavior. In L. Berkowitz (Ed.), *Advances in experimental social psychology* (Vol. 21, pp. 181–227). New York: Academic Press.

Thompson, C. P., Skowronski, J. J., Larsen, S. F., & Betz, A. (1996). *Autobiographical memory: Remembering what and remembering when.* Mahwah, NJ: Erlbaum.

Tice, D. M, Butler, J. L., Muraven, M. B., & Stillwell, A. M. (1995). When modesty prevails: Differential favorability of self-presentation to friends and strangers. *Journal of Personality and Social Psychology, 69,* 1120–1138.

Tooby, J., & DeVore, I. (1987). The reconstruction of hominid behavioral evolution through strategic modeling. In W. G. Kinzey (Ed.), *The evolution of human behavior* (pp. 183–237). New York: State University of New York Press.

Trope, Y. (1983). Self-assessment in achievement behavior. In J. M. Suls & A. G. Greenwald (Eds.), *Psychological perspectives on the self* (Vol. 2, pp. 93–121). Hillsdale, NJ: Erlbaum.

Trope, Y. (1986). Self-enhancement and self-assessment in achievement behavior. In R. M. Sorrentino & E. T. Higgins (Eds.), *Handbook of motivation and cognition: Foundations of social behavior* (Vol. 1, pp. 350–378). New York: Guilford Press.

Wilson, D. S. (1998). Hunting, sharing, and multilevel selection: The tolerated-theft model revisited. *Current Anthropology, 39,* 73–97.

Wilson, D. S., & Sober, E. (1994). Reintroducing group selection to the human behavioral sciences. *Behavioral and Brain Sciences, 17,* 585–654.

5

AN UPDATE ON COGNITIVE DISSONANCE THEORY, WITH A FOCUS ON THE SELF

EDDIE HARMON-JONES

Cognitive dissonance theory (Festinger, 1957) has enjoyed a long history in social psychology, and a rich body of research has tested and supported its central propositions (see Harmon-Jones & Mills, 1999a, for a recent update). Beginning in the 1960s, theorists began to propose revisions to the original theory, and several of these emphasized the importance of the self in dissonance processes. Within the past few years, research has questioned these revisions. In this chapter, I briefly review the original theory and its paradigmatic research and review the revisions of the original theory that emphasized the role of the self.[1] Then I discuss recent research that has

I would like to thank Richard Felson, Cindy Harmon-Jones, Jerry Suls, and Abraham Tesser for providing useful comments and suggestions on this chapter.

[1]The present discussion will be limited to revisions that propose that cognitive dissonance evokes an aversive motivational state and that the cognitive and behavioral changes that result from dissonance are genuine, because the bulk of the evidence supports these propositions. Revisions that do not support the proposals—impression management theory and self-perception theory—have been seriously challenged within recent years (for a recent review, see Harmon-Jones & Mills, 1999b).

challenged these revisions and offer a possible resolution to the inconsistencies between the theories. Finally, I present a recently proposed action-based model of cognitive dissonance, which considers the possible adaptive functions of the arousal and reduction of cognitive dissonance and which suggests that dissonance theory is concerned with self-regulation and executive function.

THE ORIGINAL VERSION OF COGNITIVE DISSONANCE THEORY

The original statement of cognitive dissonance theory (Festinger, 1957) held that cognitive discrepancy creates psychological discomfort that motivates individuals to attempt to reduce or eliminate the discrepancy between cognitions. According to the theory, cognition is defined rather broadly as an element of knowledge and, hence, attitudes, beliefs, and feelings about oneself, others, or the environment are cognitions. Cognitions can be relevant or irrelevant to each other, and if they are relevant, they can be consonant or dissonant with one another. Cognitions are dissonant (i.e., discrepant) if one cognition does not logically or psychologically follow from the other cognition, and they are consonant if one cognition follows from the other. To determine the magnitude of dissonance, a cognition must first be designated as a generative cognition (Beauvois & Joule, 1996). The generative cognition is the cognition that serves as the standard with which other relevant cognitions are judged to be consistent (consonant) or inconsistent (dissonant). The magnitude of dissonance is a function of the number of cognitions dissonant and consonant with the generative cognition, with each cognition weighted for its importance. Cognitive discrepancies can be reduced by adding consonant cognitions, subtracting dissonant cognitions, reducing the importance of dissonant cognitions, increasing the importance of consonant cognitions, or by using some combination of these routes. Resistance to change of the cognitions will influence which route of discrepancy reduction is used, with cognitions that are less resistant to change being altered more readily than cognitions that are more resistant to change. Resistance to change is based on the responsiveness of the cognition to reality and on the extent to which the cognition is consonant with many other cognitions. Resistance to change of a behavioral cognitive element depends on the extent of pain or loss that must be endured and the satisfaction obtained from the behavior.

In his writing on dissonance theory, Festinger (1957) referred to dissonance in two ways: (1) as the way in which cognitions are related and (2) and as the emotional–motivational state evoked by the existence of cognitions that are in a dissonant relationship. To clarify the presentation of these concepts, *cognitive discrepancy* will be used to refer to the dissonant relation between cognitions, and *dissonance* will be used to refer to the emotional–motivational state evoked by cognitive discrepancy.

EXPERIMENTAL PARADIGMS

To facilitate the presentation of research, I briefly review the two experimental paradigms that have been most commonly used to test predictions derived from dissonance theory. In each of these paradigms, the availability of the cognitions that serve to make the entire set of relevant cognitions more or less discrepant is manipulated. In the *induced-compliance paradigm*, participants are induced to act contrary to an attitude, and if they are provided few consonant cognitions (few reasons or little justification) for doing so, they are hypothesized to experience dissonance and be motivated to reduce it. Changing one's attitudes to be consistent with the behavior has served as the most often used measure of discrepancy reduction. In one of the first induced-compliance experiments, Festinger and Carlsmith (1959) paid participants either $1.00 (low justification) or $20 (high justification) to tell a "fellow participant" (confederate) that dull and boring tasks were interesting and exciting. After participants told this to the confederate, they were asked how interesting and enjoyable the tasks were. As predicted, participants given little justification for performing the counterattitudinal behavior rated the tasks as more interesting than did participants given much justification. In later research (Brehm & Cohen, 1962), dissonance was manipulated using perceived choice, assuming that having low choice to behave counterattitudinally is consonant with that behavior, whereas having high choice is not. These experiments revealed that participants who are given high choice, as opposed to low choice, to write counterattitudinal essays changed their attitudes to be more consistent with their behavior.

In the *free-choice paradigm*, participants are asked to choose between two alternatives. After they choose, participants report their attitudes toward the alternatives. The greater the number and importance of the positive aspects of the rejected alternative and the negative aspects of the chosen alternative (i.e., dissonant cognitions) relative to the number and importance of the negative aspects of the rejected alternative and the positive aspects of the chosen alternative (i.e., consonant cognitions), the greater should be the dissonance. To reduce the dissonance, individuals enhance the value of the chosen alternative and reduce the value of the rejected alternative. Brehm (1956) found that women given a choice between two highly desirable consumer products enhanced their ratings of the chosen product and lowered their ratings of the rejected product, whereas women given a choice between a highly desirable and a less desirable product did not.

AN OVERVIEW OF SELF-BASED REVISIONS TO THE ORIGINAL THEORY

Several revisions to the original theory of dissonance have been proposed. Some of the most influential revisions have emphasized aspects of the self as being responsible for effects produced in situations in which dissonance was ostensibly aroused. The following review will focus exclusively on those self theories that have been explicitly concerned with dissonance processes, although other self theories are concerned with similar motivational, emotional, and cognitive consequences of discrepancies between cognitions (see Aronson, 1992, for a discussion).

Self-Consistency

Aronson (1968, 1969, 1992, 1999) has proposed that dissonance results when individuals behave in ways that are inconsistent with their expectancies or beliefs about themselves. Thus, Aronson (1968) proposed that in the Festinger and Carlsmith (1959) experiment, dissonance was aroused by the discrepancy between the cognition that one is honest and the cognition that one misled another person, rather than by the discrepancy between the cognition that the task was dull and the cognition that one said that the task was interesting. Aronson argued that instead of a general need for consistency, individuals possess a specific need for self-consistency. Aronson (1992) proposed that because most individuals have positive self-concepts, dissonance usually involves threats to self-conceptions of rationality (consistent, stable, and predictable sense of self), competence, and morality.

In an interesting new experimental paradigm created by self-consistency theorists (Aronson, 1992; Aronson, Fried, & Stone, 1991; Dickerson, Thibodeau, Aronson, & Miller, 1992; Fried & Aronson, 1995; Stone, Aronson, Crain, Winslow, & Fried, 1994), it has been found that dissonance can occur even when participants engage in proattitudinal behavior that has positive consequences. For instance, Stone et al. (1994) had participants either make a persuasive speech (to be presented to high school students) about AIDS and safer sex in front of a video camera or develop a persuasive message but not deliver the speech to a video camera. The researchers also manipulated the salience of participants' past failures to use condoms (i.e., practice safe sex): Participants were either made aware of their past failures to use condoms by writing about instances where they had failed to do so, or they were not made aware of their past failures. Stone et al. (1994) hypothesized that if participants made the proattitudinal speech and were then made aware of their past failures to practice what they preached, they would experience dissonance and would attempt to reduce their dissonance by modifying their future behavior. Indeed, participants who were induced to feel hypocritical purchased more condoms than did participants in the other conditions. These findings have been interpreted to indicate that an inconsistency between one's behavior and one's self-concept is sufficient to create dissonance.

Fried (1998) recently found that following hypocrisy induction, individuals would change their behaviors to match what they had advocated in a public speech (favoring recycling) only if the reminders of past failures (to recycle) were reported in private. When the reminders of the past failures were reported publicly, individuals changed their attitudes away from their public advocacy instead of changing their behavior to match their advocacy. One interpretation of these results is that when individuals publicly reported their failures to engage in recycling, the cognition about their past failures to recycle became more resistant to change than did the cognition that one had just said that individuals should recycle. Therefore, discrepancy reduction was aimed at supporting the cognition about past failures to recycle and, hence, individuals came to have more negative attitudes toward recycling.

Self-Affirmation Theory

According to the self-affirmation theory revision (e.g., Spencer, Josephs, & Steele, 1993; Steele, 1988; Steele & Liu, 1983; Steele, Spencer, & Lynch, 1993), dissonance effects do not occur because of cognitive discrepancy, but they occur because of the need to maintain an overall image of self-integrity (i.e., moral and adaptive adequacy). Thus, when in situations thought to evoke dissonance, individuals change their attitudes not because of the aversiveness of cognitive discrepancy or even self-inconsistency but because of their need to maintain a positive self-image. That is, freely behaving counterattitudinally or making difficult decisions threatens a positive self-image. According to self-affirmation theory, freely choosing to behave counterattitudinally threatens a positive self-image because the individual realizes he or she has chosen to engage in an action that may produce negative consequences ("I chose to tell the other person that the boring tasks were interesting"). Similarly, making a difficult decision threatens a positive self-image because the negative consequences of the decision (i.e., positive aspects of the rejected decision alternative and negative aspects of the chosen alternative) challenge the individual's competence as a decision maker. When individuals behave in these ways, they are presumed to experience a threat to their overall self-image and are therefore primarily motivated to affirm the global integrity of the self. Because of this, individuals may successfully reduce the self threat by affirming "an equally important, yet different, aspect of the self-concept, without resolving the provoking threat [i.e., the cognitive discrepancy]" (Steele, 1988, p. 268).

Research on self-affirmation theory suggested that providing individuals with an opportunity to affirm their global self-integrity reduces the attitude change that typically occurs in the induced compliance paradigm (see Steele, 1988). Steele argued that these effects result because acting counterattitudinally threatens self-integrity, and the attitude change that is typically observed occurs to reduce this threat to self-integrity. Having individuals affirm their self-worth will thus reduce the need to change attitudes. Thus, when individuals are given an opportunity to reflect on an important self-relevant value (e.g., as a person who values aesthetics) unrelated to their recent counterattitudinal behavior (e.g., writing that funding for treatment of chronic illnesses and disabilities should have low priority), they do not show the typical attitude change effect (Steele & Liu, 1983).

Tesser and Cornell (1991) have extended this research by finding that increasing the accessibility of positive self-evaluations (and not only self-affirmations) decreased the discrepancy reduction (i.e., attitude change) in an induced compliance experiment. Working from Tesser's (1988) self-evaluation maintenance model, Tesser and Cornell (1991) found that increasing the accessibility of positive self-evaluation by having individuals bask in the reflected glory of a close other (i.e., they described a time when they were outperformed by a close other on a personally unimportant task) or by having individuals engage in positive social comparison (i.e., they described a time when they outperformed another on a personally important task) prior to freely choosing to behave counterattitudinally reduced attitude change relative to a high-choice control condition. The research of Tesser and Cornell (1991) extends the self-affirmation research, which has been concerned only with intrapersonal processes, by showing that enhancing self-evaluation through interpersonal feedback can decrease discrepancy reduction. Together with the research on self-affirmation theory, Tesser and Cornell's research emphasizes the importance of considering self processes.

THE ROLE OF SELF-ESTEEM IN DISSONANCE PROCESSES

Self-Consistency

One prediction that emerged from the self-consistency revision was that individuals with positive self-concepts should respond with more dissonance when they behave in ways that have typically been used to evoke dissonance, because the discrepancy between their positive self-conception and their knowledge of their behavior (e.g., lying to another person) is greater for them than it is for individuals with negative self-concepts who may have expected themselves to behave in these ways. For example, the negative consequences of a decision (the negative aspects of the chosen and the positive aspects of the rejected), which suggest that the person made an unwise decision, are inconsistent with a positive self-concept of wisdom.[2] Gibbons, Eggleston, and Benthin (1997) have recently provided evidence supporting this prediction. In their research, they found that smokers with high self-esteem who relapsed showed lowered perceptions of health risk associated with smoking and a greater decline in commitment to quitting smoking, whereas smokers with low self-esteem did not. Moreover, the decline in risk perception was related to maintenance of self-esteem for those who relapsed. These results support predictions derived from self-consistency theory by showing that individuals with high self-esteem engaged in more discrepancy reduction than did individuals with low self-esteem.

Self-Affirmation

In direct contrast to predictions derived from self-consistency theory, the self-affirmation model predicts that individuals with high self-esteem would be less likely than those with low self-esteem to engage in discrepancy reduction, because those with high self-esteem have more positive self-concepts and self resources with which to affirm and repair their perception of self-integrity. The self-consistency model predicts just the opposite, because the actions often elicited in dissonance experiments are more discrepant from a positive than from a negative self-concept. To test these competing predictions, Steele et al. (1993), using a free-choice paradigm, found that reminding individuals of their self-esteem levels by having them complete self-esteem scales prior to their decision caused individuals with low self-esteem to be more likely than individuals with high self-esteem to justify their decision. Steele et al. (1993) concluded that these effects were opposite to effects predicted by the self-consistency model, but consistent with the self-affirmation model. It is important to note that justification of the decision (i.e., change in evaluation of the decision alternatives) did not differ between individuals with high and low self-esteem in the condition in which they were not reminded of their level of self-esteem, suggesting that neither the self-consistency nor the self-affirmation model can adequately explain the data.

---

[2]The present discussion of the role of trait self-esteem in dissonance processes entails only global self-esteem or self-expectancies, because most of the research on this issue has focused on only global self-esteem. However, a consideration of self-esteem and self-expectancies for specific domains (e.g., self-expectancy for being compassionate) may assist in clarifying the research on the self in dissonance processes. Moreover, although past dissonance research has treated self-esteem, self-concept, and self expectancies as synonyms of each other, it may be frugal to consider the possibility that they are different constructs.

An Attempt to Reconcile Self-Consistency and Self-Affirmation Predictions

Stone (1999) recently conducted an experiment to further compare the self-affirmation model to the self-consistency model. He noted that making individuals more aware of their self-concept prior to the decision (and arousal of dissonance) reverses the temporal processing sequence proposed by the self-consistency model in which behavior-related cognitions are brought into consciousness first and self-related cognitions are brought into consciousness second and are used as standards by which the behavior is evaluated. In other words, to provide the most appropriate test of the self-consistency model, the self-concept should be made more accessible following the dissonant action. For the self-affirmation model, the temporal sequence should not matter, because individuals with high self-esteem, who have more positive self-views with which to reaffirm their self-integrity, will be less likely to engage in discrepancy reduction than will individuals with low self-esteem.

To empirically address these issues, Stone conducted a free-choice experiment in which individuals with high or low self-esteem were reminded of their self-esteem level (by completing a self-esteem scale) either before or after they made a difficult decision. Paralleling results obtained by Steele et al. (1993), Stone found that when reminded of their self-esteem before making a decision, individuals with low self-esteem justified their decision more than did individuals with high self-esteem. However, in marked contrast to predictions derived from self-affirmation theory, Stone also found that when reminded of their self-esteem after making a decision, individuals with low self-esteem justified their decision less than did individuals with high self-esteem. Stone argued that these latter results were consistent with self-consistency theory, which would predict that the self-concept is compared to the dissonance-producing behavior (e.g., the negative consequences of the decision) after the behavior has occurred and not before the behavior has occurred. Stone (1999) suggested that these results cast doubt on both self-affirmation and self-consistency theories, and he proposed that both the self-affirmation and self-consistency models are correct, but under different conditions.

ADDITIONAL CHALLENGES TO THE SELF-BASED REVISIONS

Self-Consistency Model

The self-consistency version of dissonance theory (Aronson, 1992) posits that dissonance effects emerge when the need to perceive oneself as competent, moral, or rational is threatened. In essence, this self-consistency view is consistent with the original theory in its reliance on cognitive inconsistency as the motivating force behind cognitive and behavioral effects. However, it does narrow the scope of the original theory by limiting it to self-concept violations. Moreover, this revision assumes that dissonance effects emerge after individuals access a metacognitive structure, the self (and whether it is rational, moral, and competent), and compare their perception or behavior to this metacognitive structure. The self-consistency version eliminates the possibility that simple discrepancies between perceptions (e.g., violations of the law of gravity) can cause dissonance effects. The self-consistency version probably would have failed to generate and to explain the interesting research by Lawrence and Festinger (1962), who found dissonance effects in white rats, which presumably do not possess a self-concept.[3]

In addition, as Brehm (1992) noted, results obtained in the hypocrisy paradigm are not easily explained by the self-consistency revision. He pointed out that there was no evidence supporting the idea that the self-concept mediated the observed effects. Moreover, he noted that it was not conceptually clear why the hypocrisy effects emerged only if one had first tried to persuade others: "If the self-concept of being a decent person were an anchor for determining what cognitions are consonant or dissonant, then being reminded of one's shortcomings should be a sufficient condition for dissonance and its effects" (p. 315). But as the Stone et al. (1994) experiment showed, dissonance-produced behavior change did not occur in the remind-only condition but occurred only in the remind-plus-persuade condition. Brehm (1992) further suggested that the results were more adequately explained by the original theory of dissonance, because the effects emerged from the discrepancy between the knowledge of recent behavior and the knowledge of past behavior (see Wicklund & Brehm, 1976), not from the discrepancy between the self-concept and the knowledge of past behavior.

Also at odds with the self-consistency revision are recent data obtained in experiments used to assess affective responses to dissonance-arousing situations. Elliot and Devine (1994) found, in two induced-compliance experiments, that individuals reported more discomfort but not more self-directed negative affect (example items included "am dissatisfied with myself", "feel guilty", and "am annoyed with myself") after being given high choice to write counterattitudinal essays. Harmon-Jones (in press-a) recently extended these findings by observing that individuals reported increased discomfort but not decreased state self-esteem (as measured by the State Self-Esteem

---

[3]The dissonance theory explanation of results obtained by Lawrence and Festinger (1962) was criticized by Amsel (1962, 1972) and Mowrer (1963), who explained the results using behavior theory. Wicklund and Brehm (1976) argued that there was much overlap between dissonance theory and behavior theory when applied to the research conducted by Lawrence and Festinger (1962) using white rats. Wicklund and Brehm (1976) further noted that behavior theory would not adequately explain results obtained in dissonance theory experiments using human participants.

Scale; Heatherton & Polivy, 1991) after freely choosing to write counterattitudinal essays that did not produce aversive consequences. If self-consistency
needs were driving the attitude change that occurred in both the Elliot and
Devine (1994) and Harmon-Jones (in press-a) experiments, then decreased
state self-esteem or increased self-directed negative affect should have resulted, because individuals are assumed to have behaved in ways discrepant
from their positive self-conceptions.[4] The data, however, are inconsistent
with this interpretation.

Of course, the self-concept and self-esteem may moderate dissonance
effects in a number of ways. First, the self-concept may moderate dissonance
effects by serving as the standard against which other cognitions are evaluated as dissonant or consonant and by determining the degree to which
they are dissonant or consonant. This might occur when individuals with
positive self-concepts view deceiving others as more dissonant with their
self-concept than would individuals with negative self-concepts. Second,
the self may moderate dissonance effects by altering perceptions of the importance of the involved cognitions, as when one is reminded of valued self-
relevant attributes (Simon, Greenberg, & Brehm, 1995). Third, the self
may alter dissonance effects by determining whether cognitions are relevant
to one another or by affecting the resistance to change of cognitions. Even
Festinger himself (Festinger & Freedman, 1964) acknowledged that the
self-concept may be a cognition against which other cognitions are compared and thus may serve as a source of dissonance. The important point,
which is supported by research (e.g., Lawrence & Festinger, 1962; Steele et
al., 1993), is that reflecting on the self-concept is not necessary for dissonance to occur.

Self-Affirmation Model

The self-affirmation model of dissonance (Steele, 1988) predicts that
dissonance effects emerge because dissonance-producing situations threaten
the individual's striving for moral and adaptive integrity. As such, the self-
affirmation model should predict that dissonance would cause increased self-
directed negative affect, a finding that did not emerge in the experiments of
Elliot and Devine (1994) and Harmon-Jones (in press-a), who found that

---

[4]The empirical relation between self-directed negative affect, as measured in Elliot and Devine's experiments (1994), and state self-esteem, as measured by Heatherton and Polivy's (1991) scale, is unknown. Both scales, however, ask participants about feelings about themselves, and therefore may be
assessing the same construct.

discrepancy did produce increased discomfort but did not produce increased self-directed negative affect.

In addition, as discussed by Thibodeau and Aronson (1992), self-affirmation manipulations may reduce dissonance because reminders of valued self-relevant attributes are cognitions that are consonant with the positive self-conceptions of most participants. In other words, the knowledge that one is creative is a cognition consonant with a positive self-concept. As Festinger (1957) discussed, one way in which dissonance can be reduced is by adding consonant cognitions. With the addition of these consonant cognitions (e.g., positive self-attributes) and hence decreased dissonance, the need to engage in cognitive discrepancy reduction (e.g., attitude change) should be lessened.

In a challenge to the self-affirmation revision, research by Simon et al. (1995) has shown that a typical self-affirmation manipulation (i.e., completing a scale reporting personally important values) causes individuals to perceive their counterattitudinal behavior and preexisting attitudes as less important, which reduces the likelihood of observing dissonance-related attitude change. In another experiment, Simon et al. (1995) found that making an important but non-self-relevant issue salient without allowing for self-affirmation caused reductions in the perceived importance of the counterattitudinal behavior and preexisting attitude rather than attitude change following freely choosing to write a counterattitudinal statement. Taken together, these results suggest that self-affirmation manipulations may exert their effects on the dissonance process by reducing an individual's perception of the importance of the cognition associated with the preexisting attitude and counterattitudinal behavior. If this is so, and the data seem to strongly support this view, then the original theory of dissonance can be used to explain the effects generated by self-affirmation theory. Moreover, self-affirmation theory does not adequately explain the findings obtained in the latter-described experiment of Simon et al. (1995), whereas the original theory does.

In addition, self-affirmation treatments may serve to simply increase positive affect and thus reduce the negative affect produced by cognitive discrepancy (see Tesser, Martin, & Cornell, 1996, for a discussion of this issue). Such an effect would be consistent with the results of Rhodewalt and Comer (1979), who found that an independent manipulation of emotion affected the degree of attitude change in an induced compliance experiment, with negative affect leading to more, and positive affect leading to less, attitude change. By showing that increased positive affect decreases discrepancy reduction and that increased negative affect increases discrepancy reduction, these findings provide an alternative explanation for the research findings generated by self-affirmation theory. In addition, Kidd and Berkowitz (1976) found that a positive mood induced by a humorous audiotape eliminated behaviors that putatively resulted from the motivation to reduce cognitive discrepancy, and Steele, Southwick, and Critchlow (1981) found that consuming small amounts of alcohol, which induces positive affect, eliminated discrepancy reduction in an induced compliance paradigm.[5]

Steele et al. (1993) attempted to rule out the mood alternative explanation by manipulating non-self-relevant mood prior to having participants make a difficult decision. Individuals in both the positive-mood and negative-mood induction conditions engaged in discrepancy reduction. However, as Steele et al. (1993) acknowledged, these findings could not rule out the mood alternative explanation because they are null findings. Moreover, the time between the mood induction and the arousal of dissonance was substantial, suggesting that the effects of the mood induction may have been diminished by the time dissonance was aroused. Supporting this speculation is the fact that only a marginally significant effect was observed on the mood manipulation check that was close in time to the decision.

Other evidence that has suggested that the self-affirmation model of dissonance may not be fully adequate comes from research by Blanton, Cooper, Skurnik, and Aronson (1997). In their induced compliance experiment, individuals were assigned to conditions in which they reflected on a positive aspect of the self that was either relevant (compassionate) or irrelevant (creative) to the counterattitudinal action (an essay that argued to reduce funding for services for students with disabilities). They replicated the basic self-affirmation effect, finding that individuals who were provided with positive personality feedback that was not relevant to the counterattitudinal action (i.e., creative) changed their attitudes in the direction of the behavior less than did control-condition participants. More important, and in contrast to self-affirmation theory, they found that when individuals were provided positive personality feedback that was relevant to but inconsistent with their counterattitudinal action (i.e., compassionate), participants changed their attitudes in the direction of their behavior even more than did control-condition participants. In a related experiment, Aronson, Blanton, and Cooper (1995) found that individuals would avoid positive personality-test feedback about their compassion after they had freely chosen to behave in an uncompassionate manner.

---

[5]In the Rhodewalt and Comer (1979) experiment, emotion was manipulated during the writing of the counterattitudinal essay by having individuals hold their faces to form either a smile, a frown, or a neutral expression. Results revealed that these facial expressions successfully induced positive, negative, and neutral affect, respectively. Rhodewalt and Comer (1979) suggested that because facial expressions were posed during the writing of the essays, commitment to the position taken in the essay rather than emotion may have caused the attitude effects. As compared to individuals who posed neutral expressions, those who frowned may have taken their essays more seriously and been more committed to them, whereas those who smiled may have taken their essays less seriously and been less committed to them. These differences in commitment to the essay may have, in turn, caused the differences in attitude change. Whereas this explanation may cast doubt on mood modulation as an explanation of the attitude change effects, it does not easily account for the effects obtained by Kidd and Berkowitz (1976) and Steele et al. (1981), because in these experiments, mood was manipulated after counterattitudinal behavior.

The effects obtained by Blanton et al. (1997) could be interpreted in original dissonance theory terms. Accordingly, the counterattitudinal behavior is the cognition most resistant to change, the conception of oneself as compassionate is dissonant with the cognition about the behavior, and thus the magnitude of dissonance is increased relative to a situation in which the conception of oneself as compassionate is not made more accessible. With increased dissonance, more attitude change should occur, and that is what resulted. To continue, the conception of oneself as creative is a cognition that is not relevant to the cognitions involved in the dissonant relationship. Hence, it should have no effect on the magnitude of dissonance. However, it may alter the amount of dissonance aroused because this cognition distracts one from the dissonance, reduces the importance of the relevant cognitions (Simon et al., 1995), or decreases the negative affect associated with the dissonance.

Stone, Wiegand, Cooper, and Aronson (1997) recently provided further evidence suggesting that the primary motive underlying dissonance reduction is the resolution of the specific cognitive discrepancy rather than the restoration of the global moral and adaptive integrity of the entire self system. When individuals were given a choice between engaging in cognitive discrepancy reduction or self-affirmation following the arousal of dissonance, they were more likely to choose cognitive discrepancy reduction. In the experiment, an hypocrisy paradigm was used in which participants delivered a public speech advocating the use of condoms to prevent AIDS and were then reminded of their failures to use condoms. Stone et al. (1997) found that when given a choice between purchasing condoms, which would reduce the specific discrepancy, and donating to a homeless project, which would restore global self-worth, more participants chose to purchase condoms. In a second experiment using an hypocrisy paradigm in which participants delivered a public speech advocating the importance of volunteering to help homeless individuals and were then reminded of their failures to volunteer, Stone et al. (1997) found that more participants chose to donate to the homeless than to purchase condoms, even when participants had rated that using condoms to prevent AIDS was more important to their global self-worth than was donating to feed homeless individuals. Results from the experiments also indicated that individuals were more likely to choose an option that would restore global self-worth in conditions in which a sufficient discrepancy was aroused (hypocrisy) than in comparison conditions. These results suggest that individuals will choose to restore global self-worth following a discrepant action if it is the only available option. However, if given a choice, individuals opt for direct discrepancy reduction, suggesting that avoiding discrepancy rather than restoring global self-worth is a more prominent concern for individuals in dissonance situations. Thus, the results from these experiments cast serious doubt on the self-affirmation explanation of dissonance effects.

Taken together, the results of recent research suggest that the self-affirmation version of dissonance theory may not adequately account for all of the data generated by dissonance theory. Self-affirmation treatments may exert their effects on discrepancy reduction by reducing the importance of cognitions (Simon et al., 1995), by distracting individuals from the discrepancy or dissonance, by adding cognitions consonant with the positive self-concept (Thibodeau & Aronson, 1992), or by reducing the negative affective state produced by dissonance. But as was shown by Stone et al. (1997), engaging in self-affirmations following dissonance-evoking behaviors seems subordinate to resolving the specific discrepancy aroused by the behavior.

Reconciling Self-Consistency and Self-Affirmation Theories

Self-affirmational and self-consistency strivings are presumably present in humans and may moderate reactions to sufficient cognitive discrepancies. However, such moderating effects of other motives or needs do not call for the abandonment of the original theory of dissonance for several reasons. First, in neither the Steele et al. (1993) nor Stone (1999) experiments did level of dispositional self-esteem moderate the amount of justification that occurred in the control (no self-focus) condition. This effect is inconsistent with both the self-consistency and self-affirmation models. These effects, however, are consistent with failed attempts to find that self-reported dispositional self-esteem moderates dissonance effects (e.g., Malewski, 1962). Other research on the relation between self-esteem and dissonance has shown contradictory effects, with high self-esteem leading to more (Gerard, Blevans, & Malcolm, 1964; Glass, 1964) and less (Steele et al., 1993; Stone, 1999) discrepancy reduction. Stone's (1999) research suggests that the relationship between self-esteem level and dissonance reduction is complex and may depend on when during the dissonance situation the self-concept is made more accessible.

The self-image is flexible and may occasionally operate as a standard for behavior, being the cognition generating the dissonance when behavior fails to meet this standard, as self-consistency theory would contend. Conversely, the self-image may occasionally operate as a resource, being able to buffer dissonance-induced threats to the self, as self-affirmation theory would contend. Factors such as the relevance (Blanton et al., 1997) and timing (Stone, 1999) of the affirmation may influence whether the self will serve as a standard or a resource (Aronson, Cohen, & Nail, 1999).

Is Dissonance a Theory of the Self?

Beauvois and Joule (1996, 1999) argued that dissonance theory is not a self theory and reported evidence that would be difficult to explain in terms of self-consistency or self-affirmation processes. They asserted that revisions concerned with a moral self would not adequately explain the results of the classic experiment by Festinger and Carlsmith (1959). They wrote, "Contrary to what the versions based on the morally good self and centered around the idea of lying would lead us to expect, dissonance can be increased by a perfectly moral act: telling the truth" (Beauvois & Joule, 1999, p. 50).

According to Beauvois and Joule (1999; Joule & Girandola, 1995), in the Festinger and Carlsmith (1959) experiment, participants engaged in two behaviors that may have generated dissonance: (a) They performed the boring task (i.e., for most individuals, performing boring tasks is inconsistent with their desires) and (b) they told a peer that the boring task was interesting (i.e., they made a counterattitudinal statement). When participants said that the task was interesting, a consonant cognition may have been added, because saying the task is interesting is consistent with having performed the task. Beauvois and Joule (1999), therefore, reasoned that the participants in Festinger and Carlsmith's (1959) experiment may have experienced less dissonance than is possible in such a situation.

Beauvois and Joule further reasoned that participants who are merely told about the boring nature of the task and do not perform it would experience even more dissonance as a result of saying that the task is interesting. This effect would occur because the participants who actually performed the task would experience less dissonance because they have one more consonant cognition ("I said that the task is interesting") than would participants who did not perform the task. In contrast, saying that the task is boring is dissonant with having performed the task. Hence, participants who say that the task is boring should experience more dissonance than do participants who say that the task is interesting. This analysis leads to the prediction that once participants have performed the boring task, those who say that the task is enjoyable should evidence less dissonance than those who say that the task is boring.

In support of this analysis, Joule and Girandola (1995) found, in addition to replicating the results of Festinger and Carlsmith (1959), that participants who performed the boring task and then said it was boring rated it as more enjoyable than did participants who performed the task and said it was enjoyable. Thus, Beauvois and Joule argued that the immorality of the "lie" did not cause the attitude change effects obtained by Festinger and Carlsmith (1959). Instead, the attitude change was caused by cognitive inconsistency. These results strongly challenge the self-consistency and self-affirmation revisions of the original theory of dissonance.

TOWARD A RESOLUTION OF THE REVISIONS OF DISSONANCE THEORY

Results from research cast doubt on the self-consistency and self-affirmation revisions of the theory of dissonance. These results suggest that dissonance effects emerge when one does not compare one's discrepant behavior to the metacognitive structure of self (Lawrence & Festinger, 1962), and when discrepant actions do not produce increased self-directed negative affect (Elliot & Devine, 1994) or decreased state self-esteem (Harmon-Jones, in press-a). These findings, as well as others that were reviewed, suggest that the revisions are not necessary. This is not to say that the revisions have not uncovered important information. Indeed, research generated by the revisions has shed light on conditions that intensify the magnitude of dissonance, on alternative ways of reducing dissonance, and more.

Perhaps the best way to conceptualize the revisions is to incorporate them into the original theory of dissonance rather than view them as competing explanations. Such would be consistent with the goal of having a cumulative social psychology (Aronson, 1992; Berkowitz & Devine, 1989). Moreover, incorporation of these self-based revisions into the original theory would be consistent with the scientific value for parsimony, which would attempt to explain the behavior of humans and nonhumans using the same psychological constructs and mechanisms. With regard to the self-consistency revision, dissonance effects can be produced and may be intensified when individuals compare their negative behavior to their positive self-concept (or vice versa), as the self-consistency revision posits. But this self-comparison is not necessary to produce dissonance effects (Lawrence & Festinger, 1962; Steele et al., 1993; Stone, 1999). With regard to the self-affirmation revision, focusing on positive self-conceptions may reduce dissonance effects by decreasing the importance of the dissonant cognitions, distracting individuals from the dissonance or the discrepancy, or by reducing the negative affective state produced by the cognitive discrepancy. But these self-affirmation effects do not indicate that dissonance is not a theory about cognitive inconsistency (e.g., Simon et al., 1995; Stone, 1999; Stone et al., 1997).

CLARIFYING THE ORIGINAL THEORY

Although the original theory can be used to explain results obtained in experiments designed to test self-affirmation and self-consistency theories, the ability of the theory to predict and explain results could be enhanced with the specification and measurement of additional variables.

Level of Abstraction of Cognitions

First, the level of abstraction at which the cognitions are mentally represented may be critical in determining the antecedents and consequences of the dissonance process. As others have proposed (e.g., Carver & Scheier, 1981; Vallacher & Wegner, 1985), cognitions, or elements of knowledge, can range from being extremely concrete (e.g., "My index finger just pressed the *e* key") to being extremely abstract (e.g., "I am writing this article to assist in fulfilling my need for self-esteem"). Lower level, concrete cognitions might not necessarily involve self-conceptions, whereas higher level, more abstract cognitions might (Carver & Scheier, 1981). However, discrepancies between cognitions can occur at each level of abstraction and presumably evoke dissonance. Thus, a simple discrepancy between an attitude toward a bitter-tasting beverage and verbal behavior opposite to that attitude (Harmon-Jones, Brehm, Greenberg, Simon, & Nelson, 1996), as well as a discrepancy between the self-concept of honesty and then lying to another person, may arouse dissonance (Aronson, 1992). The motivational, emotional, and cognitive consequences of these types of discrepancies may vary greatly but dissonance occurs nonetheless. Research examining the accessibility, content, and importance of cognitions is sorely needed.

Routes of Dissonance Reduction

Second, consideration of alternative routes of dissonance reduction need to be included in designing and interpreting dissonance experiments (Hardyck & Kardush, 1968; Leippe & Eisenstadt, 1999). Without measures of discrepancy reduction other than attitude change, it is difficult to conclude that dissonance was not aroused, for it may have been aroused and reduced in a manner other than attitude change. For instance, research has shown that under certain conditions cognitive discrepancy will be reduced by reducing the perceived strength of the counterattitudinal behavior (Scheier & Carver, 1980), by forgetting the discrepancy (Brehm & Cohen, 1962; Elkin & Leippe, 1986), by finding external justifications for the behavior (Brock & Buss, 1962; Stalder & Baron, 1998), by nonverbally distancing oneself from the behavior (Fleming & Rudman, 1993), by reducing the discrepancy between cognitions by appealing to a superordinate cognition that explains the discrepancy (Burris, Harmon-Jones, & Tarpley, 1997), by other types of cognitive restructuring (Leippe & Eisenstadt, 1999), or by reducing the importance of the relevant cognitions (Simon et al., 1995). The research by Simon et al. (1995) is a compelling example of a case where alternative routes of dissonance reduction were induced by a manipulation of self-affirmation that was intended to eliminate dissonance motivation. Simon et al. (1995) found that typical self-affirmation manipulations caused individuals to reduce dissonance by reducing the perceived importance of the dissonant cognitions. Without this assessment of alternative ways of reducing dissonance, one might interpret the self-affirmation experiments in line with the theoretical revision advanced by Steele (1988). However, with the assessment of alternative ways of reducing dissonance, Simon et al. (1995) interpreted their results as being inconsistent with self-affirmation theory but consistent with the original version of dissonance theory—that is, one way to reduce dissonance is to reduce the importance of dissonant cognitions (Festinger, 1957).

The Role of Affect

Similarly, considerations of the role of the dissonance state in producing cognitive discrepancy reduction should be included in theory construction and experimental design. Recent research has shown that when attitudes are extremely important to individuals, increases in reported negative affect but no change in attitudes result from counterattitudinal behavior (Devine, Tauer, Barron, Elliot, & Vance, 1999). Without this assessment of negative affect and with only a measure of attitude change, it might have been concluded that dissonance was not aroused in the individuals with extremely important attitudes, but this recent research suggests a different conclusion: Dissonance was aroused but was not reduced via attitude change.

Moreover, the research showing that independent manipulation of positive affect or negative affect influences discrepancy reduction (e.g., Kidd & Berkowitz, 1976; Rhodewalt & Comer, 1979; Steele et al., 1981) could be said to contradict all revisions of dissonance theory. None of the revisions of the theory has made an explicit distinction between a proximal and a distal motive for reducing discrepancy and, as such, each revision posits only one motivation to reduce discrepancy, whether it be self-affirmation or restoration of self-consistency. When an independent manipulation of affect is found to influence the magnitude of discrepancy reduction, it is not clear that these changes in affect altered the participants' feelings of self-worth or their self-concept. In fact, it would not be parsimonious to posit that such occurred. As Tesser et al. (1996) suggested, negative affect may drive self-evaluation defenses in general. They also astutely noted that self-reported negative affect may not reveal evidence of negative affect mediating self-defenses (as in, e.g., Harmon-Jones et al., 1997; Steele et al., 1993), because it may be that negative affect whose cause is unknown (as compared to known) is more likely to evoke self-regulatory processes. Such would explain why misattribution paradigms generally reveal evidence of negative affect mediating defensive responses in dissonance and self-evaluation maintenance paradigms, whereas self-reported affect fails to provide evidence of negative affect mediating these defensive responses (Greenberg et al., 1992; Harmon-Jones, in press-a; Harmon-Jones et al., 1997). In fact, the logic underlying the use of the misattribution paradigm assumes that individuals are not fully aware of the source of their affect, because if they were, they would not be able to misattribute the affect of dissonance to another source, such as a pill. Thus, other assessments of affect, such as physiological responses, are needed in dissonance research (Harmon-Jones & Gerdjikov, 1999).

Proximal and Distal Motives for Discrepancy Reduction

An adequate theory of dissonance processes needs to be able to deal with the evidence that suggests that negative affect mediates cognitive discrepancy reduction and, as such, should posit a proximal motive and distal motive to discrepancy reduction. The proximal motive would be one that would regulate the negative affective state of dissonance (emotion-focused coping), and the distal motive would explain why the negative affect resulted in response to cognitive discrepancy and what the negative affect motivated the organism to accomplish (problem-focused coping). Most current models of dissonance processes posit different distal motives, such as maintenance of global self-integrity (Steele, 1988) or self-concept consistency (Aronson, 1999).

According to one recently developed model (Harmon-Jones, 1999, in press-b), enhancing positive affect or reducing negative affect may decrease the motivation and information-seeking that motivates cognitive work aimed at resolving the cognitive discrepancy that would prevent one from behaving effectively (Jones & Gerard, 1967). In other words, the enhanced positive affect or reduced negative affect signals safety and decreases the motivation to reduce cognitive discrepancy. According to the model, the organism is not striving for consistency but is motivated to avoid inconsistency among accessible cognitions because of the maladaptive effect discrepant cognitions might have on action. Cognitive discrepancy creates negative affect because discrepancy among cognitions undermines the requirement for efficient and unconflicted action (Harmon-Jones et al., 1996). When perceptions about the environment or about oneself are dissonant, decisions cannot be implemented, and protective or facilitative action may be impeded. Indeed, Ramachandran (1994, 1995) has advanced a similar position in explaining the process by which the visual system imposes coherence. From the current perspective, the proximal motivation to reduce cognitive discrepancy stems from the need to reduce negative affect, whereas the distal motivation to reduce discrepancy stems from the requirement for effective action. When the maintenance of clear and certain knowledge and thus the potential for effective action is threatened, negative affect results, which prompts attempts at the restoration of cognitions supportive of the action (i.e., discrepancy reduction).

Jones and Gerard (1967) held a similar position when they discussed the concept of an unequivocal behavior orientation that, they argued, was an adaptive strategy that forced individuals to bring their relevant cognitions into harmony with each other. They argued that the unequivocal behavior orientation "represents a commitment to action in the face of uncertainty. Such a commitment involves the risks of acting inappropriately, but such risks are assumed to be less grave on the average than the risks of hesitant or conflicted action" (p. 185). They further posited that this process serves the

> important function of preparing the organism for effective, unconflicted action. But for action to be unconflicted, for it to occur at the proper time and with the proper coordination, there must be a minimum of

cognitive or evaluative confusion about the considerations involved. When the time comes to act, the great advantage of having a set of coherent internally consistent dispositions is that the individual is not forced to listen to the babble of competing inner forces. (p. 181)[6]

The action-based model concurs with the view that the primary focus of dissonance reduction is the rationalization of behavior (Beauvois & Joule, 1996). Rationalization generally modifies cognitions other than the one that is most resistant to change. However, according to the action-based model, the cognition most resistant to change will not necessarily be recent behavior or behavior in the present situation. At first glance, the present model may appear to advance the position that recent behavior will be the cognition most resistant to change. However, it must be remembered that cognition is for action, and most, if not all, cognitions have behavioral implications. If one possesses a cognition that has successfully guided one's behavior for years in multiple situations (e.g., a religious belief), and then one acts contrary to that belief, one will experience dissonance but will probably avoid engaging in belief change (e.g., Burris et al., 1997; Sherman & Gorkin, 1980; see Harmon-Jones, 1999, for a review).

CONCLUSION

Self-consistency and self-affirmation theories have proposed alternative theoretical explanations for the original theory of cognitive dissonance. Each revision has generated exciting research. However, recent research has challenged these revisions and provided support for the original version of the theory. The predictive, explanatory, and generative power of the theory can be improved with further considerations of the level of abstraction of the cognitions, routes of dissonance reduction, role of affect, and the proximal and distal motivations underlying dissonance processes. According to the recently proposed action-based model of cognitive dissonance, the prox-

---

[6]Although the spirit of the Jones and Gerard (1967) model is in line with the present model, it is not identical in focus. The Jones and Gerard model posits a psychological mechanism, the unequivocal behavioral orientation, that assists in decision making and thus should cause pre-decisional biased information processing (e.g., spreading of decision alternatives). However, dissonance theorists (Brehm & Cohen, 1962; Festinger, 1964) consider dissonance processes to be entirely post-decisional, and they have suggested that pre-decisional processes are not partial or biased. Evidence for the impartiality (Festinger, 1964) as well as partiality (Gerard, 1967; Mills & Ford, 1995) of pre-decisional processes has been discovered. One possible resolution to this debate is proposed by the present model. Whereas dissonance theorists have defined commitment as an overt behavior resulting from a decision, the present model does not advance such a claim. Dissonance theorists seem to have regarded commitment as a categorical (behavior vs. no behavior) rather than continuous variable. By defining commitment as a continuous variable and stating that commitment to a cognition can occur prior to overt behavior, the present model can account for both the seeming impartiality and partiality of pre-decisional processing. Whether such is observed depends on the degree of commitment evoked in the situation prior to the overt behavioral commitment.

imal motivation underlying dissonance processes is the reduction of negative affect and the distal motivation is the production and maintenance of cognitions that guide effective action. The action-based model of dissonance thus proposes that dissonance reduction serves the adaptive function of assisting with the execution of effective action. When one considers dissonance reduction in this light, it becomes evident that dissonance theory is a theory concerned with self-regulation, and it thus becomes imperative for current theorists concerned with self-regulation and executive function to carefully consider the theory and research developed by dissonance researchers over the past four decades.

REFERENCES

Amsel, A. (1962). Frustrative nonreward in partial reinforcement and discrimination learning: Some recent history and a theoretical extension. *Psychological Review, 69*, 306–328.

Amsel, A. (1972). Behavioral habituation, counterconditioning, and a general theory of persistence. In A. H. Black & W. F. Prokasy (Eds.), *Classical conditioning II: Current research and theory* (pp. 409–426). New York: Appleton-Century-Crofts.

Aronson, E. (1968). Dissonance theory: Progress and problems. In R. P. Abelson, E. Aronson, W. J. McGuire, T. M. Newcomb, M. J. Rosenberg, & P. H. Tannenbaum (Eds.), *Theories of cognitive consistency: A sourcebook* (pp. 5–27). Chicago: Rand McNally.

Aronson, E. (1969). The theory of cognitive dissonance: A current perspective. In L. Berkowitz (Ed.), *Advances in experimental social psychology* (Vol. 4, pp. 1–34). New York: Academic Press.

Aronson, E. (1992). The return of the repressed: Dissonance theory makes a comeback. *Psychological Inquiry, 3*, 303–311.

Aronson, E. (1999). Dissonance, hypocrisy, and the self concept. In E. Harmon-Jones & J. Mills (Eds.), *Cognitive dissonance: Progress on a pivotal theory in social psychology* (pp. 103–126). Washington, DC: American Psychological Association.

Aronson, E., Fried, C., & Stone, J. (1991). Overcoming denial and increasing the intention to use condoms through the induction of hypocrisy. *American Journal of Public Health, 81*, 1636–1638.

Aronson, J., Blanton, H., Cooper, J. (1995). From dissonance to disidentification: Selectivity in the self-affirmation process. *Journal of Personality and Social Psychology, 68*, 986–996.

Aronson, J., Cohen, G., & Nail, P. R. (1999). Self-affirmation theory: An update and appraisal. In E. Harmon-Jones & J. Mills (Eds.), *Cognitive dissonance: Progress on a pivotal theory in social psychology* (pp. 127–147). Washington, DC: American Psychological Association.

Beauvois, J. L., & Joule, R. V. (1996). *A radical dissonance theory*. London: Taylor and Francis.

Beauvois, J. L., & Joule, R. V. (1999). A radical point of view on dissonance theory. In E. Harmon-Jones & J. Mills (Eds.), *Cognitive dissonance: Progress on a pivotal theory in social psychology* (pp. 43–70). Washington, DC: American Psychological Association.

Berkowitz, L., & Devine, P. G. (1989). Research traditions, analysis, and synthesis in social psychological theories: The case of dissonance theory. *Personality and Social Psychology Bulletin, 15*, 493–507.

Blanton, H., Cooper, J., Skurnik, I., & Aronson, J. (1997). When bad things happen to good feedback: Exacerbating the need for self-justification with self-affirmations. *Personality and Social Psychology Bulletin, 23*, 684–692.

Brehm, J. W. (1956). Postdecision changes in the desirability of alternatives. *Journal of Abnormal and Social Psychology, 52*, 384–389.

Brehm, J. W. (1992). An unidentified theoretical object. *Psychological Inquiry, 3*, 314–315.

Brehm, J. W., & Cohen, A. R. (1962). *Explorations in cognitive dissonance*. New York: Wiley.

Brock, T. C., & Buss, A. H. (1962). Dissonance, aggression, and evaluation of pain. *Journal of Abnormal and Social Psychology, 65*, 197–202.

Burris, C. T., Harmon-Jones, E., & Tarpley, W. R. (1997). "By faith alone": Religious agitation and cognitive dissonance. *Basic and Applied Social Psychology, 19*, 17–31.

Carver, C. S., & Scheier, M. F. (1981). *Attention and self-regulation: A control-theory approach to human behavior*. New York: Springer-Verlag.

Devine, P. G., Tauer, J. M., Barron, K. E., Elliot, A. J., & Vance, K. M. (1999). Moving beyond attitude change in the study of dissonance-related processes. In E. Harmon-Jones & J. Mills (Eds.), *Cognitive dissonance: Progress on a pivotal theory in social psychology* (pp. 297–323). Washington, DC: American Psychological Association.

Dickerson, C. A., Thibodeau, R., Aronson, E., & Miller, D. (1992). Using cognitive dissonance to encourage water conservation. *Journal of Applied Social Psychology, 22*, 841–854.

Elkin, R. A., & Leippe, M. R. (1986). Physiological arousal, dissonance, and attitude change: Evidence for a dissonance-arousal link and a "don't remind me" effect. *Journal of Personality and Social Psychology, 51*, 55–65.

Elliot, A. J., & Devine, P. G. (1994). On the motivation nature of cognitive dissonance: Dissonance as psychological discomfort. *Journal of Personality and Social Psychology, 67*, 382–394.

Festinger, L. (1957). *A theory of cognitive dissonance*. Evanston, IL: Row, Peterson.

Festinger, L. (1964). *Conflict, decision, and dissonance*. Stanford, CA: Stanford University Press.

Festinger, L., & Carlsmith, J. M. (1959). Cognitive consequences of forced compliance. *Journal of Abnormal and Social Psychology, 58*, 203–210.

Festinger, L., & Freedman, J. L. (1964). Dissonance reduction and moral values. In P. Worchel & D. Byrne (Eds.), *Personality change* (pp. 220–243).

Fleming, J. H., & Rudman, L. A. (1993). Between a rock and a hard place: Self-concept regulating and communicative properties of distancing behaviors. *Journal of Personality and Social Psychology, 64,* 44–59.

Fried, C. B. (1998). Hypocrisy and identification with transgressions: A case of undetected dissonance. *Basic and Applied Social Psychology, 20,* 145–154.

Fried, C. B., & Aronson, E. (1995). Hypocrisy, misattribution, and dissonance reduction. *Personality and Social Psychology Bulletin, 21,* 925–933.

Gerard, H. B. (1967). Choice difficulty, dissonance and the decision sequence. *Journal of Personality, 35,* 91–108.

Gerard, H. B., Blevans, S. A., & Malcolm, T. (1964). Self-evaluation and the evaluation of choice alternatives. *Journal of Personality, 32,* 395–410.

Gibbons, F. X., Eggleston, T. J., & Benthin, A. C. (1997). Cognitive reactions to smoking relapse: The reciprocal relation between dissonance and self-esteem. *Journal of Personality and Social Psychology, 72,* 184–195.

Glass, D. C. (1964). Changes in liking as a means of reducing cognitive discrepancies between self-esteem and aggression. *Journal of Personality, 32,* 531–549.

Greenberg, J., Solomon, S., Pyszczynski, T., Rosenblatt, A., Burling, J., Lyon, D., Simon, L., & Pinel, E. (1992). Why do people need self-esteem? Converging evidence that self-esteem serves an anxiety-buffering function. *Journal of Personality and Social Psychology, 63,* 913–922.

Hardyck, J. A., & Kardush, M. (1968). A modest modish model for dissonance reduction. In R. P. Abelson, E. Aronson, W. T. McGuire, T. M. Newcomb, M. J. Rosenberg, & P. H. Tannenbaum (Eds.), *Theories of cognitive consistency: A sourcebook* (pp. 684–692). Chicago: Rand-McNally.

Harmon-Jones, E. (1999). Toward an understanding of the motivation underlying dissonance processes: Is feeling personally responsible for the production of aversive consequences necessary to cause dissonance effects? In E. Harmon-Jones & J. Mills (Eds.), *Cognitive dissonance: Progress on a pivotal theory in social psychology* (pp. 71–99). Washington, DC: American Psychological Association.

Harmon-Jones, E. (in press-a). Cognitive dissonance and experienced negative affect: Evidence that dissonance increases experienced negative affect even in the absence of aversive consequences. *Personality and Social Psychology Bulletin.*

Harmon-Jones, E. (in press-b). A cognitive dissonance theory perspective on the role of emotion in the maintenance and change of beliefs and attitudes. In N. H. Frijda, A. R. S. Manstead, & S. Bem (Eds.), *The effects of emotions upon the formation and strength of beliefs.* Cambridge: Cambridge University Press.

Harmon-Jones, E., Brehm, J. W., Greenberg, J., Simon, L., & Nelson, D. E. (1996). Evidence that the production of aversive consequences is not necessary to create cognitive dissonance. *Journal of Personality and Social Psychology, 70,* 5–16.

Harmon-Jones, E., & Gerdjikov, T. (1999). *An examination of affective mediators of dissonance effects.* Unpublished manuscript.

Harmon-Jones, E., & Mills, J. (1999a). *Cognitive dissonance: Progress on a pivotal theory in social psychology*. Washington, DC: American Psychological Association.

Harmon-Jones, E., & Mills, J. (1999b). An introduction to cognitive dissonance theory and an overview of current perspectives on the theory. In E. Harmon-Jones & J. Mills (Eds.), *Cognitive dissonance: Progress on a pivotal theory in social psychology* (pp. 3–21). Washington, DC: American Psychological Association.

Harmon-Jones, E., Simon, L., Greenberg, J., Pyszczynski, T., Solomon, S., & McGregor, H. (1997). Terror management and self-esteem: Evidence that self-esteem reduces mortality salience effects. *Journal of Personality and Social Psychology, 72*, 24–26.

Heatherton, T. F., & Polivy, J. (1991). Development and validation of a scale for measuring state self-esteem. *Journal of Personality and Social Psychology, 60*, 895–910.

Jones, E. E., & Gerard, H. B. (1967). *Foundations of social psychology*. New York: Wiley.

Joule, R. V., & Girandola, F. (1995). Tâche fastidieuse et jeu de rôle dans le paradigme de la double soumission. *Revue Internationale de Psychologie Sociale, 8*, 101–116.

Kidd, R. F., & Berkowitz, L. (1976). Effect of dissonance arousal on helpfulness. *Journal of Personality and Social Psychology, 33*, 613–622.

Lawrence, D. H., & Festinger, L. (1962). *Deterrents and reinforcement*. Stanford, CA: Stanford University Press.

Leippe, M. R., & Eisenstadt, D. (1999). A self-accountability model of dissonance reduction: Multiple modes on a continuum of elaboration. In E. Harmon-Jones & J. Mills (Eds.), *Cognitive dissonance: Progress on a pivotal theory in social psychology* (pp. 201–232). Washington, DC: American Psychological Association.

Malewski, A. (1962). The influence of positive and negative self-evaluation on post-decision dissonance. *Polish Sociological Bulletin, 3*, 39–49.

Mills, J., & Ford, T. E. (1995). Effects of importance of a prospective choice on private and public evaluations of the alternatives. *Personality and Social Psychology Bulletin, 21*, 256–266.

Mowrer, O. H. (1963). Cognitive dissonance or counterconditioning?—A reappraisal of certain behavioral "paradoxes." *Psychological Record, 133*, 197–211.

Ramachandran, V. S. (1994). Phantom limbs, neglect syndromes, repressed memories, and Freudian psychology. *International Review of Neurobiology, 37*, 291–333.

Ramachandran, V. S. (1995). Anosognosia in parietal lobe syndrome. *Consciousness and Cognition, 4*, 22–51.

Rhodewalt, F., & Comer, R. (1979). Induced-compliance attitude change: Once more with feeling. *Journal of Experimental Social Psychology, 15*, 35–47.

Scheier, M. F., & Carver, C. S. (1980). Private and public self-attention, resistance to change, and dissonance reduction. *Journal of Personality and Social Psychology, 39*, 390–405.

Sherman, S., & Gorkin, L. (1980). Attitude bolstering when behavior is incon-sistent with central attitudes. *Journal of Experimental Social Psychology, 16,* 388–403.

Simon, L., Greenberg, J., & Brehm, J. W. (1995). Trivialization: The forgotten mode of dissonance reduction. *Journal of Personality and Social Psychology, 68,* 247–260.

Spencer, S. J., Josephs, R. A., & Steele, C. M. (1993). Low self-esteem: The uphill struggle for self-integrity. In R. F. Baumeister (Ed.), *Self-esteem: The puzzle of low self-regard* (pp. 21–36). New York: Plenum Press.

Stalder, D. R., & Baron, R. S. (1998). Attributional complexity as a moderator of dissonance-produced attitude change. *Journal of Personality and Social Psychology, 75,* 449–455.

Steele, C. M. (1988). The psychology of self-affirmation: Sustaining the integrity of the self. In L. Berkowitz (Ed.), *Advances in experimental social psychology* (Vol. 21, pp. 261–302). San Diego, CA: Academic Press.

Steele, C. M., & Liu, T. J. (1983). Dissonance processes as self-affirmation. *Journal of Personality and Social Psychology, 45,* 5–19.

Steele, C. M., Southwick, L. L., & Critchlow, B. (1981). Dissonance and alcohol: Drinking your troubles away. *Journal of Personality and Social Psychology, 41,* 831–846.

Steele, C. M., Spencer, S. J., & Lynch, M. (1993). Self-image resilience and disso-nance: The role of affirmational resources. *Journal of Personality and Social Psychology, 64,* 885–896.

Stone, J. A. (1999). What exactly have I done? The role of self-attribute accessi-bility in dissonance. In E. Harmon-Jones & J. Mills (Eds.), *Cognitive dissonance: Progress on a pivotal theory in social psychology* (pp. 175–200). Washington, DC: American Psychological Association.

Stone, J., Aronson, E., Crain, A. L., Winslow, M. P., & Fried, C. B. (1994). Inducing hypocrisy as a means for encouraging young adults to use condoms. *Personality and Social Psychology Bulletin, 20,* 116–128.

Stone, J., Wiegand, A. W., Cooper, J., & Aronson, E. (1997). When exemplifica-tion fails: Hypocrisy and the motive for self-integrity. *Journal of Personality and Social Psychology, 72,* 54–65.

Tesser, A. (1988). Toward a self-evaluation maintenance model of social behavior. In L. Berkowitz (Ed.), *Advances in experimental social psychology* (Vol. 21, pp. 181–227). New York: Academic Press.

Tesser, A., & Cornell, D. P. (1991). On the confluence of self processes. *Journal of Experimental Social Psychology, 27,* 501–526.

Tesser, A., Martin, L. L., & Cornell, D. P. (1996). On the substitutability of self-protective mechanisms. In P. M. Gollwitzer & J. A. Bargh (Eds.), *The psychol-ogy of action* (pp. 48–68). New York: Guilford Press.

Thibodeau, R., & Aronson, E. (1992). Taking a closer look: Reasserting the role of the self-concept in dissonance theory. *Personality and Social Psychology Bulletin, 18,* 591–602.

Vallacher, R. R., & Wegner, D. M. (1985). *A theory of action identification*. Hillsdale, NJ: Erlbaum.

Wicklund, R. A., & Brehm, J. W. (1976). *Perspectives on cognitive dissonance*. Hillsdale, NJ: Erlbaum.

III

The Self in Interpersonal Processes

6

OUTSTANDING ROLE MODELS: DO THEY INSPIRE OR DEMORALIZE US?

PENELOPE LOCKWOOD
ZIVA KUNDA

One of Canada's brightest hopes for a gold medal at the 1998 Nagano Winter Olympic games was figure skater Elvis Stojko. Shortly before the games began, however, Stojko developed a serious groin injury. Despite this setback, he skated a difficult program, landing eight triple jumps, and won a silver medal. Stojko was lauded in the press as a striking example of courage under adversity (Deacon, 1998). The media hype reached a fever pitch when a five-year-old girl sent Elvis a letter in which she described him as her hero; his example had inspired her to skate in her first competition despite the fact that she had the flu (Wilkes, 1998).

We frequently encounter examples of such role models—individuals whose spectacular achievements are expected to inspire others to achieve comparable excellence. However, such superior individuals can also exert the opposite effect. In a recent newspaper article describing her lunch with author Anna Quindlen, reporter Jan Wong (1998) commented, "Anna Quindlen induces nausea. She's so successful, so has-it-all, you can hardly choke down your grilled salmon at Acqua" (p. A12). Wong, a well-respected

147

journalist and author in her own right, evidently felt that her own accomplishments paled in contrast to those of Quindlen. When one encounters an individual whose achievements seem to far outstrip one's own, one may feel inferior by comparison and become demoralized rather than inspired.

Thus, a superior other may be self-enhancing and inspiring or self-deflating and demoralizing. It is also possible that if one sees an outstanding other as irrelevant, the other will have no impact whatsoever on the self. For example, an aspiring musician may be unaffected either by Stojko's stellar skating or by Quindlen's literary accomplishments, viewing such successes as irrelevant to his or her own artistic skills.

THE EFFECT OF ROLE MODELS ON SELF-PERCEPTIONS OF SUCCESS

What determines whether role models have any impact on the self and, if they do, what determines whether that impact is positive or negative? Our research program suggests that two key factors play a role. First, an outstanding other will exert an effect on the self—positive or negative—only if one compares oneself to the star other. One will draw a such a comparison only when the role model is considered *relevant* (cf. Major, Testa, & Bylsma, 1991). Second, the direction of a relevant role model's impact will depend on the perceived *attainability* of the role model's success. If the role model's success appears attainable, one will be self-enhanced and inspired by the comparison. If the role model's success appears unattainable, one will be self-deflated and demoralized.

Relevance

What determines the relevance of a role model? Our answer has been informed by research on analogical reasoning. In forming analogies, people use a familiar *source* to understand or make inferences about a less familiar *target*. For example, students can learn about atomic structure by using the analogy of the atom as a tiny solar system; their familiarity with the structure of the solar system, the source, can help them understand the unfamiliar atom, the target (Reeves & Weisberg, 1994). Similarly, when individuals make social comparisons to role models, using their knowledge of another person to make inferences about themselves, they are also applying analogical reasoning: They are mapping themselves onto another person, the source, to glean information about themselves, the target.

People are most likely to form analogies when there are coherent correspondences between the source and target; the analogy is constrained by the extent to which there is a good fit between the sets of elements involved. One such constraint on analogical coherence is the extent to which the attributes or features of the elements are similar (Holyoak & Thagard, 1997). Greater similarity provides a better correspondence between the target and the source, increasing the likelihood that an analogy will be drawn. Thus, a more similar role model will be more relevant, making a social comparison more likely. Similarity in the domain of achievement may be particularly important in determining the relevance of role models: One may be more influenced by a role model who has succeeded in one's own field of interest than by one who has succeeded in a different field. A psychologist, for example, may be more likely to draw an analogy between herself and another psychologist than between herself and an athlete.

The influential Self-Evaluation Maintenance (SEM) model also assumes that the self-relevance of the comparison domain will influence the outcome of a social comparison (e.g., Tesser & Campbell, 1983). However, the SEM model distinguishes between self-relevance and psychological closeness, and these play different roles in the model. Psychological closeness refers to the extent to which individuals are in a "unit-relation" (Heider, 1958) with each other. Individuals are psychologically close if they are from a similar background or family, or if they are similar in such dimensions as age, race, or gender. Psychological closeness determines whether another person will have an impact on the self. Relevance determines the direction of a close other's impact. If a close other outperforms one on a self-relevant dimension, the impact will be threatening, and one's own performance will seem inferior by comparison. If, however, a close other outperforms one on a dimension that is not self-relevant, one can "bask in the reflected glory" of the other person's achievements (Cialdini et al., 1976), experiencing pride in the other's achievements without questioning the quality of one's own accomplishments (Tesser & Collins, 1988).

We have identified a different role that domain self-relevance can play in social comparison: The self-relevance of a star's domain of excellence can, like psychological closeness, contribute to the determination of whether the star is relevant. When a superior other is successful in a domain that is important to one, this increases the similarity between oneself and a star, thereby increasing the likelihood that one will draw an analogy. Thus, if an outstanding other is perceived as relevant to oneself, one can draw an analogy and make inferences about oneself.

Attainability

If individuals can form an analogy between themselves and an outstanding other, a social comparison can take place. Its impact will depend on the perceived attainability of the role model's achievements. To be inspired by a superior other, one must be able to imagine a self who is as outstanding as the other (Markus & Nurius, 1986). If the role model's success seems attainable, one will be inspired, drawing the inference that one will be able to achieve a similar level of success. If the role model's success seems unattainable, one will be demoralized; one will not be able to imagine a future self like the star, and one's own achievements will seem inferior in contrast.

If models of attainable success inspire people by leading them to imagine more successful future selves, then anything that constrains the extent to which one can generate a "better" self will probably undermine the models' inspirational impact. To wit, in studies in which participants were outperformed by another individual but had no opportunity to improve on their own performance, the impact of the social comparison was negative (cf. Aspinwall, 1997; Major et al., 1991). This was the case in a series of studies by Tesser and his colleagues on the negative implications of upward comparisons to close others. Participants were typically informed that they had been outperformed on a test for which the superior other's achievements were probably perceived as unattainable—they either received their score on a test they did not expect to take again (Pleban & Tesser, 1981; Tesser & Cornell, 1991; Tesser & Paulhus, 1983) or received several scores in quick succession with no opportunity to practice between scores (Tesser, Millar, & Moore, 1988). In either case, participants did not have an opportunity to improve on their scores and so could not hope to achieve a future success like that of the superior other. These are precisely the conditions under which an upward comparison can be be demoralizing.

In contrast, in studies in which a superior other's achievements seemed more attainable, participants were more positively affected by the comparison (for a review, see Major et al., 1991). In one study, participants who were outperformed on an essay-writing task but believed that they could improve their scores on a second test reported less hostility and depression than did participants who believed that improvement was not possible (Testa & Major, 1990). However, because this study did not include a no-comparison control group, it is impossible to determine the overall impact of the upward comparison. Studies assessing the self-reported impact of past comparisons also suggest that upward comparisons are inspiring only when the other's achievements appear attainable. For example, cancer patients may find comparisons to better-off others pleasing and inspiring only when they believe that improvement is possible (cf. Wood & Van der Zee, 1997). However, patients' self-reports can be influenced by their theories about how they should respond to a better-off other (cf. Collins, 1996) and may not reflect the actual impact of social comparisons. Thus, research on social comparison provided suggestive but inconclusive evidence that the perceived attainability of a superior other's achievements determines whether one will be inspired or deflated by this person.

We have been exploring how relevance and attainability jointly determine the impact of role models on the self. We have examined the extent to which relevance determined whether a role model had any effect on self-perceptions and also examined whether the perceived attainability of a relevant model's achievements determined whether the impact of the role model on self-views was positive or negative. In each study, we exposed individuals to a richly detailed description of an outstanding role model, a high-achiever who had accomplished a meaningful degree of success, and assessed this role model's impact on participants' self-views.

Study 1: Career-Matched Role Models Are More Relevant

In one study, we created a role model whose achievements would appear attainable to participants, and we examined the effect of the model's relevance in terms of career matching (Lockwood & Kunda, 1997, Study 1). We exposed students to a star who had excelled either in his or her own intended profession or in a different profession. We expected that matching on occupation would increase the surface correspondence between participants and the role model, thus increasing the likelihood that participants would draw an analogy between themselves and the model.

We invited female students who were planning to become either teachers or accountants to take part in a study on the impact of journalistic styles on social perception. Participants were told that we were studying whether the style of a newspaper article would affect their perceptions of the person described in the article. Participants read a bogus newspaper article about either an outstanding teacher (described by her principal as "one of the most talented, creative, and innovative teachers" he had ever worked with) or an outstanding accountant (described by her supervisor as "one of the most extraordinarily talented and innovative individuals" he had ever worked with).

Participants rated how relevant the target was to them for the purpose of comparison. As expected, future teachers rated an outstanding teacher as more relevant than an outstanding accountant, and future accountants rated an outstanding accountant as more relevant than an outstanding teacher. Thus, individuals themselves indicated that the role model who shared their intended profession was more relevant to them than the one who did not.

Participants also explained their responses to the relevance question in open-ended form, and we coded these explanations for reports of inspiration. Participants were considered to have experienced inspiration if they described the target as inspiring (e.g., "This type of dedication and success in the teaching field is quite inspirational"), if they indicated greater motivation (e.g., "If I judge myself by her standards I will work harder to achieve my goals, so that I can have what she has [only better]"), if they indicated that their goals had been enhanced (e.g., "Moving up the ranks so quickly is something I can try to aim for figuring that an example has already been set"), or if they explicitly referred to the target as a role model. The percentage of participants experiencing inspiration was considerably higher among those exposed to the relevant role model (45%) than among those exposed to the irrelevant model (15%). Thus, one may subjectively experience inspiration by an outstanding role model, particularly if that model is in one's own career area.

Were participants' self-evaluations also affected by the relevant role model? After reading the article, participants rated themselves on a set of 10 positive (e.g., "bright," "successful") and 10 negative (e.g., "inadequate," "incompetent") success-related items. These were averaged into an index of how successful participants perceived themselves to be (after reverse-scoring the negative items). As may be seen in Figure 6.1, both future teachers and future accountants viewed themselves more positively after exposure to a career-matched role model than after exposure to a role model in a different career area. We also included a control group of future teacher participants who rated themselves on the success-related items without first reading about either target (there were too few available accounting students to permit a control group of future accountants). As may be seen in Figure 6.1, the star accountant exerted no impact on the self-ratings of future teachers: The self-evaluations of future teachers exposed to the irrelevant accountant were almost identical to those of future teachers exposed to no role model.

Thus, the finding that participants exposed to a star who had excelled at their own intended profession rated themselves more positively than did those exposed to a star who had excelled at a different profession was due entirely to the self-enhancing impact of the matched star. Results of a mediation analysis (Baron & Kenny, 1986) also suggested that the differential impact of the career-matched and mismatched stars on self-ratings was due to the differences in the star's perceived relevance. The impact of the star's occupation on participants' self-ratings was eliminated when we controlled for the targets' relevance, which provides further evidence that role models will affect self-perceptions only if they are perceived as relevant.

In Study 1, individuals were positively affected by the relevant role model. But will this always be the case? We have suggested that individuals will be inspired by a role model only if they view the successful other's achievements as attainable; if the role model's achievements seem out of reach, individuals may be demoralized instead. To examine this possibility, we created a role model who had achieved success in a domain relevant to participants and varied the perceived attainability of that role model's achievements in a series of studies.

Study 2: Attainability Is Varied as a Function of Career Stage

In Study 1, the role model was a professional who had completed university several years earlier. Participants would have an opportunity to improve and become more like this model in the future and so could perceive her accomplishments as attainable. In contrast, when one is at the same ca-

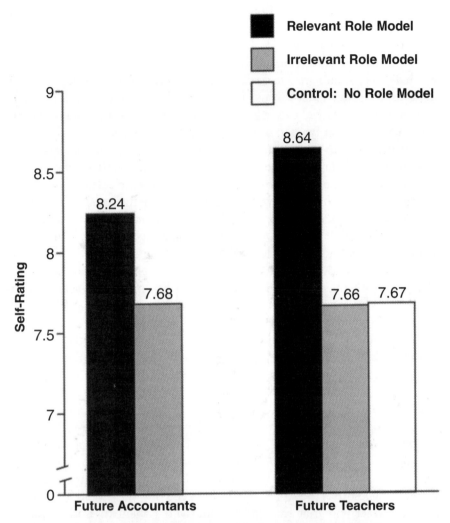

Relevant Role Model

Irrelevant Role Model

Control: No Role Model

Figure 6.1. Future accountants' and teachers' self-ratings of success after exposure to role models matched (relevant) or mismatched (irrelevant) by career. (Study 1) Adapted from Lockwood and Kunda (1997, table 1, p. 95). Copyright 1997 by the American Psychological Association. Adapted with permission of the publisher and author.

reer stage as a role model, an upward comparison may be more threatening. A superior peer may lead one to feel incompetent, without offering the hope that one may catch up in the future; it is already too late for one to achieve what the peer has achieved, and one consequently feels inferior and demoralized. Thus, one's own career stage may constrain one's ability to imagine a self as successful as an outstanding role model.

To examine this possibility, we created a role model whose achievements would appear either attainable or unattainable depending on participants' year in school (Lockwood & Kunda, 1997, Study 2). The role model was an outstanding fourth-year accounting student who had won a prestigious academic award. Participants were accounting students in their first or fourth year. We expected that first-year students, who had four years ahead of them in which to become similarly successful, would perceive the role model's achievements as attainable and so would be inspired. We expected that fourth-year students would be forced to recognize that the role model was more successful than they could ever hope to be and so would be demoralized.

Participants in the experimental condition read a bogus newspaper article about a stellar fourth-year accounting student of their own gender. They then rated the extent to which they viewed the target as relevant for comparison and provided a written explanation of their response. Participants then rated themselves on the same success-related items used in Study 1. Participants in the control condition completed the self-rating items without first reading the article.

First-year students rated the target as more relevant than did fourth-year students. This is somewhat surprising, given that fourth-year students were more similar to the target in age and academic stage. Fourth-year students, who should have perceived the target's achievements as unattainable, may have been trying to reduce the negative impact of the comparison by construing the target as less relevant (Pleban & Tesser, 1981). First-year students, who should have perceived the target's achievements as attainable, were more comfortable claiming the star graduating student as a relevant role model.

The open-ended explanations of relevance ratings shed further light on this finding. As in Study 1, we coded responses for reports of inspiration. Among first-year students, 82% reported being inspired, whereas only 6% of fourth-year students reported being inspired. The explanations of first-year students suggest that these participants believed that they could become like the star target and that the star had motivated them to work harder to achieve their goals. For example, one student commented,

> It is almost spooky how much alike Walker and I are: Firstly, I am in Arts Accounting Co-op and am an overachiever just like she is. Therefore, because we are both female [and] planning on becoming Accountants, I almost now want to work super-hard so that I can get that award that she got. . . . I just decided that I will go to the ASA [Accounting Students' Association] meeting tomorrow now because it is probably a good idea to get involved like Jennifer did. (Lockwood & Kunda, 1997, p. 98)

Other first-year students indicated that the star helped them clarify their own goals. For example, another first-year student noted,

> Jeffrey Walker is very relevant to me for the purpose of comparison because what he has done is what my goals are. My goal is to become a CA

and more important, I want to be at the top of my class. I also want to be well-rounded and have a life outside academics. Jeffrey Walker has done this through his athletics and volunteer work, and I would like to do the same. After seeing what Jeffrey has accomplished, I know what I must strive for. (Lockwood & Kunda, 1997, p. 98)

Thus, the star graduating student served as a guide for other first-year students hoping to achieve comparable success.

Fourth-year students, who showed little inspiration, tended to focus instead on the pointlessness of comparing oneself to another person, by stating that they had too little information to make a comparison, that they preferred to judge themselves by their own standards rather than by examples set by others, or that they believed comparisons to another person are pointless, as is illustrated in the following examples:

> I try to improve myself, but using who I was yesterday as a model for that comparison. Jeffrey is unknown to me . . . I have a set of special circumstances unique only to me and so does everyone else. To think otherwise is absurd. You can't compare "success" between any two people on the planet because we are all different and successful in our own right.

> * * *

> He is in the same program and has the same career plans. However, I do not know enough of his personal character for him to be relevant.

> * * *

> JW is like a classmate to me. I'm usually influenced more by how I view myself than by how well I'm compared to my classmates. I'm more influenced by my own standards. (Lockwood & Kunda, 1997, p. 98)

Fully 50% of fourth-year students denigrated the comparison process, whereas only 6% of first-year students did so. Thus, whereas first-year students indicated that they had been inspired and motivated by the star, fourth-year students appeared to be attempting to reduce the threat posed by the comparison by focusing on why they could learn nothing meaningful about themselves from the star.

The self-ratings provided additional evidence that first- but not fourth-year students were inspired by the star. As may be seen in Figure 6.2, first-year students exposed to the role model rated themselves more positively than did first-year control participants.[1] In contrast, fourth-year students exposed to the role model rated themselves somewhat less positively than did fourth-year control participants, although this effect was not significant.

---

[1]Unlike in Study 1, the impact of the target on participants' self-perceptions was limited to the positive items. There were no significant effects on the negative items, possibly because the students' negative self-ratings were already so low that the role model could not diminish them any further.

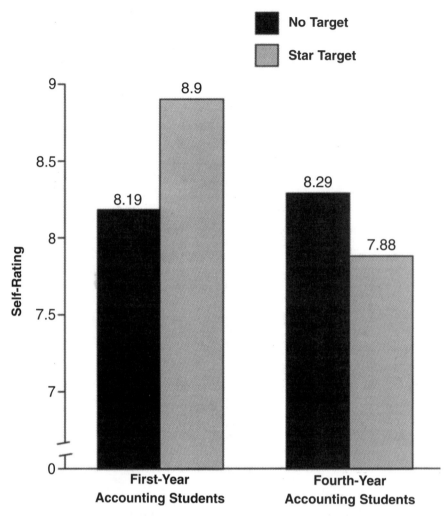

Figure 6.2. First- and fourth-year accounting students' self-ratings of success after exposure to a successful role model (star target). (Study 2) Adapted from Lockwood and Kunda (1997, table 2, p. 97). Copyright 1997 by the American Psychological Association. Adapted with permission of the publisher and author.

Overall, the role model had a positive impact on first-year participants. These students still had four years to achieve similar success and so could perceive the target's achievements as attainable. In contrast, the role model's impact on fourth-year students was, if anything, negative. Because the fourth-year students were already at the same career stage as the star, they would be unable to achieve similar success. Therefore, fourth-year participants were threatened by the comparison to the role model and focused on reducing this threat by denigrating the comparison process. Only those participants who could view the model's achievements as attainable experienced inspiration.

Study 3: Attainability Is Varied as a Function of
Theories of Intelligence

We sought convergent evidence that attainability determined the impact of relevant models by designing another study with individuals who
were likely to differ in their perceived attainability of academic excellence
by virtue of their theories about the stability of academic achievement
(Lockwood & Kunda, 1997, Study 3). People differ in their beliefs about
whether intelligence is fixed and unalterable or malleable and improvable
(Dweck & Leggett, 1988). We reasoned that participants who viewed intelligence as malleable would see the achievements of an outstanding academic role model as attainable; they would believe that they too could improve and become like the role model. As a result, these individuals should
be inspired. In contrast, participants who viewed their intelligence as un-
changeable would see the achievements of the role model as unattainable;
they would think they would be unable to increase their own academic
standing and achieve the success of the role model. These individuals should
be demoralized by a role model.

At the beginning of term, we administered a pretest designed to assess
theories of intelligence. Participants rated the extent to which they agreed
with 6 items indicating that intelligence is fixed (e.g., "extra schooling cannot make a person more intelligent") and 6 items indicating that intelligence is malleable ("intelligence is influenced by the environment a person
lives in"). We reverse-scored the fixed items and averaged all the items to
form an index of how malleable participants believed intelligence to be.

We randomly selected first-year participants among those who had
completed the pretest and divided them into "fixed-theory" and "malleable-
theory" groups based on a median split. Participants were invited to take
part in a study on journalism and social perceptions. As in the previous studies, participants read a newspaper article about a highly successful fourth-
year student. To ensure that this role model was relevant, we individually
tailored the articles so that all participants read about a high achiever in
their own major. After reading the article, participants rated the target and
then themselves on the success-related items. Participants in the control
condition rated themselves without first reading about a target.

As may be seen in Figure 6.3, participants holding malleable theories
of intelligence were positively affected by the role model. Those exposed to
the model rated themselves more positively than did participants in the
control group. In contrast, participants holding fixed theories of intelligence
showed no evidence of inspiration. If anything, those exposed to the role
model rated themselves less positively than did those in the fixed-theory
control group, although this effect was not significant. As in Study 2, only
those participants who could imagine a similarly successful future self were
positively affected.

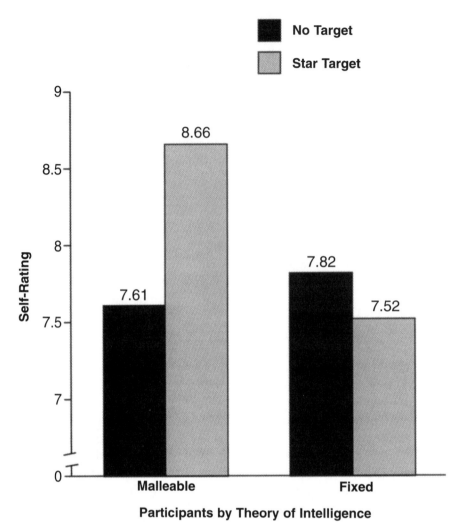

Taken together, Studies 2 and 3 provide strong evidence that a role model with attainable achievements can inspire people to generate more positive possible selves. If so, then anything that constrains participants' ability to imagine more positive future selves will undermine the inspirational impact of a role model. We explored this possibility in another set of studies.

Study 4: Reality Constraints Can Undermine a Role Model's Inspirational Impact

Typically, individuals may be able to generate unrealistically positive possible selves after exposure to a superstar; one can imagine a heroic self, a brilliant self, or a glamorous superstar self. If, however, one is forced to consider how one might realistically become like the superstar, it may be more difficult to imagine this spectacular self. Individuals can tolerate inconsistencies among their beliefs, but only as long as such inconsistencies are not made salient (for a review, see McGregor, Newby-Clark, & Zanna, in press). Thus, individuals may have a realistic understanding of their own weaknesses and inadequacies, but as long as they are not forced to dwell on these limitations, they are able to imagine overly optimistic future selves. Once these limitations are made salient, however, it becomes more difficult to generate more positive possible selves, and this may undermine inspiration from the role model. To explore this possibility, we exposed participants to a highly successful role model and then asked them to generate a realistic scenario in which they could become like the role model. We reasoned that, because of the difficulty of generating feasible scenarios, this exercise would undermine the inspirational impact of the role model (Lockwood, 1999).

We recruited first-year introductory psychology students for a study on adjustment to university life. We told them that we were interested in their intuitions about how other students coped well or poorly with university life and also how they themselves were adjusting. First, participants were asked to read a description ostensibly written by a more advanced student who was adjusting extremely well, achieving both social and academic success. In the scenario condition, students were then asked to imagine a detailed scenario in which they could become like the person they read about. In the no-scenario condition, participants were asked to imagine how they spent a typical day. Participants then rated their own adjustment on the success-related items used in the previous studies. Participants in the control condition rated themselves without first reading about a target.[2]

How did generating the scenario affect reactions to the role model? No-scenario participants who had read about the role model rated themselves more positively than did those in the control group. This replicates our finding that students are inspired when they are exposed to a more advanced high achiever (see Figure 6.4). However, this inspiration was undermined for participants who had generated scenarios: Their self-ratings did not differ from those in the control group. These students had been asked to consider exactly what they would have to accomplish to become like the

---

[2]This study also included scenario and no-scenario downward comparison conditions that are not relevant to the issues addressed in this chapter.

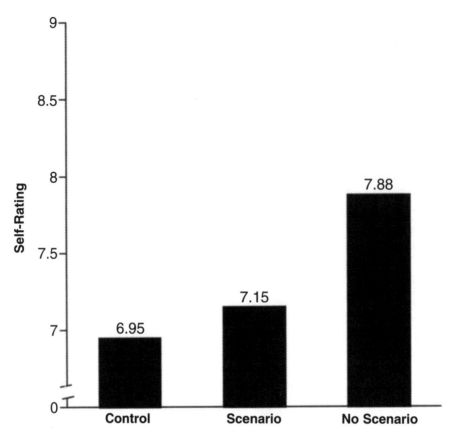

Figure 6.4 First-year psychology students' self-ratings of success after exposure to a successful role model (star target). (Study 4).

star student. In doing so, they were forced to recognize that it would be difficult, if not impossible, for them to achieve the star's success. It may be inspiring to learn of the success of an outstanding role model, but if one attempts to envision exactly how one will go about pursuing this brilliant outcome, one's dreams of a spectacular future may be dimmed. The achievements of the star role model will seem unattainable, and inspiration will be undermined.

Study 5: Salience of Best Past Selves Constrains the Positivity of Possible Future Selves

Even if individuals do not explicitly consider the likelihood that they will match the role model's achievements, they may still be negatively affected if they are made aware of their limitations indirectly. Ironically, reminding individuals of their best achievements may restrict their ability to imagine a self as positive as an outstanding role model. Awareness of one's highest accomplishments will ground one in reality, setting limits on the kind of self that one can imagine becoming. This will in turn undercut the inspiration that a role model normally produces. If a well-defined image of a best self is salient, it may be difficult to generate a better self. For example, an aspiring junior track and field runner may be inspired when she hears about the success of a senior school athlete who has just set a new sprinting record. If, however, she is reminded of her own best time, which is considerably less impressive, she may perceive her likelihood of becoming a future track star as less feasible. Her awareness of her own best accomplishment undermines her ability to imagine a self as spectacular as the star. Instead, her own achievement will seem inferior, and she will feel discouraged rather than inspired.

To examine this possibility, we exposed participants to an outstanding role model after first reminding them of their best past accomplishments, and then we assessed the impact of the role model on their self-perceptions (Lockwood & Kunda, 1999, Study 1). Participants were recruited for a study on journalism and social perception. They were greeted by a research assistant who indicated that she was an honors student and asked if they would mind completing a pilot questionnaire for her honors thesis research. This bogus pilot questionnaire served as a priming manipulation. In the success prime condition, participants were asked to write about an academic experience of which they were pleased and proud. In the neutral prime condition, participants were asked to write about their activities on the previous day.

Participants then went on to the "journalism and social perception" questionnaire. In the star target condition, participants read a bogus newspaper article about a highly successful fourth-year student in their own academic major. In the no-target condition, participants read a bogus newspaper article about an animal recently acquired by the local zoo. Next, participants rated themselves on the success-related items used in the previous studies.

As may be seen in Figure 6.5, among participants not exposed to a star target, success-primed participants rated themselves more positively than did neutral-primed participants, suggesting that we were successful in reminding participants of their best selves. But did this success priming also set participants up for a fall when they encountered the star? In the neutral prime condition, those participants exposed to the role model rated themselves more positively than did those in the no-target condition. This replicates our findings in Studies 2, 3, and 4 that a role model with attainable achievements can be inspiring. However, among participants in the success prime condition, inspiration was undercut. Those participants exposed to the role model rated themselves somewhat less positively than did those in the no-target condition. Reminding these participants of their best achievements had undermined the inspiration that the role model normally provided. Thus, the role model had a positive impact on individuals focused on their

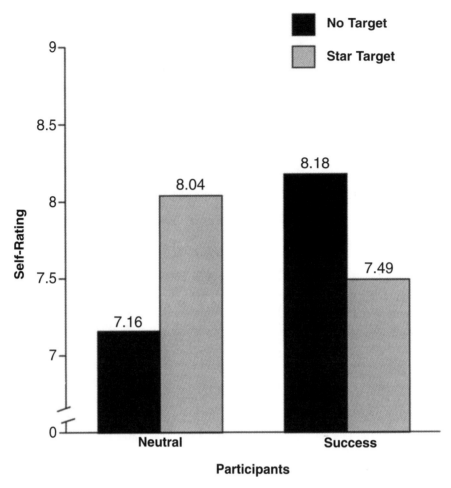

Figure 6.5. Self-ratings of success among participants primed versus not primed for success prior to exposure to a successful role model (star target). (Study 5) From Lockwood and Kunda (1999, figure 1, p. 217). Copyright 1999 by the American Psychological Association. Adapted with permission of the publisher and author.

typical selves but had a negative impact on individuals focused on their best selves. Increasing the salience of best past selves set limits on the future selves that these individuals could imagine becoming, undermining the positive impact of the role model.

Study 6: Salience of Best Future Selves Constrains the Positivity of Possible Selves

If priming one's best past self undercuts the inspirational effect of a role model, will a focus on one's hoped-for ideal self have a similar impact?

Articulating the achievements that one hopes to achieve should also make one aware of what one realistically can accomplish, thus constraining the positivity of the future self that one can imagine becoming. If one's ideal future accomplishments are inferior to those of a role model, this should undermine the inspiration that the role model would otherwise provide.

In another study, participants described either their current-actual selves or the selves they hoped to become and were then exposed to a role model (Lockwood & Kunda, 1999, Study 2). We expected that participants focused on their actual selves would be inspired by the role model: They would be free to imagine a more successful future self. In contrast, participants focused on their ideal future selves would be discouraged; articulating their hoped-for achievements would constrain their ability to generate a still more positive future self, undermining their ability to draw inspiration from the star.

Participants were first asked if they would complete a brief pilot questionnaire on adjustment to student life to help the experimenter with her honors thesis. This questionnaire served as a priming manipulation. Present-primed participants were asked to write about their current level of academic success. Future-primed participants were asked to describe the academic and career achievements they hoped to accomplish over the next 10 years. Neutral-primed participants were asked to describe the typical leisure activities of the average student.

After the priming task, participants were randomly assigned to either a star-target or a no-target group. Star-target participants read a bogus newspaper article about a highly successful fourth-year student in their own major. No-target participants read an article about an animal recently acquired by the local zoo. Participants then rated themselves on the success-related scale.

As may be seen in Figure 6.6, participants in both the neutral prime and present prime conditions were positively affected by the role model; those exposed to the star target rated themselves more positively than did no-target participants. In contrast, among participants primed with their future ideal selves, this positive effect was undermined. If anything, participants exposed to the star target rated themselves less positively than did no-target participants.

Thus, as in Study 5, reminding participants of their best selves undermined the inspiration provided by a role model. Those focused on their best past or hoped-for accomplishments were constrained in their ability to imagine a more positive future self. As a result, they were self-deflated by the star. Those focused on their actual, more typical selves were free to generate a self as outstanding as the star and so were self-enhanced by the role model.

Study 7: Role Models Can Inspire Individuals to Generate More Positive Future Selves

The idea that role models inspire people to generate more positive future selves than they would spontaneously imagine is central to our explanation of

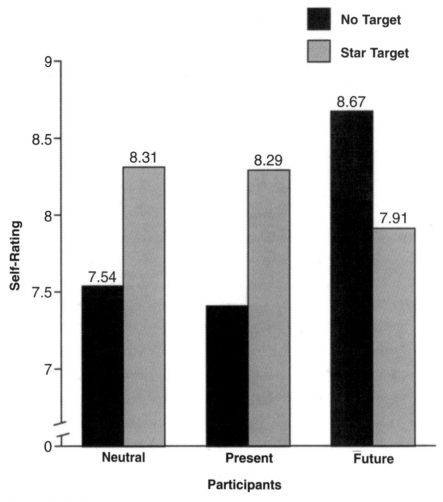

Figure 6.6. Self-ratings of success among participants primed for present versus future success before exposure to a successful role model (star target). (Study 6) From Lockwood and Kunda (1999, figure 3, p. 220). Copyright 1999 by the American Psychological Association. Adapted with permission of the publisher and author.

why priming best selves undermines inspiration. We could strengthen this argument by showing that the future selves that individuals typically envision are not nearly as spectacular as those that they imagine after encountering a role model. In one study, we did just that: We asked individuals to describe their ideal future selves either just before or just after reading about a role model, and then we coded the positivity of the future selves that they generated (Lockwood & Kunda, 1999, Study 3). We expected that individuals exposed to a role model would generate more outstanding future selves than would individuals who generated future selves before exposure to a role model.

As in Studies 5 and 6, the experiment involved a bogus two-study design. Participants were randomly assigned to a pre-target or post-target condition. Pre-target participants were asked to describe their ideal future selves as part of a pilot questionnaire on student life and then read a bogus newspaper article about a highly successful student in their own academic major. This condition was essentially the same as the ideal future prime condition in Study 6. Post-target participants read the article about the star student first and then described their ideal future selves. Next, participants in both groups completed the self-ratings of success items.

Participants' descriptions of their ideal future selves were coded by three independent raters who were unaware of participants' experimental condition. Raters assessed the overall positivity of participants' responses on a 5-point scale ranging from 1 (below average) to 5 (above average). These positivity ratings are presented in the top row of Table 6.1. As expected, the future-self descriptions of participants who described themselves after reading about the role model were rated as more positive than those of participants who described themselves before reading about the role model. Exposure to the outstanding other did indeed lead participants to generate more spectacular future selves. In addition, as may also be seen in Table 6.1, following the exposure to the role model, the self-ratings of pre-target participants were less positive than those of post-target participants. Participants who described their ideal selves before reading about the star were constrained in their ability to imagine more positive future selves. Like the participants in the future prime condition of Study 6, they were unable to generate still more positive selves after exposure to the star. Those who described themselves only after reading about the star were not constrained in this way. The star had encouraged them to generate more positive future selves, and they therefore also had more positive self-perceptions.

Reminding participants in advance of their best hoped-for selves also served to undercut their belief in their ability to attain the star's level of success. At the end of the questionnaire, participants rated how their own future

TABLE 6.1

Mean Coding of Hoped for Future Selves, Self-Ratings, and Success Ratings of Participants Who Described Their Future Goals Before or After Exposure to a Star Target (Study 7)

	Pre-target condition	Post-target condition
Coding of future selves positivity	2.89	3.32
Objective measures self-ratings	7.38	8.26
success ratings	−2.31	−0.84

Note. Higher numbers indicate more positive ratings. From Lockwood and Kunda (1999, table 1, p. 222). Copyright 1999 by the American Psychological Association. Reprinted with permission.

success would compare to that of the target, on a 13-point scale ranging from −6 (I will be much less successful than Jennifer/Jeffrey Walker), through 0 (I will be about as successful as Jeffrey/Jennifer Walker), to +6 (I will be much more successful than Jennifer/Jeffrey Walker). Pre-target participants viewed themselves as less likely to become as successful as the star than did post-target participants, as is shown in Table 6.1. Reminding participants of their best hopes in advance appears to have grounded them in reality, making it difficult for them to imagine a self as successful as the star. Those participants who described themselves after reading about the star did not experience this constraint; they believed that they could become as successful as the star.

CONCLUSION

Taken together, these studies suggest that outstanding others will only affect self-perceptions if they are considered relevant. The impact of a relevant star will depend on the perceived attainability of the star's achievements. If these achievements seem attainable, one can imagine an equally successful future self and thus draw inspiration from the star's accomplishments. If, however, the star's success seems out of reach because one has already missed the chance of achieving comparable success, because one believes one's abilities cannot improve, or because one is reminded of one's own limitations, then the inspirational impact of the role model will be undermined, and one may feel demoralized rather than inspired.

Inspiration Versus Reflection

The notion that upward comparisons on self-relevant dimensions can be inspiring and self-enhancing has received little previous attention. Earlier theorists suggested that individuals could be self-enhanced by superior others through "basking in the reflected glory" of a close other's achievements (e.g., Cialdini et al., 1976; Tesser & Campbell, 1983). Such reflection occurs when the other's achievements do not threaten the self because they are in a domain that is not self-relevant. In addition, reflection may occur when one is focusing on one's social or group identity rather than on one's personal identity (Brewer & Weber, 1994). One can feel proud to be a member of a successful group, such as one's baseball team or sorority, without experiencing a change in one's personal goals and ambitions. We have found that role models can also exert a different kind of positive impact on the self: inspiration. Inspiration can occur even (indeed, especially) if the star's domain of excellence is highly self-relevant, so that the star becomes a role model that one hopes and wishes to emulate. People are inspired by role models not because they are reveling in the models' achievements, but rather because they are imagining a similar level of future success for themselves. They are not experiencing self-enhancement based on their membership in a successful group; instead, their sense of themselves as unique individuals striving to achieve personal ambitions has been engaged. Thus, the role model can enhance their personal rather than their group identity.

It could be argued that, in these studies, we have not demonstrated inspiration, but rather have merely provided another example of reflection. After all, in most cases, participants were positively affected by role models who were or had been members of their in-group, high-achievers in their own academic program or career area. Perhaps participants experienced self-enhancement merely because their group identity was boosted by the accomplishments of the role model, not because they perceived themselves to be any more likely to achieve personal success.

We have several reasons for believing otherwise. First, participants' own descriptions of their reactions to the role model (Studies 1 and 2) provide vivid examples of inspiration. Participants reported feeling inspired and motivated, modifying and enhancing their goals, and hoping for comparable achievements. Moreover, they were especially likely to do so in the those conditions that prompted self-enhancement. Study 7 demonstrated further that role models can indeed affect personal goals; individuals described more positive future selves after than before they were exposed to a relevant star. If individuals were experiencing only reflection, we would not expect their individual academic and career goals to be boosted by the superior other. Finally, the reflection process cannot account for the role of perceived attainability in determining the star's impact. If a role model makes one feel good merely because a member of one's group has achieved success, the extent to which one perceives that success to be within one's own grasp should be irrelevant. The fact that perceived attainability determined whether the outcome of the comparison was positive or negative suggests that participants' personal ambitions and aspirations were involved.

In proposing that role models can inspire individuals, we do not wish to dispute the importance of the reflection process. There is ample evidence that people can come to feel better about themselves through basking in the reflected glory of outstanding others (Brewer & Weber, 1994; Cialdini et al., 1976; Tesser & Campbell, 1983). We have found that outstanding others can also prompt self-enhancement through a different route—inspiration. Moreover, inspiration occurs in circumstances where reflection is unlikely, namely, when the other excelled at a highly self-relevant domain, and when one's personal self is salient.

Social Comparison as Analogy

By applying principles of analogical reasoning to social comparison processes, this research also enhances our understanding of what makes others relevant for the purpose of comparison. In his original article on social comparison theory, Festinger (1954) argued that people prefer to compare themselves to similar others, but he provided no clear definition of similarity. Since then, researchers have wrestled with the question of what determines whether individuals will compare themselves to others (cf. Wood, 1989). Analogical reasoning provides a valuable framework for understanding when and how social comparison processes occur: Individuals will be influenced by others only when they can map themselves onto another person, drawing parallels between their own experience and that of the other.

In our research to date, we have focused on surface or attribute similarities in determining the relevance of role models. For example, in Study 1, we found that a role model who shared participants' career interests was more relevant than one with different career interests. However, analogies can also be guided by more complex, structural similarities that are based on elaborate patterns of relations among elements (Holyoak & Thagard, 1997). In some cases, structural similarities may even overcome superficial dissimilarities. For example, in one study (Markman & Gentner, 1993), participants were shown two cartoon frames, one in which a woman receives food from a food bank employee, and another in which a woman feeds a squirrel. When asked to reflect on the two frames, participants mapped the woman in the first frame onto the squirrel rather than onto the woman in the second frame. The features of the woman and the squirrel are clearly highly dissimilar, but the underlying structure of the relationship, "receives food," is the same.

Similarly, individuals may be able to draw comparisons between themselves and role models based on structural rather than surface similarities (Lockwood, 1998). If one can perceive more abstract, relational similarities that one shares with a successful other, one may draw an analogy between oneself and the other despite surface dissimilarities. For example, a White feminist may map herself onto Martin Luther King, despite the differences in race, gender, and occupation type, because of their shared interest in overcoming discrimination. Thus, mismatches on surface attributes may be overcome if deeper, structural parallels between individuals and a role model are highlighted. If one perceives these deeper shared patterns, one may be influenced by a superficially dissimilar role model.

The relevance of role models may be determined not only by a combination of surface and structural similarities, but also by one's goals. Analogical reasoning is constrained not only by similarities between the target and source, but also by the purpose of the individual drawing the analogy: Individuals tend to form analogies that are congruent with their goals (Holyoak & Thagard, 1997). Goals may influence both the kinds of social analogies that are drawn and the outcomes of such analogies. For example, individuals with primarily achievement and self-promotion goals may be especially likely to draw comparisons between themselves and superior others who can serve as guides for self-improvement. In contrast, individuals with primarily self-protection and harm prevention goals may prefer to compare themselves to inferior others whose misfortunes may contain lessons about how to avoid a similar fate (cf. Higgins, 1998; Taylor & Lobel, 1989). People may be most strongly affected by comparisons that are congruent with their motivation. If a comparison supports one's goals, one may develop a more elaborate and convincing analogy between oneself and the other than he or she would if the comparison does not serve such a purpose.

Overall, this research has important practical as well as theoretical implications regarding the potential effects of role models on their target audiences. It is a cultural cliché that role models will be inspirational, that their superlative accomplishments will encourage those around them to strive for a similar degree of excellence. These studies, however, suggest that the effects of such outstanding others will not always be beneficial. First, if the role model is perceived as irrelevant, there may be no impact whatsoever on the audience. Second, the impact of a relevant role model will be positive only if the achievements of that model appear attainable. If one believes that one will not be able to become like the star in the future, because of external circumstances, beliefs about the malleability of one's abilities, or reminders of what one is realistically likely to achieve, then one may in fact be demoralized by the outstanding other. Only if one can imagine a future self as outstanding as the role model will one be inspired.

REFERENCES

Anderson, S. M., Glassman, N. S., Chen, S., & Cole, S. W. (1995). Transference in social perception: The role of chronic accessibility in significant-other representations. *Journal of Personality and Social Psychology, 69,* 41–57.

Aspinwall, L. G. (1997). Future-oriented aspects of social comparison: A framework for studying health-related comparison activity. In B. P. Buunk & F. X. Gibbons (Eds.), *Health and coping: Perspectives from social comparison theory* (pp. 125–165). Hillsdale, NJ: Erlbaum.

Baron, R. M., & Kenny, D. A. (1986). The moderator–mediator variable distinction in social psychological research: Conceptual, strategic, and statistical considerations. *Journal of Personality and Social Psychology, 51,* 1173–1182.

Brewer, M. B., & Weber, J. G. (1994). Self-evaluation effects on interpersonal versus intergroup social comparison. *Journal of Personality and Social Psychology, 66,* 268–275.

Cialdini, R. B., Borden, R. J., Thorne, A., Walker, M. R., Freeman, S., & Sloan, L. R. (1976). Basking in reflected glory: Three (football) field studies. *Journal of Personality and Social Psychology, 34,* 366–375.

Collins, R. L. (1996). For better or worse: The impact of upward social comparisons on self-evaluations. *Psychological Bulletin, 119,* 51–69.

Deacon, J. (1998, February 23). Profile in courage. *Macleans, 111,* 36–37.

Dweck, C. S., & Leggett, E. L. (1988). A social-cognitive approach to motivation and personality. *Psychological Review, 95*, 256–273.

Festinger, L. (1954). A theory of social comparison processes. *Human Relations, 7*, 117–140.

Heider, F. (1958). *The psychology of interpersonal relations.* New York: Wiley.

Higgins, E. T. (1998). Promotion and prevention: Regulatory focus as a motivational principle. *Advances in Experimental Social Psychology, 30*, 1–46.

Holyoak, K. J., & Thagard, P. (1997). The analogical mind. *American Psychologist, 52*, 35–44.

Lockwood, P. (1998). *How do people respond to role models? The role of analogical reasoning and self-esteem in comparisons to superior others.* Unpublished doctoral dissertation, University of Waterloo, Waterloo, Ontario, Canada.

Lockwood, P. (1999). [Self-perceptions following social comparisons]. Unpublished data.

Lockwood, P., & Kunda, Z. (1997). Superstars and me: Predicting the impact of role models on the self. *Journal of Personality and Social Psychology, 73*, 91–103.

Lockwood, P., & Kunda, Z. (1999). Salient best selves can undermine inspiration by outstanding role models. *Journal of Personality and Social Psychology, 76*, 214–228.

Major, B., Testa, M., & Bylsma, W. H. (1991). Responses to upward and downward social comparisons: The impact of esteem-relevance and perceived control. In J. Suls & T. A. Wills (Eds.), *Social comparison: Contemporary theory and research* (pp. 237–260). Hillsdale, NJ: Erlbaum.

Markman, A. B., & Gentner, D. (1993). Structural alignment during similarity comparisons. *Cognitive Psychology, 25*, 431–467.

Markus, H., & Nurius, P. (1986). Possible selves. *American Psychologist, 41*, 954–969.

McGregor, I., Newby-Clark, I. R., & Zanna, M. P. (in press). "Remembering" dissonance: Simultaneous accessibility of inconsistent cognitive elements moderates epistemic discomfort. In E. Harmon-Jones & J. Mills (Eds.), *Cognitive dissonance: Progress on a pivotal theory in social psychology* (pp. 325–353). Washington, DC: American Psychological Association.

Pleban, R., & Tesser, A. (1981). The effects of relevance and quality of another's performance on interpersonal closeness. *Social Psychology Quarterly, 44*, 278–285.

Reeves, L. M., & Weisberg, R. W. (1994) The role of content and abstract information in analogical transfer. *Psychological Bulletin, 115*, 381–400.

Taylor, S. E., & Lobel, M. (1989). Social comparison activity under threat: Downward evaluation and upward contacts. *Psychological Review, 96*, 569–575.

Tesser, A., & Campbell, J. (1983). Self-definition and self-evaluation maintenance. In J. Suls & A. Greenwald (Eds.), *Social psychological perspectives on the self* (pp. 1–31). Hillsdale, NJ: Erlbaum.

Tesser, A., & Collins, J. E. (1988). Emotion in social reflection and comparison situations: Intuitive, systematic, and exploratory approaches. *Journal of Personality and Social Psychology, 55*, 695–709.

Tesser, A., & Cornell, D. P. (1991). On the confluence of self processes. *Journal of Experimental Social Psychology, 27*, 501–526.

Tesser, A., Millar, M., & Moore, J. (1988). Some affective consequences of social comparison and reflection processes: The pain and pleasure of being close. *Journal of Personality and Social Psychology, 54*, 49–61.

Tesser, A., & Paulhus, D. (1983). Self-definition of self: Private and public self-evaluation strategies. *Journal of Personality and Social Psychology, 44*, 672–682.

Testa, M., & Major, B. (1990). The impact of social comparison after failure: The moderating effects of perceived control. *Basic and Applied Social Psychology, 11*, 205–218.

Thagard, P., & Kunda, Z. (1998). Making sense of people: Coherence mechanisms. In S. J. Read & C. C. Miller (Eds.), *Connectionist models of social reasoning and social behavior* (pp. 3–26). Mahwah, NJ: Erlbaum.

Wilkes, J. (1998, February 17). Jessica just wanted to make him feel better. *The Toronto Star*, p. 1.

Wong, J. (1998, October 6). The grass is always greener in Anna Quindlen's yard. *The Globe and Mail*, p. A12.

Wood, J. V. (1989). Theory and research concerning social comparisons of personal attributes. *Psychological Bulletin, 106*, 231–248.

Wood, J. V., & Van der Zee, K. (1997). Social comparisons among cancer patients: Under what conditions are comparisons upward and downward? In B. P. Buunk & F. X. Gibbons (Eds.), *Social comparison, health, and coping* (pp. 299–328). Hillsdale, NJ: Erlbaum.

7

SEEING THE SELF THROUGH A PARTNER'S EYES: WHY SELF-DOUBTS TURN INTO RELATIONSHIP INSECURITIES

SANDRA L. MURRAY
JOHN G. HOLMES

The most peculiar social self which one is apt to have is in the mind of the person one is in love with. The good or bad fortunes of this self cause the most intense elation and dejection. . . . To his own consciousness he *is* not, so long as this particular social self fails to get recognition, and when it is recognized his contentment passes all bounds.

The Principles of Psychology, William James, 1910

When individuals look into a romantic partner's eyes, what image of themselves do they see? Does the image that reflects back affirm their hopes and aspirations for themselves and their relationships? Or does it confirm their own self-doubts or uncertainties? As James intuited, such looking-glass selves are critical because individuals seem to base personal feelings of self-esteem on the degree of acceptance they perceive from others (e.g., Baldwin & Sinclair, 1996; Cooley, 1902; Felson, 1989; Leary, Tambor, Terdal, & Downs, 1995; Mead, 1934).

We are grateful for the assistance of Lorne Campbell, Christine Celnar, Dan Dolderman, Mary Dooley, Julie Haniszewski, Geoff MacDonald, Tonia Schlicker, and Amy Sullivan in the conduct of this research. This research was prepared with the support of a Social Sciences and Humanities Research Council of Canada (SSHRC) research grant to John Holmes and Sandra Murray and NIMH B/START and UB Social Sciences Research Foundation grants to Sandra Murray.

It is perhaps a happy accident of romantic life, then, that both low and high self-esteem individuals possess romantic partners who typically see them in more generous or idealized ways than they see themselves (Murray, Holmes, & Griffin, 1996a, 1996b). The existence of such positive reflected appraisals raises the possibility that close, romantic attachments might provide one special context where low self-esteem individuals function relatively free of their own self-doubts. In fact, seeing themselves through their partners' more forgiving and accepting eyes might even provide an effective remedy for more chronic insecurities.

Despite the ready availability of an affirming partner, however, dispositional insecurities appear to pose a significant relationship vulnerability. Individuals with lower self-esteem are involved in less satisfying marriages (Fincham & Bradbury, 1993; Murray et al., 1996a) and less satisfying (Murray et al., 1996a) and stable dating relationships than high self-esteem individuals (Hendrick, Hendrick, & Adler, 1988). Similarly, individuals troubled by greater neuroticism (and thus lower self-esteem) are involved in less satisfying (Karney & Bradbury, 1997) and less stable marriages (Kelly & Conley, 1987) than are less neurotic individuals. Why does this occur?

Growing evidence suggests that relationship satisfaction and stability depend on intimates seeing each other's behaviors and attributes in the most generous or positive light possible (e.g., Murray et al., 1996a, 1996b; Murray & Holmes, 1997; Simpson, Ickes, & Blackstone, 1995; Van Lange & Rusbult, 1995). However, the possession of personal insecurities appears to interfere with such generous perceptions. For instance, individuals troubled by greater neuroticism (and thus lower self-esteem) are more likely to make blaming attributions for their spouses' behaviors (Karney, Bradbury, Fincham, & Sullivan, 1994). Dating intimates high on attachment-related anxiety or fear of rejection (and thus lower self-esteem) also interpret their partners' hypothetical (Collins, 1996) and actual transgressions in suspicious ways that are likely to exacerbate feelings of distress (Simpson, Rholes, & Phillips, 1996). More generally, low self-esteem dating and married individuals see less virtue in their partners concurrently (Murray et al., 1996a), and low self-esteem dating individuals grow even less generous over time (Murray et al., 1996b).

Why do low self-esteem individuals find less to value in their partners and relationships than high self-esteem individuals? The most obvious answer might seem to be that low self-esteem individuals actually possess less virtuous, less desirable partners. In both dating and married couples, however, the partners of low and high self-esteem individuals do not differ significantly in self-esteem (Murray et al., 1996a, 1996b). Married intimates are not even all that similar in terms of basic personality dimensions, such as neuroticism (Lykken & Tellegen, 1993). It seems unlikely, then, that self-doubt poses a relationship vulnerability simply because lows attract lower self-esteem, more neurotic partners than high self-esteem individuals.

THE LOOKING-GLASS SELF AND THE REGULATION OF INTERPERSONAL DEPENDENCY

Maybe the answer lies in the way that low and high self-esteem individuals respond to the experience of dependency and vulnerability in their romantic relationships. Low and high self-esteem individuals alike are uniquely vulnerable in their relationships. In perhaps no other context is the anticipation of another's acceptance more self-affirming and the possibility of rejection more self-threatening (e.g., Baumeister, Wotman, & Stillwell, 1993; Hazan & Shaver, 1994). Such high personal stakes necessitate a certain degree of caution in the social inference process. In fact, attachment and interdependence theorists believe that individuals actively regulate closeness (and thus dependence) with felt security, not letting themselves feel fully in love and committed until they are reasonably assured that their feelings are reciprocated (e.g., Berscheid & Fei, 1977; Bowlby, 1982; Holmes & Rempel, 1989; Kelley, 1983).

For low self-esteem individuals, though, this level of confidence in a partner's positive regard may be difficult to attain even when it is warranted. In this chapter, we explore the hypothesis that self-doubt turns into relationship insecurities because perceptions of a partner's love and regard for the self are largely projections, reflecting self-perceived worthiness of love rather than accurately mirroring the partner's regard. We argue that such looking-glass selves play a crucial role in relationships, because individuals regulate processes of attachment and relationship-valuing in a self-protective fashion, seeing the best in their partners and relationships only when they feel confident that their partners also see special qualities in them. Feeling unsure of their partners' regard, then, low self-esteem individuals might defensively find fault in their partners or relationships to protect themselves from the prospect of rejection. In contrast, feeling more confident of their partners' regard, high self-esteem individuals might safely risk greater vulnerability and see their relationships in a more generous light than lows.

Figure 7.1 presents our conceptual model of the dependency regulation process (Murray, Holmes, & Griffin, in press; Murray, Holmes, MacDonald, & Ellsworth, 1998). It reflects our assumption that reflected appraisals—perceptions of a partner's regard and continuing acceptance—provide a critical mechanism linking self-esteem to relationship perceptions.[1] In this chapter, we first describe the evidence linking self-esteem to perceptions of others' regard for the self (path *a* in Figure 7.1). We then discuss the evidence linking these reflected selves to processes of attachment and relationship-valuing (path *b* in Figure 7.1). We conclude by offering a conceptualization of self-

---

[1]For the sake of simplicity, we refer to perceived reflected appraisals as perceived regard or perceptions of a partner's regard throughout this chapter.

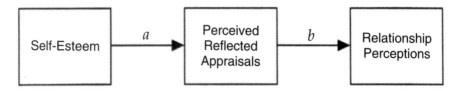

Figure 7.1. The dependency regulation model.

esteem maintenance and change that emphasizes its roots in processes of interpersonal attachment.

Seeing the Self as Imagined Through a Partner's Eyes

What are the implications of the hypothesized link between self-esteem and perceptions of a partner's regard for achieving a sense of felt security in a partner's affections? Attachment theorists have argued that models of self as being worthy of love develop through experiences with more or less responsive caregivers in early childhood (e.g., Bartholomew, 1990; Bowlby, 1982; Collins & Read, 1994; Hazan & Shaver, 1994). Experiences with consistently responsive caregivers are thought to foster personal feelings of self-worth, whereas experiences with less consistently responsive or even rejecting caregivers are thought to foster feelings of personal inadequacy. From an attachment perspective, then, models of self reflect internalized expectancies regarding others' positive or negative orientations to the self (e.g., Baldwin, 1992).

Carried into adult romantic relationships, more or less positive models of self may function as heuristics that color perceptions of others' regard for the self in a reciprocal fashion. Consistent with this hypothesis, individuals simply seem to assume that most others see them in roughly the same way as they see themselves (e.g., Kenny, 1994; Shrauger & Schoeneman, 1979). Imagine the likely consequences if such biases also extend to romantic relationships. Low self-esteem individuals generally possess less positive, less certain, and more conflicted beliefs about themselves than high self-esteem individuals (e.g., Baumeister, 1993, 1998; Baumgardner, 1990; Campbell, 1990; Campbell et al., 1996). If most individuals assume that their romantic partners see them just as they see themselves, low self-esteem individuals should then chronically feel less positively regarded than high self-esteem individuals. Rather accidentally, then, people with high self-esteem may accurately estimate their partners' positive regard, but the identical tendency toward naïve realism might lead individuals with low self-esteem to underestimate how positively their partners see them.

The potential threat to felt security imposed by such inaccurate perceptions of a partner's regard may be further compounded by differences in the working models that regulate the inner and interpersonal worlds of low and high self-esteem individuals. Low self-esteem individuals possess a more contingent or conditional sense of others' regard than highs (Baldwin & Sinclair, 1996; Roberts, Gotlib, & Kassel, 1996). That is, low self-esteem individuals believe that others' acceptance (and affections) depends on them possessing valued attributes and living up to certain standards. In contrast, high self-esteem individuals tend to see others' acceptance (and affections) as being relatively unconditional in nature.

A sense of felt security in a partner's affections may therefore prove to be a readily attainable goal for high self-esteem individuals because it is so easy for them to generate reasons why their partners should care for them. In a sense, a partner's love is no mystery to them. It is more than adequately explained by the assumption that their partners see as many virtues in them as they see in themselves. However, the same sense of felt security may prove to be an elusive goal for low self-esteem individuals if they believe that others' love and acceptance is conditional and that their partners see as many faults in them as they see in themselves.

Such doubts about a romantic partner's regard may be particularly self-threatening or hurtful for low self-esteem individuals. Interpersonal theorists on self-esteem have argued that feelings of self-worth are directly calibrated to a sense of connection to others and that low self-esteem (both acute and chronic) reflects a state of deprivation that activates the need for approval and interpersonal connections (Kernis, Cornell, Sun, Berry, & Harlow, 1993; Leary et al., 1995). Thus, in the unique context for self-affirmation that relationships provide, low self-esteem individuals may entertain the hope that their partners' admiration might help them realize certain ideals for the self. In fact, they might be especially dependent on their partners' positive regard for a sense of self-esteem because they possess relatively few other self-affirmational resources (Steele, Spencer, & Lynch, 1993), and they also tend to feel isolated from others (Leary et al., 1995). However, the combination of pessimistic expectations and unfulfilled needs for acceptance may leave them more vigilant for signs of rejection than acceptance (e.g., Downey & Feldman, 1996; Nezlek, Kowalski, Leary, Blevins, & Holgate, 1997).

The Role of Perceived Regard in Regulating Dependency

The preceding arguments suggest that low self-esteem individuals may be caught in an uncomfortable approach–avoidance conflict in romantic relationships, needing their partners' positive regard and acceptance, but doubting its existence. What are the implications of such insecurities for processes of attachment and relationship-valuing? The dependency regulation path in Figure 7.1 (path *b*) reflects our assumption that perceived regard constrains feelings of attachment in ways that leave individuals who feel less valued or affirmed in their partners' eyes defensively perceiving less virtue or value in their partners and relationships than do individuals who feel more affirmed (regardless of self-esteem).

Accordingly, low self-esteem individuals may react to the implicit threat to the self posed by relatively negative perceptions of a partner's regard by maintaining a safe distance in their relationships, seeing their partners and relationships in a less positive light. In contrast, feeling more confident of their partners' regard, high self-esteem individuals can generally afford to risk greater vulnerability, by seeing their partners and relationships in a more generous, virtuous light. To translate these dynamics into mediational terms, perceptions of a partner's regard for the self may mediate the link between the perceiver's self-esteem and perceptions of the partner. More generally, perceived regard may also mediate the link between the perceiver's self-esteem and feelings of satisfaction in the relationship.

The idea that low self-esteem individuals react to insecurity by leaning toward avoidance, by valuing their relationships less, rather than more, than highs, might seem counterintuitive. After all, Leary et al. (1995) argued that self-esteem acts as a gauge or sociometer that monitors interpersonal acceptance. A basic assumption of this model is that low self-esteem individuals are especially motivated to seek inclusion and interpersonal connections to bolster self-esteem. More generally, many theorists on the self (Sedikides, 1993; Steele, 1988; Taylor & Brown, 1988) have argued that low, just like high, self-esteem individuals possess basic needs for self-affirmation (although some debate exists concerning the priority of self-enhancement over self-verification needs; see Swann, 1987). Surely, then, individuals with low self-esteem have the most to gain intrapersonally by valuing their relationships and the sense of interpersonal connection they provide.

In fact, growing evidence suggests that close attachments function in part as a self-affirmational resource. Intimates are happier in their relationships the closer they feel their partners bring them to their ideal selves (Drigotas, Rusbult, Wieselquist, & Whitton, 1996; Ruvolo & Brennan, 1997). Dating and married individuals are also happier in their relationships when their partners see virtues in them that they do not see in themselves (Murray et al., 1996a), and dating individuals who are idealized in this way actually show increases in self-esteem and security of attachment over time (Murray et al., 1996b). Therefore, enhancing the value of the relationship (and thus the value of the partner's regard) might seem to provide a direct means of affirming the self for both lows and highs.

Although the sociometer model maintains that the need for acceptance generally motivates such approach behaviors, our dependency regulation perspective suggests that a sense of inclusion needs to be secured before intimates are willing to take the risk of relying on their relationships for self-esteem. That is, individuals allow themselves to feel close and attached to others only in circumstances where the possibility of rejection is perceived to be relatively minimal. If that is the case, enhancing the value of the relationship is likely to be seen as a viable or safe strategy of self-enhancement only by individuals who trust in the continued stability of their relationships. For lows, enhancing the value of the relationship may pose more potential threats than boosts to the self because they cannot escape doubts about their partners' continuing positive regard and affections. For highs, though, enhancing the value of the relationship may pose more potential boosts than threats to the self because they possess a sense of trust in their partners' continued acceptance.

Prior theorizing and research on self-evaluation motives suggest that low self-esteem individuals react to situations that pose the potential for gain and loss to the self in a self-protective or risk-averse fashion. Typically, they take only those opportunities for self-enhancement that seem sure to affirm the self and avoid those that might pose a further threat to their already impoverished sense of self (see Baumeister, 1993, 1998, for reviews). In contrast, high self-esteem individuals are relatively more risk-seeking because their resource rich self-concept can easily absorb the effects of occasional losses. Troubled by chronic doubts about their partners' regard, affirming the self through a sense of connection to the relationship may simply seem to be too risky a strategy of self-enhancement for lows (because it increases the value of a self-concept resource they anticipate losing).

To summarize these dynamics, low self-esteem individuals may be caught in an uncomfortable approach–avoidance conflict in romantic relationships where embracing the relationship poses a potential boost to the self, but the process of becoming closer also activates fears of rejection, and thus poses a potential loss to the self. We believe that the resulting motive to protect the self from the possibility of loss typically interferes with processes of attachment and relationship-valuing for low self-esteem individuals.[2]

Of course, these hypothesized dynamics are not occurring in a vacuum. Dating and married partners are interdependent in that the feelings, thoughts, and behaviors of one member of the couple affect the other (see Kelley, 1983, for a review). Consequently, the partners of lows may be caught in the unfortunate cross-fire between the conflicting motivations of low self-esteem individuals. Speaking to this possibility, the partners of lows reported less satisfaction in both dating and marital relationships than the partners of highs (Murray et al., 1996a; in press). They have also reported less satisfaction, greater conflict, and greater ambivalence as dating relationships progress (Murray et al., 1996b). It seems easy to imagine how low

---

[2]Although projection processes will typically ensure that valuing a partner seems psychologically safe to individuals with high self-esteem, we are not trying to argue that these individuals are immune to insecurities. Instead, there may be times in a relationship, such as in its initial stages, when even they may experience doubts about their partners' regard and find themselves self-protectively regulating a sense of connection.

self-esteem individuals' perhaps constant demands for reassurance, overreactions to conflicts, and relatively negative views of their partners might undermine their partners' satisfaction over time, effectively creating the potential for a self-fulfilling prophecy to occur (e.g., Snyder, 1992). If that is the case, perceptions of a partner's regard for the self may also mediate the link between the perceiver's self-models and the partner's reports of satisfaction.

A CORRELATIONAL TEST OF THE DEPENDENCY REGULATION MODEL

The dynamics that we have outlined imply that perceptions of a partner's regard mediate the link between self-esteem and relationship perceptions. As our first correlational test of the mediational model depicted in Figure 7.1, we asked dating ($n = 121$) and married ($n = 105$) couples to rate themselves and their partners on a variety of interpersonal virtues and faults, such as responsive, critical, lazy, and warm (Murray et al., in press). They also rated how they thought their partners saw them on these same qualities (to provide a measure of perceived regard), as well as how they wanted their partners to see them (to provide a measure of desired regard). Partners' ratings of the participants on these same qualities indexed their actual regard. Each member of the couple also completed a global measure of relationship satisfaction (e.g., "I am perfectly satisfied in my relationship"). The couples in the two samples had been dating an average of 19.0 months and married an average of 10.9 years, respectively.

Figure 7.2 presents the structural model we used to test our hypotheses that self-esteem structures perceived regard, and such reflected selves in turn

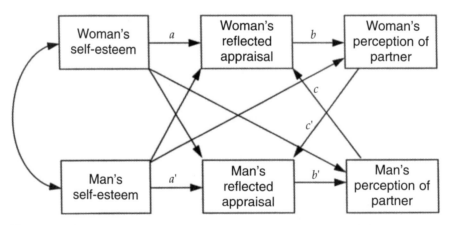

Figure 7.2. The role of perceived reflected appraisals in regulating the link between self-esteem and perceptions of the partner. From Murray, Holmes, & Griffin, in press.

regulate the value intimates see in their partners. At first glance, the model of dependency regulation depicted in Figure 7.2 might not seem to remotely resemble the conceptual model we presented in Figure 7.1. Incorporating dyadic data (i.e., the partner's self-esteem and perceptions) necessitated a causal structure that appears more complex on its surface. However, the basic elements of our conceptual model are still represented. First, the naïve realism paths a and a' represent the link between self-esteem and perceptions of the partner's regard for the self. Second, the regulated regard paths b and b' index the role that perceived regard plays in regulating how positively individuals see their partners. The additional backwards paths c and c' index the extent to which perceived regard is rooted in an interpersonal reality (i.e., the partner's actual regard). Including these backwards paths allows us to see whether naïve realism results in perceptions of a partner's regard that are not warranted by the partner's actual appraisals (i.e., paths a and a', controlling for paths c and c').[3]

To test this model, we used the structural equation modeling program within the AMOS procedure of SPSS for Windows. This program allowed us to test for both gender and relationship status (i.e., dating vs. married) differences in the size of the path coefficients (for detailed descriptions of these procedures, see Kenny, 1996; and Murray et al., 1996a; in press). When we conducted our analyses, we found strong and parallel support for the basic model presented in Figure 7.2 for both dating and married men and women. Accordingly, we present standardized coefficients that are pooled across both gender and relationship status.

Not surprisingly, perceptions of a partner's regard partly reflected the partner's actual appraisal (paths c and $c' = .21$). The more positive their partners' regard, the more valued or positively regarded individuals felt. Even when we controlled for the kernel of truth in perceptions of a partner's regard, the naïve realism paths were strong and significant (a and $a' = .69$), suggesting that personal feelings of self-esteem distort the image individuals see in the looking glass. Low and high self-esteem dating and married individuals used their own self-images as templates for constructing their partners' impressions of them, consistent with a basic tenet of self-verification theory (Swann, 1987). Consequently, individuals with high self-esteem believed that their partners saw them relatively positively, whereas lows believed that their partners saw them relatively negatively.

---

[3]All the paths indicated on Figure 7.2 were included in the estimation of the model (although we simply focus on the paths of greatest conceptual interest for the sake of simplicity). Including the backwards paths also necessitated the placement of two additional constraints on the model: (a) the inclusion of correlated errors between perceived regard and perceptions of the partner and (b) constraining the direct effect of the perceiver's self-models on perceptions of the partner to be zero. Freeing these paths would have made this model underidentified because of the correlated residuals introduced by the backwards paths. We examine the direct effects of self-esteem shortly in a recursive version of Figure 7.2.

Ironically, though, the relatively negative image of themselves that low self-esteem individuals saw in the looking glass was not warranted by their partners' actual regard. A comparison of the means for perceived regard and the partner's actual regard revealed that both dating and married low self-esteem individuals dramatically underestimated just how positively their partners saw them. In contrast, high self-esteem individuals more accurately appreciated their partners' positive regard. Moreover, the greater insecurities of lows seemed to arise despite their hopes: They still reported wanting their partners to see them much more positively than they saw themselves. In fact, the discrepancy between self-perceptions and desired regard was greater for low than high self-esteem individuals, suggesting that lows need romantic partners more for self-affirmation than do highs (just as the sociometer model of self-esteem predicts). Despite their greater dependency, though, lows were less likely to perceive the affirmation they sought in their partners' eyes (even though this resource existed).

Turning the Looking Glass Outward

Did the image that intimates saw in the looking glass then constrain the amount of value they could safely risk seeing in their partners? Consistent with our dependency regulation hypothesis, perceptions of a partner's regard for the self appeared to regulate the value individuals found in their partners (paths b and $b' = .48$). Generally, when dating and married perceivers found greater evidence of virtue in their partners, the more positively regarded they felt when they looked at themselves through their partners' eyes. More specifically, feeling more positively regarded by their partners, high self-esteem individuals saw their partners in a more positive, more generous light than lows. Conversely, feeling less affirmed in their partners' eyes, low self-esteem individuals saw their partners in a less positive, less generous light.

A recursive version of Figure 7.2 also revealed that perceived regard completely mediated the link between self-esteem and perceptions of the partner. In this model, we reversed the direction of paths c and c' and estimated the direct effects of self-models on perceptions of the partner. Our analyses revealed that the direct paths for self-esteem were close to zero, and the regulated regard paths were again strong and significant. Finding an effect of perceived regard on perceptions of the partner in this revised model is particularly impressive, because this regulation effect emerged after we controlled for the component of perceived regard that is rooted in the perceiver's self-esteem. This suggests that reflected selves—the images individuals see of themselves in their partners' eyes—play a unique and important role in constraining interpersonal generosity in dating and marital relationships.

Although these results provided encouraging support for our dependency regulation framework, there are at least two possible alternative explanations for these effects. The first comes from the fact that the measures of self-esteem, perceived regard, and perceptions of the partner were all based on the identical set of attributes. As a result, shared method variance may have artificially inflated the magnitude of the naïve realism and regulated regard paths. However, we found an identical mediational pattern when we used a different indicator of self-models: global self-esteem on the Rosenberg (1965) scale. The second comes from the possibility that low self-esteem individuals might feel less admired and find less virtue in their partners simply because they are involved in less satisfying relationships. In other words, self-esteem, perceived regard, and partner perceptions might be related only through a shared, spurious correlation with satisfaction (i.e., a third variable model). However, perceptions of a partner's regard still mediated the link between self-esteem and interpersonal generosity when we included satisfaction as an exogenous variable in the model illustrated in Figure 7.2.

Did the image individuals saw in the looking glass also constrain the amount of happiness they were able to find in their relationships? Figure 7.3 presents the structural model that we used to examine the role of perceived regard in mediating the link between the perceiver's self-esteem and the perceiver's and partner's reports of satisfaction. Focusing on the paths from self-esteem to satisfaction, paths a and a' tap the direct effects of perceivers' self-esteem on their own feelings of satisfaction. Paths b and b' tap the direct effects of perceivers' self-esteem on their partners' satisfaction. Turning to the paths from reflected selves to satisfaction, paths c and c' index the effects of feeling positively regarded by a partner on the perceiver's satisfaction. Paths d and d' index the effects of possessing a partner who feels more positively regarded on the perceiver's satisfaction.

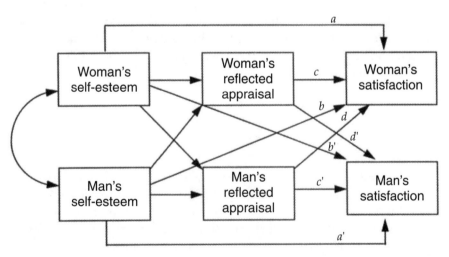

Figure 7.3. The role of perceived reflected appraisals in regulating the link between self-esteem and satisfaction.

When we obtained estimates for this model, we found strong support for the benefits of feeling valued or affirmed in a partner's eyes. Dating and married intimates reported greater satisfaction in their relationships, the more positively they believed their partners saw them (c and $c' = .45$). Individuals were also happier the more positively their partners felt they were regarded (d and $d' = .29$). Thus, satisfaction seems to reflect a shared, dyadic sense of felt security. Moreover, perceived regard completely mediated the link between self-esteem and reports of satisfaction. Such findings suggest that low self-esteem individuals are less happy in their relationships in part because they possess unwarranted and unwanted insecurities about their partners' regard for them.

The Benefits of Feeling Understood

Our arguments about the benefits of feeling valued, however, are inconsistent with a basic prediction of self-verification theory—that individuals prefer others who verify and confirm their self-concepts (e.g., Swann et al., 1994; Swann & Predmore, 1985). This reasoning suggests that individuals should be happiest in their relationships when they believe their partners see them as they see themselves, even if this involves confirming more negative self-concepts. To explore the potential benefits of feeling understood or verified, we conducted a series of regression analyses predicting satisfaction from self-perceptions on the interpersonal qualities scale, perceptions of the partner's regard, and the interaction (i.e., the match between the two perceptions). If intimates prefer self-verifying over self-affirming perceptions of a partner's regard, we should find a significant interaction in these regression analyses. However, we did not find any such interactions. Intimates were simply happier the more positively regarded that they felt. Crucially, then, low self-esteem individuals who perceived the least self-verifying images in the looking glass—that is, lows who felt most admired and affirmed in their partners' eyes—were actually happiest in both dating and marital relationships.

A SAFE HAVEN? WHEN SELF-PROTECTION AND RELATIONSHIP-VALUING MOTIVES COLLIDE

The results of the cross-sectional study suggest that low self-esteem individuals respond to the implicit self-threat posed by unwanted and unwarranted insecurities about their partners' regard by self-protectively finding less evidence of value in their relationships. In contrast, high self-esteem individuals seem to possess sufficient confidence in their partners' regard to risk greater vulnerability, seeing their partners and relationships in a more generous light. Although these effects were impressively robust across both dating and marital samples, the correlational nature of these findings limited our ability to draw support for the causal connections illustrated in Figure 7.1. Accordingly, we conducted four experiments to provide a more stringent test of our dependency regulation model (Murray et al., 1998).

According to Bowlby (1982), the experience of self-threat activates the attachment system (and its component models of self and other). If that is the case, the dynamics we observed in our cross-sectional study should be exacerbated whenever some sort of threat to the self is posed. Under such circumstances, romantic partners should provide a safe haven for high self-esteem individuals—a place where they can turn for self-affirmation and comfort in the face of inevitable stresses (see Collins & Read, 1994). However, a miscalibrated sociometer and the vulnerabilities implicit in their working models may make this same potential source of acceptance fraught with risk for low self-esteem individuals.

A Contamination Hypothesis

For people with low self-esteem, the activation of self-doubts posed by a critical remark from a friend, a poor evaluation at work, or moments of intemperance with their partners might only accentuate relationship insecurities. How might this occur? First, low self-esteem individuals are less certain of who they are than highs and, consequently, treat incoming information as being more self-diagnostic. This hypothesis-testing orientation thus leaves them with a more labile or reactive sense of self-esteem, because everyday stresses threaten their more vulnerable sense of self (e.g., Baumeister, 1993, 1998; Baumgardner, 1990; Campbell, 1990; Campbell et al., 1996). On such occasions of self-doubt, lows may wish they could turn to their partners for support. In fact, they may be especially dependent on their partners for support and approval in such instances because they possess fewer internal self-affirmational resources (e.g., Fritz & Helgeson, 1998; Leary et al., 1995; Steele et al., 1993). As a result, they might continually monitor their partners' behavior for information that might affirm their sense of self, such as hoped-for signs of positive appraisals and caring.

However, an expectation-guided search is likely only to thwart their hopes and confirm their doubts. Mirroring their more chronic perceptions, low self-esteem individuals might project any new self-doubts onto their partners, imagining that their partners will share their own sense of disappointment (an acute instance of naïve realism). Moreover, the insecurity-inducing effects of such perceptions are likely to be compounded by their tendency to see others' regard as conditional in nature (Baldwin & Sinclair, 1996). Given these contingencies, occasional failures or disappointments might activate concerns that their romantic partners will eventually discover their "true" selves and then their affections might diminish. In the face of personal failures, then, low self-esteem individuals should find little comfort in their partners' regard. Instead, they should react to such failings by fearing and perhaps anticipating rejection.

Rather than leaving themselves vulnerable to a painful loss (and a further threat to the self), lows might actively defend against this possibility by devaluing and distancing themselves from their relationships, thereby reducing their dependency on this threatened resource. In a sense, acute self-doubt might put them on the interpersonal offense, leading them to try to find fault in their partners before their partners have the chance to reject them. Such a seemingly self-defeating strategy might actually soothe their anxieties if it makes the prospect of rejection seem less threatening (because the partner now seems less desirable). Ironically, however, it also results in low self-esteem individuals undercutting the resource of a loving, admiring partner that—if appreciated—could bolster their self-esteem.

A Compensation Hypothesis

Now imagine the likely thoughts of a high self-esteem individual in response to a self-threat such as a negative evaluation at work or a critical remark from a friend. Occasional self-doubts or failures rarely seriously threaten feelings of self-worth for such individuals (Baumeister, 1993, 1998; Baumgardner, 1990; Blaine & Crocker, 1993; Campbell, 1990; Campbell et al., 1996; Nezlek et al., 1997; Taylor & Brown, 1988). Instead, they find some means of fending off such threats and enhancing the self (see Baumeister, 1998, for a review). For instance, high self-esteem individuals compensate for intellectual self-doubts by embellishing their interpersonal strengths (Brown & Smart, 1991; Dunning, Leuenberger, & Sherman, 1995).

For high self-esteem individuals, a partner's perceived regard may function as a chronically accessible resource for self-affirmation. Unlike lows, high self-esteem individuals typically anticipate others' acceptance (Leary et al., 1995) and view this acceptance as unconditional in nature (Baldwin & Sinclair, 1996). This interpersonal template or schema should facilitate their use of relationships as a self-affirmation resource, preventing self-doubts from turning into relationship insecurities. In terms of the sociometer model, they might soothe self-doubts by affirming a sense of social or relational inclusion. Accordingly, we expect these individuals to compensate for their own personal disappointments or failures by becoming even more convinced of their partners' continued positive regard and acceptance and by enhancing the value of their relationships.

Overview of the Methodology

The basic paradigm in each of our experiments was similar. Our goal was to first activate the attachment system (and thus the need for a safe haven) by threatening low and high self-esteem dating individuals' feelings of self-worth. We then assessed their confidence in their partners' positive regard and continuing acceptance (as a measure of perceived regard) and, next, their self-perceived dependence on their relationships for self-esteem, perceptions of their partners' attributes, and predictions for their partners' future behaviors (as measures of relationship-valuing). Participants in all experiments were involved in dating relationships averaging 19.5 months in length. Low and high self-esteem dating individuals were identified on the basis of their scores on the Rosenberg (1965) self-esteem scale.

In our first three experiments, we introduced a relationship-based threat to self-worth. The self-threat in Experiments 1 and 2 centered around feelings of guilt over a past, seemingly isolated transgression. We induced this doubt by asking experimental participants to provide a vivid, written description of an important time in their relationships when they disappointed their partners. Then they completed the dependent measures. Control participants completed the dependent measures before they described a disappointment episode.

We created a new relational self-doubt in Experiment 3 by leading individuals to doubt their own considerateness. Experimental participants first completed a purported measure of considerateness deliberately designed to elicit low considerateness scores. They answered questions such as, "How often do you seem a little bit impatient with your partner? How often do you say something that ends up irritating or hurting your partner a bit?" (1 = never, 7 = once or more a week). They were then told that their score suggested that they were behaving inconsiderately toward their partners fairly often. Control participants completed a more balanced considerateness inventory (containing both positive and negative items), and they did not receive any feedback. All participants then completed the dependent measures.

In Experiment 4, we introduced a seemingly nonrelational threat to self-esteem by leading individuals to question their own intellectual abilities. Experimental participants first completed a difficult version of a purported measure of integrative ability (described as the ability to perceive interconnections among diverse pieces of data) and then received failure feedback. Control participants completed a mixture of easy and difficult test items that they believed were nondiagnostic of ability. In both conditions, the test items asked individuals to provide the concept (e.g., memory) that links three other concepts (e.g., elephant–lapse–vivid). All participants then completed the dependent variables.

Our dependent measures tapped the use of the relationship as a safe haven or compensatory resource to buffer the impact of the self-threat. As one measure of anticipated acceptance or perceived regard, we asked participants to spend a moment imagining a hypothetical scenario where they had transgressed (i.e., lying to their partners or criticizing their partners publicly). They then described their partners' likely reaction to this transgression on scales tapping anticipated acceptance versus rejection (e.g., forgiving, angry, accepting, distant from me). For a more global measure of perceived regard, participants also completed items tapping their overall feelings of confidence in their partners' continued positive regard and unconditional acceptance (e.g., "I am confident that my partner will always want to look beyond my faults and see the best in me"; "My partner sees special qualities in me, qualities that other people might not see"; "I couldn't do anything that would make my partner think less of me").

As one measure of relationship-valuing, we asked participants to respond to items tapping their dependence on their romantic relationships as a resource for self-affirmation and identity (e.g., "I wouldn't be myself without my partner"; "If I couldn't be in this relationship, I would lose an important part of myself"). Participants then described their partners on the Interpersonal Qualities Scale (Murray et al., 1996a), a series of interpersonally oriented virtues and faults, to provide an overall index of the value perceived in their partners (e.g., warm, responsive, critical, demanding). They also rated the likelihood of their partners engaging in positive and negative behaviors to provide an index of optimism about the future (e.g., "My partner will do something that really upsets and angers me").

Through the Looking Glass Darkly?

Did low self-esteem individuals react to self-doubt with increased relationship insecurities, and did high self-esteem individuals react to manifestly similar self-doubts with greater confidence? Table 7.1 presents a summary of our findings. It contains the results of a meta-analysis assessing the size and consistency of the hypothesized contrast effects (threat vs. control condition) for each dependent measure separately for low and high self-esteem in-

TABLE 7.1.
Meta-Analytic Results Across Four Experiments

Variable	Participants Low self-esteem		Participants High self-esteem	
	Threat condition (Average d)	Control condition (Z)	Threat condition (Average d)	Control condition (Z)
Reflected appraisals				
forgiving a transgression	−.43	3.16***	.24	1.75**
global reflected appraisal	−.58	4.58***	.30	2.48***
Relationship-valuing				
dependence	−.29	2.22**	.26	1.69**
optimism for partner	−.34	2.59***	.20	0.81
perceptions of partner	−.61	4.88***	.19	1.49

Note. Contamination effects are reflected in negative ds, whereas compensation effects are reflected in positive ds.

$^*p < .10$, $^{**}p < .05$, $^{***}p < .01$, one-tailed.

Adapted from Murray, Holmes, MacDonald, & Ellsworth, 1998.

dividuals. We calculated the average d as a measure of effect size and used the method of combining unweighted ts described by Rosenthal (1984) to assess the overall significance of the contrasts. Contamination effects are reflected in negative ds (i.e., participants in the threat condition scoring lower than those in the control condition), whereas compensation effects are reflected in positive ds (i.e., participants in the threat condition scoring higher than control participants).

As the perceived regard findings illustrate, low self-esteem individuals reacted to acute self-doubt by expressing less confidence in their partners' continued positive regard and acceptance. For instance, individuals with low self-esteem reacted to doubts about their intellectual abilities by concluding that their partners would not forgive them if they transgressed in their relationships. Similar doubts about the likelihood of their partners' continued positive regard and acceptance also emerged on the more global measure of perceived regard. Moreover, low self-esteem individuals in the self-threat conditions then seemed to defend against the heightened risks of rejection by finding less to value in their relationships (a contamination effect). They expressed less need for their relationships on the dependence scale, found less evidence of virtues in their partners' attributes, and were less optimistic about the future of their relationships. Thus, low self-esteem individuals seem to react to self-doubt and consequent fears of rejection by diminishing the value of the very resource—a close interpersonal attachment—that they might have relied on as a source of comfort.

In contrast, high self-esteem individuals reacted to manifestly similar self-doubts by using their relationships as a resource for self-affirmation (a compensation effect). These individuals reacted to self-doubt by becoming more convinced of their partners' willingness to forgive their specific transgressions. Highs in the self-threat conditions also expressed greater confidence in the security of their partners' positive regard. In fact, high self-esteem individuals seemed to react to self-doubt by valuing their relationships more rather than less. For instance, they seemed to compensate for self-threats by expressing greater need for their relationships as a resource for self-affirmation on the dependence scale. Moreover, acute self-doubt did not diminish the value they saw in their partners (presumably because they found the affirmation they sought when they looked at themselves through their partners' eyes).

Why did the contamination effects occur for low self-esteem individuals? Were they diminishing the value of their relationships to protect themselves against the prospect of rejection, as our dependency regulation model predicts? If this dynamic occurred, perceived regard should mediate the interactive effect of self-esteem and acute self-doubt on the relationship-valuing indices. Accordingly, we conducted a set of mediational analyses, testing the hypothesis that perceived regard mediated the link between the condition by self-esteem interaction and relationship-valuing. These analyses revealed strong evidence of mediation (see Murray et al., 1998, for further details). Such results suggest that self-doubts turn into doubts about the relationship for low, but not high, self-esteem individuals because self-doubts activate anxieties about a partner's possible rejection among lows.

The results of the experimental studies provide further support for our dependency regulation model, but there are at least two possible alternative explanations for the effects. The first is that the self-doubt manipulations primed insecurities for low, but not high, self-esteem individuals simply because the threat was more effective for lows. However, lows and highs did not differ in the amount of guilt they reported feeling on recounting their transgressions. They also received comparably low scores on the considerateness and integrative complexity tests.

The second is that it was not the self-doubt itself that magnified the anxieties of individuals with low self-esteem, but the threat this imperfection posed to a more fragile relationship. After all, three of the self-threats we posed could also be construed as signs of relationship difficulties—a potential threat to the relationship. Maybe then it was lows' insecurities linked to the state of their relationships that triggered their anxieties about rejection, not their insecurities about themselves. Such causal dynamics are naturally difficult to untangle because only personal failings that threaten social inclusion may activate the self-affirmation motive (Leary et al., 1995). However, all of the effects remained consistent when we controlled for satisfaction, a well-used proxy for relationship quality. Second, we also found contamination effects using a self-threat, low integrative ability, that had no necessary relation to the well-being of the relationship. These findings suggest that low self-esteem individuals simply projected personal insecurities onto their relationships, contaminating this potential safe haven by defending against a rejection that might not have materialized.

More generally, these findings suggest that the sociometer may not be as accurate and as functional a barometer of acceptance as Leary et al. (1995) described. Instead, the sociometers of low self-esteem individuals appear to be calibrated in ways that reinforce rather than alleviate self-doubts. These individuals seem to be overly sensitized to possible cues to rejection, actually anticipating rejection in advance of its occurrence. They then react to such anxieties by minimizing the personal value of interpersonal connections rather than engaging in approach behaviors that might reaffirm feelings of self-worth. In contrast, high self-esteem individuals seem relatively immune to such anxieties, actually perceiving greater acceptance on occasions of self-doubt.

A Window to Security

We suspect that low self-esteem individuals are so susceptible to doubts about a partner's regard because their more mixed store of self-knowledge and conditional sense of others' acceptance provide a tenuous evidential basis for a sense of felt security in a partner's continuing devotion (e.g., Baldwin & Sinclair, 1996; Baumeister, 1993, 1998). Based on this logic, we reasoned that it might be possible to increase low self-esteem individuals' confidence in their partners' regard by providing a boost to their self-esteem—that is, by providing the beginnings of a rationale for their own worthiness of love and their partners' admiration. We included self-esteem boost conditions in Experiments 3 and 4 to explore this possibility. In Experiment 3, participants completed a considerateness inventory designed to elicit high scores and then received feedback attesting to their considerateness. In Experiment 4, participants completed an easy version of the integrative complexity test and received success feedback.

If an impoverished sense of their own virtues is the only barrier to security, low self-esteem individuals might react to this potential boost to self-esteem by expressing greater confidence in their partners' regard and by placing greater value on their relationships. Much to our surprise, these intended boosts to self-esteem had the unintended effect of exacerbating the insecurities of low self-esteem individuals. They reacted to even these potential affirmations by becoming less confident of their partners' continuing regard and by finding less to value in their relationships. Why did this occur? For lows, focusing on a personal strength or weakness might only highlight the perception that a partner's regard is conditional. Such if–then contingencies are activated automatically when low self-esteem individuals are primed to think of personal successes or failures (Baldwin & Sinclair, 1996).

Compounding this vulnerability, low self-esteem individuals tend to organize self-knowledge in such a way that their virtues serve only to remind them of their faults (Showers, 1992), and they actively self-verify and recruit evidence of faults to counter self-boosts (Swann, 1987). Therefore, even entertaining the thought of being smarter or more considerate than they thought they were might only remind them of more serious faults, thereby threatening rather than affirming their sense of self. Because of their contingent sense of others' acceptance, it may be simply too much of a risk for these individuals to conclude that their partners' positive regard and acceptance is secure when they can easily think of personal faults that might put this regard in peril.

WHEN IMAGES BECOME REALITY

According to interpersonal theorists on self-esteem, the satisfaction of belongingness needs serves to bolster personal feelings of self-worth (e.g., Leary et al., 1995). However, our findings suggest that low self-esteem individuals may inadvertently construct relationship realities that reinforce rather than alter their self-models, frustrating basic needs for belongingness and thus self-affirmation. How might this occur?

Self-expansion theorists have argued that intimates adjust, update, and revise their working models of self by incorporating features of their partners into their self-representations (Aron, Aron, Tudor, & Nelson, 1991; Aron, Paris, & Aron, 1995). Imagine the likely consequences for self-esteem maintenance and change if individuals also incorporate this private audience's perceived perspective on the self (e.g., Cooley, 1902; Felson, 1989; McNulty & Swann, 1994; Mead, 1934; Shrauger & Schoeneman, 1979). For highs, this inclusion might only affirm the self because they correctly assume that their partners see them just as generously as they see themselves. For lows, however, this inclusion might only limit the self if they incorrectly assume that their partners see them no more generously than they see themselves. As time passes, then, the image seen in the looking glass might increasingly reinforce existing feelings of self-esteem.

We recently examined the evidence for this looking-glass self hypothesis in a longitudinal follow-up of the dating couples involved in our correlational study (Murray et al., in press). At Time 1, both members of the couple described themselves, their partners, and their perceptions of their partners' regard on a series of interpersonal virtues and faults. One year later couples in stable relationships again described themselves and their partners on these interpersonal attributes. This data allowed us to predict changes in self-esteem from initial perceptions of a romantic partner's regard for the self.

Supporting the looking-glass self hypothesis, low and high self-esteem intimates accommodated their models of self to incorporate the image of themselves they saw in their partners' eyes. For highs, feeling more positively regarded by the partner initially predicted relatively greater self-esteem at year end. Conversely, for lows, feeling less valued in the partner's eyes initially predicted relatively less self-esteem at year end. Such findings suggest that self-models are constructed and anchored in a top-down fashion, incorporating images in the looking glass that are themselves distorted by existing levels of self-esteem.

Are the prospects for self-esteem change among lows really as pessimistic as the findings for perceptions of a partner's regard suggest? Bowlby (1982) argued that working models are tolerably accurate, adapting in response to changes in the contingencies surrounding others' perceived responsiveness to the self. Similarly, Leary et al. (1995) argued that the sociometer has evolved to accurately monitor signs of interpersonal rejection or acceptance. Such bottom-up perspectives suggest that close, secure, and continuing attachments should at least have the potential to remedy dispositional insecurities. Illustrating this potential, our longitudinal study also revealed that actually being idealized by a romantic partner—that is, the image that actually should have existed in the looking glass—predicted long-term increases in self-esteem among both low and high self-esteem individuals (Murray et al., 1996b).

Which image in the looking glass will become reality—the one individuals perceive, or the one that actually exists? Intriguingly, perceived and actual partner regard each had independent effects on changes in self-esteem (Murray et al., in press). Such findings suggest that the self-esteem benefits of possessing an admiring partner may not always be mediated by individuals' conscious awareness of this admiration. Instead, self-esteem change may occur through both more explicit and implicit routes, avenues that may sometimes contain contradictory messages. Although speculative, our reasoning is based on growing evidence that suggests that self-esteem is multidimensional in nature, including both explicit and implicit self-evaluations (e.g., Pelham & Hetts, 1999) and feelings of both self-liking and self-competence (Tafarodi, 1998). At an explicit level, individuals may incorporate the image of themselves they perceive in their partners' eyes, thereby verifying their existing self-concepts and self-competencies in most instances. At an implicit level, however, individuals may respond to the admiration and tolerance they receive from their partners, slowly growing to like themselves more, perhaps without their complete conscious awareness.

Of course, the continued existence of such potentially self-affirming behavioral interaction sequences (and thus the likelihood of implicit feelings becoming explicit) may be easily disrupted by the relatively automatic, self-protective defenses of lows. For instance, the results in the self-esteem boost conditions in our experiments suggest that an individual's well-meaning attempt to soothe a low self-esteem partner's insecurities—perhaps by pointing to his or her various virtues—might only have the unintended effect of exacerbating them. Feeling unsure of their partners (but still needing their acceptance), lows might also behave in overly needy or demanding ways that actually diminish their partners' regard for them. Moreover, the experimental findings suggest that such insecurities may surface in more explicit criticisms of the partner that might have the eventual effect of undermining the partner's commitment to the relationship (e.g., Downey, Freitas, Michaelis, & Khouri, 1998; Mongrain, Vettese, Shuster, & Kendal, 1998).

We found some tentative evidence of the potential for such self-fulfilling effects in our prior research. For instance, individuals' impressions of their partners much more closely mirrored their partners' self-perceptions in married than in dating couples (Murray et al., in press). Similarly, dating intimates were less able to continue idealizing their partners over time, the lower their partners' initial self-esteem. Even perceivers' global reports of satisfaction were more strongly tied to their partners' level of self-esteem in married than in dating couples. In a real sense, then, individuals with low self-esteem may gradually contaminate the very resource—a partner's positive regard—that they might have used for self-affirmation. In such ways, these individuals may actually create the image in the looking glass that they initially, incorrectly, perceived.

REFERENCES

Aron, A., Aron, E. N., Tudor, M., & Nelson, G. (1991). Close relationships as in-cluding other in the self. *Journal of Personality and Social Psychology, 60,* 241–253.

Aron, A., Paris, M., & Aron, E. N. (1995). Falling in love: Prospective studies of self-concept change. *Journal of Personality and Social Psychology, 69,* 1102–1112.

Baldwin, M. W. (1992). Relational schemas and the processing of social informa-tion. *Psychological Bulletin, 112,* 461–484.

Baldwin, M. W., & Sinclair, L. (1996). Self-esteem and "if . . . then" contingencies of interpersonal acceptance. *Journal of Personality and Social Psychology, 71,* 1130–1141.

Bartholomew, K. (1990). Avoidance of intimacy: An attachment perspective. *Journal of Social and Personal Relationships, 7,* 147–178.

Baumeister, R. F. (1993). *Self-esteem: The puzzle of low self-regard.* New York: Plenum Press.

Baumeister, R. F. (1998). The self. In D. T. Gilbert, S. T. Fiske, & G. Lindzey (Eds.), *Handbook of social psychology* (4th ed., pp. 680–740). New York: McGraw-Hill.

Baumeister, R. F., Wotman, S. R., & Stillwell, A. M. (1993). Unrequited love: On heartbreak, anger, guilt, scriptlessness, and humiliation. *Journal of Personality and Social Psychology, 64,* 377–394.

Baumgardner, A. H. (1990). To know oneself is to like oneself: Self-certainty and self-affect. *Journal of Personality and Social Psychology, 58,* 1062–1072.

Berscheid, E., & Fei, J. (1977). Romantic love and sexual jealousy. In G. Clanton & L. G. Smith (Eds.), *Jealousy* (pp. 101–109). Englewood Cliffs, NJ: Prentice-Hall.

Blaine, B., & Crocker, J. (1993). Self-esteem and self-serving biases in reactions to positive and negative events: An integrative review. In R. F. Baumeister (Ed.), *Self-esteem: The puzzle of low self-regard* (pp. 55–85). New York: Plenum Press.

Bowlby, J. (1982). *Attachment and loss: Vol. 1. Attachment.* London: Hogarth Press.

Brown, J. D., & Smart, S. A. (1991). The self and social conduct: Linking self-representations to prosocial behavior. *Journal of Personality and Social Psychol-ogy, 60,* 368–375.

Campbell, J. D. (1990). Self-esteem and clarity of the self-concept. *Journal of Personality and Social Psychology, 59,* 538–549.

Campbell, J. D., Trapnell, P. D., Heine, S. J., Katz, I. M., Lavallee, L. F., & Lehman, D. R. (1996). Self-concept clarity: Measurement, personality correlates, and cultural boundaries. *Journal of Personality and Social Psychology, 70,* 141–156.

Collins, N. L. (1996). Working models of attachment: Implications for explanation, emotion and behavior. *Journal of Personality and Social Psychology, 71,* 810–832.

Collins, N. L., & Read, S. J. (1994). Cognitive representations of attachment: The structure and function of working models. *Advances in Personal Relationships, 5,* 53–90.

Cooley, C. H. (1902). *Human nature and the social order*. New York: Scribner.

Downey, G., & Feldman, S. I. (1996). Implications of rejection sensitivity for intimate relationships. *Journal of Personality and Social Psychology, 70*, 1327–1343.

Downey, G., Freitas, A. L., Michaelis, B., & Khouri, H. (1998). The self-fulfilling prophecy in close relationships: Rejection sensitivity and rejection by romantic partners. *Journal of Personality and Social Psychology, 75*, 545–560.

Drigotas, S. M., Rusbult, C. E., Wieselquist, J., & Whitton, S. (1996). Close partner as sculptor of the ideal self: Behavioral affirmation and the Michelangelo phenomenon. *Journal of Personality and Social Psychology, 77*, 293–323.

Dunning, D., Leuenberger, A., & Sherman, D. A. (1995). A new look at motivated inference: Are self-serving theories of success a product of motivational forces? *Journal of Personality and Social Psychology, 69*, 58–68.

Felson, R. B. (1989). Parents and the reflected appraisal process: A longitudinal analysis. *Journal of Personality and Social Psychology, 56*, 965–971.

Fincham, F. D., & Bradbury, T. N. (1993). Marital satisfaction, depression and attributions: A longitudinal analysis. *Journal of Personality and Social Psychology, 64*, 442–452.

Fritz, H. L., & Helgeson, V. S. (1998). Distinctions of unmitigated communion from communion: Self-neglect and over-involvement with others. *Journal of Personality and Social Psychology, 75*, 121–140.

Hazan, C., & Shaver, P. R. (1994). Attachment as an organizational framework for research on close relationships. *Psychological Inquiry, 5*, 1–22.

Hendrick, S. S., Hendrick, C., & Adler, N. L. (1988). Romantic relationships: Love, satisfaction, and staying together. *Journal of Personality and Social Psychology, 54*, 980–988.

Holmes, J. G., & Rempel, J. K. (1989). Trust in close relationships. In C. Hendrick (Ed.), *Review of personality and social psychology: Close relationships* (Vol. 10, pp. 187–219). Newbury Park, CA: Sage.

James W. J. (1910). *Principles of psychology*. New York: Holt.

Karney, B. R., & Bradbury, T. N. (1997). Neuroticism, marital interaction, and the trajectory of marital satisfaction. *Journal of Personality and Social Psychology, 72*, 1075–1092.

Karney, B. R., Bradbury, T. N., Fincham, F. D., & Sullivan, K. T. (1994). The role of negative affectivity in the association between attributions and satisfaction. *Journal of Personality and Social Psychology, 66*, 413–424.

Kelley, H. H. (1983). Love and commitment. In H. H. Kelley, E. Berscheid, A. Christensen, J. H. Harvey, T. L. Huston, G. Levinger, E. McClintock, L. A. Peplau, & D. R. Peterson (Eds.), *Close relationships* (pp. 265–314). New York: Freeman.

Kelly, E. L., & Conley, J. J. (1987). Personality and compatibility: A prospective analysis of marital stability and marital satisfaction. *Journal of Personality and Social Psychology, 52*, 27–40.

Kenny, D. A. (1994). *Interpersonal perception: A social relations analysis*. New York: Guilford Press.

Kenny, D. A. (1996). Models of non-independence in dyadic research. *Journal of Social and Personal Relationships, 13*, 279–294.

Kernis, M. H., Cornell, D. P., Sun, C. R., Berry, A., & Harlow, T. (1993). There's more to self-esteem than whether it is high or low: The importance of stability of self-esteem. *Journal of Personality and Social Psychology, 65*, 1190–1204.

Leary, M. R., Tambor, E. S., Terdal, S. K., & Downs, D. L. (1995). Self-esteem as an interpersonal monitor: The sociometer hypothesis. *Journal of Personality and Social Psychology, 68*, 518–530.

Lykken, D. T., & Tellegen, A. (1993). Is human mating adventitious or the result of lawful choice? A twin study of mate selection. *Journal of Personality and Social Psychology, 65*, 56–68.

McNulty, S. E., & Swann, W. B. (1994). Identity negotiation in roommate relationships: The self as an architect and consequence of social reality. *Journal of Personality and Social Psychology, 67*, 1012–1023.

Mead, G. H. (1934). *Mind, self and society.* Chicago: University of Chicago Press.

Mongrain, M., Vettese, L. C., Shuster, B., & Kendal, N. (1998). Perceptual biases, affect, and behavior in the relationships of dependents and self-critics. *Journal of Personality and Social Psychology, 75*, 230–241.

Murray, S. L., & Holmes, J. G. (1997). A leap of faith? Positive illusions in romantic relationships. *Personality and Social Psychology Bulletin, 23*, 586–604.

Murray, S. L., Holmes, J. G., & Griffin, D. (1996a). The benefits of positive illusions: Idealization and the construction of satisfaction in close relationships. *Journal of Personality and Social Psychology, 70*, 79–98.

Murray, S. L., Holmes, J. G., & Griffin, D. W. (1996b). The self-fulfilling nature of positive illusions in romantic relationships: Love is not blind, but prescient. *Journal of Personality and Social Psychology, 71*, 1155–1180.

Murray, S. L., Holmes, J. G., & Griffin, D. W. (in press). Self-esteem and the quest for felt security: How perceived regard regulates attachment processes. *Journal of Personality and Social Psychology.*

Murray, S. L., Holmes, J. G., MacDonald, G., & Ellsworth, P. (1998). Through the looking glass darkly? When self-doubts turn into relationship insecurities. *Journal of Personality and Social Psychology, 75*, 1459–1480.

Nezlek, J. B., Kowalski, R. M., Leary, M. R., Blevins, T., & Holgate, S. (1997). Personality moderators of reactions to interpersonal rejection: Depression and trait self-esteem. *Personality and Social Psychology Bulletin, 23*, 1235–1244.

Pelham, B. W., & Hetts, J. J. (1999). Implicit and explicit personal and social identity: Toward a more complete understanding of the social self. In T. Tyler, R. Kramer, & O. John (Eds.), *The psychology of the social self* (pp. 115–143). New York: Lawrence Erlbaum.

Roberts, J. E., Gotlib, I. H., & Kassel, J. D. (1996). Adult attachment security and symptoms of depression: The mediating roles of dysfunctional attitudes and low self-esteem. *Journal of Personality and Social Psychology, 70*, 310–320.

Rosenberg, M. (1965). *Society and the adolescent self-image.* Princeton, NJ: Princeton University Press.

Rosenthal, R. (1984). *Meta-analytic procedures for social research*. Beverly Hills, CA: Sage.

Ruvolo, A., & Brennan, C. J. (1997). What's love got to do with it? Close relationships and perceived growth. *Personality and Social Psychology Bulletin, 23,* 814–823.

Sedikides, C. (1993). Assessment, enhancement, and verification determinants of the self-evaluation process. *Journal of Personality and Social Psychology, 65,* 317–338.

Showers, C. (1992). Compartmentalization of positive and negative self-knowledge: Keeping bad apples out of the bunch. *Journal of Personality and Social Psychology, 62,* 1036–1049.

Shrauger, J. S., & Schoeneman, T. J. (1979). Symbolic interactionist view of the self-concept: Through the looking glass darkly. *Psychological Bulletin, 86,* 549–573.

Simpson, J. A., Ickes, W., & Blackstone, T. (1995). When the head protects the heart: Empathic accuracy in dating relationships. *Journal of Personality and Social Psychology, 69,* 629–641.

Simpson, J. A., Rholes, W. S., & Phillips, D. (1996). Conflict in close relationships: An attachment perspective. *Journal of Personality and Social Psychology, 71,* 899–914.

Snyder, M. (1992). Motivational foundations of behavioral confirmation. In M. P. Zanna (Ed.), *Advances in experimental social psychology* (Vol. 25, pp. 67–114). San Diego, CA: Academic Press.

Steele, C. M. (1988). The psychology of self-affirmation: Sustaining the integrity of the self. In L. Berkowitz (Ed.), *Advances in experimental social psychology* (Vol. 21, pp. 261–302). New York: Academic Press.

Steele, C. M., Spencer, S. J., & Lynch, M. (1993). Self-image resilience and dissonance: The role of self-affirmational resources. *Journal of Personality and Social Psychology, 64,* 885–896.

Swann, W. B. (1987). Identity negotiation: Where two roads meet. *Journal of Personality and Social Psychology, 53,* 1038–1051.

Swann, W. B., De La Ronde, C., & Hixon, J. G. (1994). Authenticity and positive strivings in marriage and courtship. *Journal of Personality and Social Psychology, 66,* 857–869.

Swann, W. B., & Predmore, S. C. (1985). Intimates as agents of social support: Sources of consolation or despair? *Journal of Personality and Social Psychology, 49,* 1609–1617.

Tafarodi, R. W. (1998). Paradoxical self-esteem and selectivity in the processing of social information. *Journal of Personality and Social Psychology, 74,* 1181–1196.

Taylor, S. E., & Brown, J. D. (1988). Illusion and well-being: A social psychological perspective on mental health. *Psychological Bulletin, 103,* 193–210.

Van Lange, P. A. M., & Rusbult, C. E. (1995). My relationship is better than—and not as bad as—yours is: The perception of superiority in close relationships. *Personality and Social Psychology Bulletin, 21,* 32–44.

8

THE STRATEGIC CONTROL OF INFORMATION: IMPRESSION MANAGEMENT AND SELF-PRESENTATION IN DAILY LIFE

BARRY R. SCHLENKER
BETH A. PONTARI

The area of self-presentation has witnessed considerable growth and acceptance within mainstream social psychology during the past 25 years. A quarter century ago, the term *self-presentation* did not appear in the index of major social psychology texts. To most social psychologists, it evoked negative images of superficiality rather than substance, and deception rather than authenticity. It was relegated to minor, fringe status in social psychology and was seen as a specific subtype of social behavior through which people could satisfy their needs for social approval by making a socially desirable impression on others. In his pioneering work on ingratiation, Jones (1964; Jones & Wortman, 1973) used self-presentation to describe one of four types of behavior—along with opinion conformity, flattery, and favor doing—through which people could try to be liked by others.

In this limited role, self-presentation was seen by most researchers in one or both of two ways. First, it was seen as a limited social skill whose mastery may be desirable for practitioners in business and politics but that comprised more of an art than a science. Social psychologists were usually content to leave the topic to nonscientists who wanted tips on how to win friends and influence people. Second, it was seen as an annoying contaminant of research that obscured the more fundamental and important processes that were of major concern to researchers. It was felt that if researchers could eliminate participants' attempts to make a good impression, via techniques like assuring anonymity, using the bogus pipeline, or creating "lie" scales, they would have a better appreciation of the "real" processes underlying social behavior. In retrospect, it seems rather naive and myopic to try to eliminate, in the name of understanding social conduct, a process that is fundamental to social conduct. Yet, for those who wanted to understand attribution, person perception, attitude change, and many other topics, self-presentation was a contaminating nuisance that provided alternative interpretations of what could otherwise be important findings.

The intervening years have seen the concept of self-presentation integrated more directly into mainstream social psychology. Virtually all social psychology texts now include a chapter on the self and feature a discussion of self-presentation in the context of the construction and protection of public identity. Self-presentation has emerged as an important theme in other disciplines, too, including counseling (Friedlander & Schwartz, 1985; Kelly & McKillop, 1996), developmental psychology (Aloise-Young, 1993; Elkind, 1980; Hatch, 1987), and organizational behavior (Rosenfeld, Giacalone, & Riordan, 1995). Despite this increased recognition of the utility and importance of the concept, there is still a lingering reluctance to embrace it fully. The connotations of superficiality, pretense, deceit, and immoral manipulativeness persist, giving it something of the status of the black sheep in the social psychological family. Although researchers can no longer deny it membership in the group of important social psychological concepts, neither do they seem to regard it as a source of pride around the family dinner table.

Our goal in this chapter is twofold. First, we want to examine some of the recurring issues in the impression management literature. We selected three key questions for discussion: (a) Does impression management occur only under restricted social conditions, such as during job interviews and first dates? (b) Is impression management inherently superficial and duplicitous? and (c) Is impression management inherently selfish and power oriented? To many social psychologists, including some who are otherwise sympathetic to impression management research, these questions seem to have the following straightforward answers: Impression management occurs only under special conditions, it is inherently duplicitous, and it is inherently selfish. We propose different answers to each question. By examining these questions, we hope to provide a stronger conceptual foundation for further theoretical development. Second, by addressing these questions, we hope to dispel many of the lingering misconceptions and prejudices that exist about impression management. These misconceptions can themselves impede theoretical refinement.

THE SCOPE OF IMPRESSION MANAGEMENT AND SELF-PRESENTATION

We define *impression management* as the goal-directed activity of controlling information about some person, object, idea, or event to audiences. People try to control information about themselves, friends or associates, enemies, ideas (e.g., their political ideologies and opinions), organizations (e.g., their companies, political parties), and events (e.g., activities in which they were engaged). *Self-presentation* is a more specific term that refers to the control of information about self.

How pervasive is self-presentation? Many researchers regard self-presentation as a type of social behavior that occurs only under limited conditions. Buss and Briggs (1984) proposed that self-presentation occurs primarily when conditions focus consciousness on the type of impression one is making on others. It is relevant (a) to important, evaluative situations that prompt people to behave pretentiously, such as on a job interview; (b) to formal situations that cue well-established social roles and interaction rituals, such as at a wedding; and (c) to situations in which the actor feels like the center of an audience's attention and may experience shyness or stage fright, such as when giving a speech. Buss and Briggs also suggested that some people, by virtue of personality characteristics such as high self-monitoring or public self-consciousness, are chronically more likely to self-present across a variety of situations. According to Buss and Briggs, most other times people are simply expressing their genuine qualities and not trying to package information for audiences. In parallel fashion, Jones and Pittman (1982) listed four types of situations in which people do not seem to engage in strategic self-presentation. These included (a) situations involving high task involvement, as when people are absorbed in a task (e.g., athletics, knitting); (b) situations involving purely expressive behavior, such as exhibiting anger or joy; (c) situations involving "overlearned, ritualized social exchanges" (p. 234), such as when checking out library books; and (d) situations in which people are "concerned with the integrity or authenticity of their actions" (p. 234), as when talking to a therapist.

One can debate the categories in these lists. Many of the categories are open to counterexamples that seem to involve clear self-presentation strategies. For example, one cannot watch a contemporary athletic contest without thinking that athletes are often as proud of their theatrical skills as their physical ones. Similarly, self-presentation, on the part of both the client and therapist, seems to play an important role in the therapy process (Kelly & McKillop, 1996). Furthermore, expressions of emotion are laden with self-presentational implications and are clearly influenced by the nature and proximity of important audiences (e.g., DePaulo, 1992; Fridlund, 1991a, 1991b). In addition, are ritualized interactions self-presentation? Buss and Briggs proposed that they are, at least if they are formal, whereas Jones and Pittman proposed that they are not, if they are overlearned. In our view, these categories are useful in pointing out dimensions that may make people more or less conscious of their self-presentations, more or less likely to devote cognitive effort to their self-presentations, and more or less likely to have self-presentation scripts activated and implemented automatically by cues outside of awareness. They do not, however, clearly distinguish self-presentation from other types of social behavior.

Our definitions of impression management and self-presentation are broader than are sometimes found in the literature. Schlenker and Weigold (1992) distinguished between restrictive and expansive approaches to impression management. Restrictive approaches, like those taken by Jones and Pittman (1982) and Buss and Briggs (1984), limit the concepts by associating them with specific interpersonal motives (e.g., gaining power or approval) and suggesting that deceit or pretense characterize the behavior. In contrast, expansive positions regard impression management and self-presentation as more ubiquitous features of social behavior (Goffman, 1959; Hogan, 1982; Schlenker, 1980, 1985). Communications are not simply descriptive or expressive, they are actions with their own ends and effects on others. The concept of impression management explicitly focuses on these goal-directed aspects of communication. Goffman (1959), who pioneered and popularized the concepts of impression management and self-presentation in the sociology literature, regarded self-presentation as a condition of interaction, one that is inherent in the fundamental nature of social life. Schlenker and Weigold (1992) argued that asking "When do people engage in self-presentation during social interaction?" is like asking "When do people engage in cognition during social interaction?" It is always going on, but its characteristics change depending on the actor's goals, audience, and circumstances. In this chapter we take the expansive approach and, by addressing the three key questions mentioned earlier, try to demonstrate the heuristic appeal of this view.

Goals and Scripts

In dealing with the scope of self-presentation, we prefer to focus on the multiple goals people try to pursue in daily life. We assume that people are purposive and planning agents who are always thinking, always acting, and always trying to achieve valued objectives in life. The actor's goals in the situation may be important or mundane (e.g., getting a job or checking out a library book), specific or vague (e.g., passing a test or becoming a scholar), immediate or long term (e.g., enjoying a date or starting a family), and overt or hidden (e.g., clear to the audience or lurking as an ulterior motive). These goals provide the objectives that the individual works toward on the occasion.

Scripts and plans are used in the pursuit of goals. These are cognitive representations that describe the operations or steps that are required to go from the present state to goal achievement, with scripts being preformulated and plans being concocted to deal with less routine situations (Schank & Abelson, 1977). They can be conscious or unconscious and, once activated, direct the individual's thoughts and actions, much as a program guides the operations of a computer in the pursuit of particular objectives. They act as templates that guide information processing and behavior. We will use the term *agenda* to refer to the combination of a goal and its associated script or plan for goal achievement.

Multiple Agendas

Social life is not so simplistic that people have the luxury of pursuing just one goal at a time. In any given situation, multiple agendas must be coordinated. Several goals are activated, and people work toward them more or less simultaneously. For instance, in the workplace, an individual may approach a co-worker with several agendas. She may have a job-relevant question that needs an answer, want to make a lunch date for later and negotiate a mutually acceptable restaurant, share the latest gossip so that each can keep up with company events, display the appropriate respect and concern that the co-worker feels is her due, and present herself in ways that maintain the respect and approval of the co-worker. Some of these goals require immediate attention, cognitive effort, and monitoring, so they are in the forefront of her awareness. Other goals may be less important or more routinized so that they are operating behind the scenes, without her awareness. These multiple agendas can be viewed as hierarchically stacked, with some consciously salient and others less so. An analogy is a computer running several programs simultaneously (Schlenker, Britt, & Pennington, 1996). Some programs may be open and their contents displayed prominently in windows on the screen. Others are minimized and operating behind the scenes, busy working on their designated tasks but not distracting the computer operator until they are needed.

Self-presentation agendas, which involve constructing, maintaining, and protecting desired images of self, are not always the sole or even primary objectives in interaction. We propose that they are necessary components of all social interactions, though. Often, they are simply less likely to be in the foreground of attention as compared to other agendas. To deal with others, people must present and maintain a coherent identity (Cheek & Hogan, 1983; Goffman, 1959; McCall & Simmons, 1978; Schlenker, 1980, 1985).

"Doing" social interaction involves taking a participant role in it and behaving in accord with the scripts associated with the relevant identity images.

Not just any role will be satisfactory, of course. People are not indifferent to the impressions they create and to the images that are associated with their identities. Research on egotism and the self-serving bias (e.g., Brown, 1998; Greenwald, 1980) evidences people's capacities to construct, in their own minds and for presentation to others, images of self that are self-glorifying yet bound by the limitations of reality. These images are influenced in part by values and expectations of salient audiences (Schlenker, 1980). Some images of self are far more desirable than others in that they are associated with more beneficial consequences (e.g., approval, respect, material rewards), while still being believable representations of self. These beneficial yet believable images have been termed *desirable identity images* (Schlenker, 1980, 1985; Schlenker & Weigold, 1989, 1992) and represent the type of person one thinks one can and should be on the occasion. They represent a balance between what one would like to express about oneself, based on self-schemas, relevant roles, and expectations of what might produce a personally beneficial impact on the audience, and what one expects to be able to convey effectively to that audience. It is these desirable images of self, which fuse private and public concerns, that people attempt to construct and maintain in their self-presentations.

Foreground and Background Modes

Given multiple agendas, which ones will receive greater conscious attention and monitoring? With limited cognitive resources, people cannot attend closely to every agenda and all the associated activities. Some agendas must therefore take a back seat to others in the agenda hierarchy. Agendas that receive greater attention and monitoring will be called *foreground agendas*, whereas those that receive less attention and monitoring will be called *background agendas* (Schlenker et al., 1996).

We propose that an agenda will receive greater attention and monitoring when (a) it is more important in the given situation or (b) the actor anticipates or encounters difficulties that would impede accomplishing the particular goal, as when the actor has low self-efficacy expectations because of inexperience, lack of ability, or the anticipation of obstacles to success. In the case of self-presentation agendas, performances can be important for at least three reasons. First, they may be relevant to images that are highly valued and central to the actor's identity (e.g., a performance involving an intellectual task is more important to the person who has pretensions of being an intellectual than to one who wants to be seen as an athlete). Second, they may involve potentially valuable outcomes (e.g., the performance can affect pay raises, promotions, dismissals, or respect from an admired other). Third, they may be relevant to highly valued prescriptions for conduct (e.g., the performance is relevant to matters of personal principles rather than to more trivial social conventions).

Anticipated difficulties for self-presentation agendas should increase conscious attention and monitoring of the agenda and its associated activities. These difficulties are created by uncertainties, doubts, conflicts, or threats that are relevant to the performance (see Schlenker, 1985, 1987; Schlenker & Leary, 1982b). The problem can spring from characteristics of the situation or task, as when a task is novel or difficult, causing actors to contemplate how to act and plan their self-presentation. It can arise from characteristics of the audience, as when an audience is seen as intimidating, expert, powerful, attractive, or otherwise difficult to impress. And it can arise from personal characteristics of the actor, such as when chronically high levels of social anxiety, low self-esteem, or high fears of failure prompt people to worry about how they will come across. These personal, audience, and task or situational factors focus people on possible ways to eliminate or circumvent the problem. Cognitive resources become marshaled to address the difficulty.

Self-presentation agendas often operate in the foreground and consume cognitive resources. People then expend cognitive effort in assessing and planning their performances, such as before an important date or business meeting. People gather relevant information about the occasion, plan and rehearse what they might do and say, try to anticipate the actions of others who are involved and develop contingent strategies, and remain alert during the performance itself by closely monitoring their own actions and those of others. People then become consciously focused on the goal of creating a desired impression on audiences. These are the occasions when people are most likely to report being self-conscious and perhaps "on stage." It is also these occasions that researchers are most likely to list as involving impression management and self-presentation rather than simply self-expression and "natural" behavior.

In contrast, an agenda will receive less attention and monitoring when it is less important or seen as unlikely to encounter problems. Often, and in some ways ideally, self-presentation agendas can reside in the background and not consume precious cognitive resources, such as during familiar, easy, or trivial tasks; among audiences with whom one feels secure and comfortable; among insignificant audiences whose opinions are a matter of relative indifference because they are low in power, unattractive, or gullible; and with interpersonally confident actors who regard themselves as high in acting skill and are high in self-esteem, low in social anxiety, and low in fear of failure.

In background mode, self-presentation agendas can guide the individual automatically, without thought and planning, based on scripts that have been used repeatedly and successfully in the past. The behaviors consist of modulated, habit-formed patterns of action that flow without self-consciousness and seem natural. These behaviors may once have been carefully and deliberately practiced. Many children and adults rehearse upcoming performances before a mirror, trying out gestures, facial expressions, lines, and retorts until they find combinations they think will make the right impression. Although these behaviors once were deliberate and self-conscious, eventually they become habitual components of personality and identity. William James (1890/1952, p. 79) emphasized the importance of such self-identifying habits in committing people to a continuation of the identities they have enacted over a lifetime. To James, one of the functions of thought is to produce habits of action, so that optimal behavior patterns can be engaged without having to go back and reconsider them each time a similar situation is encountered.

In background mode, self-presentation agendas involve some degree of automaticity. Automatic processes are characterized as ones that occur outside of awareness, in that the actor is unaware of the initiation or flow of the activity; that are effortless, in that the actor does not expend current cognitive resources; that are autonomous, in that the activities do not have to be consciously monitored once initiated; and that are involuntary, in that the activities are initiated by certain cues or prompts in the situation (Bargh, 1989; Fiske & Taylor, 1991). Automatic processes also can be intentional, in that they are dependent on specific goals (Bargh, 1989). Bargh suggested that most well-learned social scripts and action sequences are guided by intended, goal-dependent automaticity and argued that the actor need not be aware of the actions producing goal attainment. Self-presentation agendas that operate in the background mode appear to be guided by precisely such intended, goal-dependent, automatic processes.

In this mode, people's self-presentations are responsive to impression-relevant cues, but people are unaware of the extent to which their activities are shaped by the social context and their self-presentation agendas. There are many well-documented changes in self-presentations that seem to be shaped by social cues without the actor's awareness of being influenced (see Jones, 1990). Examples include the exaggeration of one's positive qualities to match the claims of a braggart or the underplaying of one's qualities to match the claims of a modest other (Jones, Rhodewalt, Berglas, & Skelton, 1981) or shifts in one's attitudes to conform to the preferences of a salient, attractive audience (Cialdini, Levy, Herman, Kozlowski, & Petty, 1976; Jones & Wortman, 1973; Tetlock, 1992). These shifts are often triggered automatically and guided by oft-used scripts replete with overlearned behaviors. Unless problems are encountered during the performance, self-presentation proceeds routinely in the background. To the actor, such behavior seems natural and expressive of self, even though it has been triggered and shaped by social contingencies that are related to the impression made on others.

If problems are encountered, however, the self-presentation agenda again becomes salient and people's attention is focused on the impression they are making on others. During an otherwise routine interaction, the actor may commit a faux pas or realize that the audience is not responding as desired. These potential impediments to desired impressions then move the self-presentation agenda to the foreground, at which time automaticity is replaced by controlled processes characterized by awareness and conscious self-monitoring. The actor then becomes motivated to take action to protect the desired impression.

Should background activities be called self-presentation? We strongly advocate that they should. In background mode, the actor's conduct is guided by the goal of creating a desired set of identity images that are contained in the pertinent self-presentation script; the actor monitors his or her behaviors and the reactions of the audience to ensure that the appropriate impression is being created and that deviations from the script do not occur; goal-dependent shifts in behavior take place to capitalize on cues in the situation; and if problems develop during the performance, the individual becomes self-conscious and takes action to correct the undesired impression that otherwise might be created. If people did not have agendas that include presenting and protecting desired identities, they would not become upset when discovering that audiences form the "wrong" impression or when "out-of-character" behaviors are noticed. Background activities seem effortless and un-self-conscious because that is the nature of automatic processes, not because they are unguided by personal goals and impression-relevant contingencies.

A computer analogy might help clarify the argument that such background behavior should be considered self-presentation. Many computer programs contain components that are activated automatically when the computer is turned on and that monitor the system for certain contingencies. Anti-virus programs and programs that guard against crashes are examples of such software. These automatic program components are largely invisible to the user. They are busy working below the surface on their assigned tasks, monitoring and sometimes controlling system activities with little intrusiveness. They are often forgotten until something happens that triggers a visible event, such as when the software encounters a virus. Just because the user does not think about the program's existence and activities until a problem occurs does not imply that the program is not there and fully functioning. The existence and functioning of the program can be checked empirically in numerous ways, such as by introducing a virus to determine whether the program catches it and responds appropriately. Similarly, even in background mode, the existence of self-presentation agendas is empirically corroborated by the goal-dependent nature of such behavior, as when people shift their self-descriptions in response to goal-relevant social contingencies and become upset when undesired impressions are created. In our view, self-presentation agendas are an inherent component of social interaction. The question is whether they are operating in foreground or background mode, not whether self-presentation occurs under some conditions but not others.

EXPLORING AUTOMATIC AND CONTROLLED
SELF-PRESENTATIONS

Because cognitive resources are limited, people have difficulty handling more than one cognitively effortful task at once (Bargh, 1989; Gilbert & Osborne, 1989). People's limited capacity for dealing with multiple controlled tasks provides researchers with the opportunity to examine automatic versus controlled activities empirically. If a process is controlled rather than automatic, it should be more likely to interfere with the ability to accomplish simultaneously other cognitively effortful tasks of lower priority, and it should be more likely to be disrupted if people are asked to accomplish a second high-priority controlled task simultaneously.

By manipulating cognitive load, Paulhus and his colleagues (Paulhus, 1988, 1993; Paulhus, Graf, & van Selst, 1989; Paulhus & Levitt, 1987) found that people's self-descriptions became more positive and socially desirable when they were made automatically. Paulhus et al. (1989), for example, asked participants to classify positive and negative trait adjectives (e.g., cheerful or defensive) as "me" or "not me" as the adjectives appeared on a computer monitor. Participants also were given a second effortful task to perform, that of monitoring digits that appeared on the screen at varying speeds. They found that people's self-descriptions became more positive when the extra cognitive load was increased. Paulhus (1988) suggested that automatic self-presentation limits the capacity to perform a more thorough search through memory for relevant information and produces a default mode that is socially desirable. This level of social desirability is higher than what would be obtained if people were not cognitively overloaded but lower than how they might describe themselves if they were highly motivated to fake an extremely positive self-presentation.

Tice and her colleagues (Tice, Butler, Muraven, & Stillwell, 1995) proposed that different self-presentation strategies are commonly associated with different audiences, such as interactions with strangers versus friends. When interacting with strangers, the more common and automatic style is self-enhancement, designed to try to impress the strangers; whereas with friends it is modesty, because people are relatively secure in their friends' regard. Indeed, Tice et al. found that people were more self-enhancing with strangers and modest with friends. If a level of self-presentation other than this familiar one is needed in the situation, it should require greater cognitive effort and disrupt the capacity to accomplish other cognitive tasks, such as remembering information from the interaction.

To test these ideas, Tice et al. asked participants to present themselves either to a stranger or a friend and either as favorably or as modestly as possible without actually misrepresenting themselves. When later asked to recall information about the interaction, participants who interacted with strangers and who had been modest remembered less than did those who had been self-enhancing. This finding that modesty to strangers interfered with recall, which also was obtained by Baumeister, Hutton, and Tice (1989), supports the idea that, with strangers, modesty requires greater cognitive effort than does self-enhancement, a conclusion that is consistent with Paulhus's results. In contrast, participants who interacted with friends and who had been self-enhancing remembered less than did those who had been modest, thus supporting the idea that self-enhancement to friends requires greater cognitive effort than does modesty. As these findings suggest, a particular self-presentation style is more appropriate and familiar in some social situations than in others. If the style and context match, the self-presentation requires relatively little conscious thought and cognitive effort; it can be placed in background mode. If the style and context are incompatible, the self-presentation requires cognitive effort and is placed in foreground mode.

Different self-presentation roles also can be more or less compatible with the actor's self-schemas and personality characteristics. Compatible roles should be more familiar and routine; hence they should be less likely to be disrupted by other cognitive tasks. To test this hypothesis, Pontari and Schlenker (in press) preselected highly extraverted and highly introverted participants and had them go through an interview in which they played an extraverted or introverted role. To add an extra cognitive load, half of the participants were asked to rehearse an 8-digit number during the interview, thus limiting the cognitive resources available to portray the assigned role. If presenting familiar versus unfamiliar images requires different amounts of cognitive effort, this extra task should disrupt the more effortful process, producing a less effective portrayal, but have less impact on the less effortful process. The interviewer's impressions of the participants' introversion or extraversion provided the measure of how effectively they played the role.

As expected, participants who played the familiar role—extraverts who played extraverts and introverts who played introverts—created the desired impression on the interviewer and seemed to be appropriately extraverted or introverted. More important, the additional cognitive task had no effect on the impression they were able to create. In contrast, the additional cognitive task did affect the impressions created by those who played unfamiliar roles. As expected, extraverts were less effective in conveying the impression of being introverts if they were cognitively busy, suggesting that the unfamiliar self-presentation was guided by controlled cognitive processes that were disrupted by the number task. Curiously, though, introverts who played the extraverted role actually were more effective in conveying the desired impression when they were cognitively busy than when they were not. This effect may have been due to the fact that these high-scoring introverts were also found to be very high in social anxiety. Prior research suggests that people high in social anxiety are aided by distracting tasks, which direct attention away from the otherwise disruptive thoughts associated with anxiety (Carver & Scheier, 1981), and which provide an excuse for possible poor performance (Brodt & Zimbardo, 1981; Leary, 1986). Introverts faced with the challenge of behaving in an unfamiliar way during a social interaction may have confronted a particularly nerve-wracking task. For those who rehearsed the number, the distracting task shifted the focus from their self-doubts and negative self-thoughts, thereby allowing their self-presentation to be more effective than that of those who had the cognitive resources available not only to think about the presentation, but also to ruminate about their inability to successfully convey extraversion. Indeed, in a follow-up study, Pontari and Schlenker (in press) found that introverts who were asked to play the role of extraverts listed fewer negative thoughts about self and expressed less public self-consciousness when they were cognitively busy rather than not busy. These findings suggest that distracting tasks will harm the performance of those who might otherwise be able to concentrate better on a demanding agenda but aid the performance of those who might otherwise have their cognitive resources overwhelmed by social anxiety and its attendant self-deflating thoughts.

Researchers have just begun to explore the implications of automatic versus controlled self-presentations. It is clear, however, that self-presentational activities are not simply self-conscious, unnatural, effortful actions that occur only occasionally when people interact. Much self-presentation is guided by automatic processes, seems perfectly natural to the actor and audience, and therefore goes unnoticed. Whether in the foreground or background, however, it is still self-presentation.

IS SELF-PRESENTATION INHERENTLY DUPLICITOUS?

To some researchers, self-presentation is inherently pretentious and duplicitous. They reason that if information is controlled to have a desired impact, it cannot be genuine or sincere. We find this to be an odd argument. It fails to acknowledge that the communication process itself necessitates shaping and tailoring information for consumption by audiences, and it ignores the dynamic, reconstructive nature of memory. In both domains, the argument overlooks the impact that social factors, including interpersonal goals and salient audiences, have on shaping people's thoughts, feelings, and public expressions. It is our thesis that the regulation and control of information is a component of effective communication and takes place independently of whether the actor is being truthful. The idea that self-presentation can be used to acquire and support desired identities that the actor perceives as either genuine or duplicitous has been discussed by Schlenker (1980), Baumeister (1982), and Hogan (1982).

Communicating Effectively to Audiences

Effective communication involves packaging information to have a desired impact on an audience. To communicate effectively, one must put oneself in the place of the audience; take into account their perspective, including their competencies, interests, and attitudes; gauge how they are likely to interpret and react to alternative message possibilities; and then edit, package, and transmit the information in a way that leads the audience to draw the desired conclusion. There are always alternative ways information can be presented. These alternative constructions can differ considerably in their effectiveness in communicating the desired ideas, regardless of the truth of the information contained in the communication. For example, think about the many ways, some boring and some memorable, in which a teacher can present a particular topic to students. Many people may associate packaging with falsehood and spontaneity with truth, but these are conceptually and empirically distinct dimensions.

Prior thought and planning about a performance can even improve its accuracy, in that (a) the "take home" message may be conveyed more clearly to the audience, and (b) the communicator may take the time to recheck the elements or details of the message to ensure their factual correctness, thus reducing the chance of mistakenly recalling incorrect information. Professors look over their notes prior to class to refresh their memories for how they want to make the points on that day's agenda and for the details they will present. Business consultants advise job-seekers to do their homework about the company, contemplate working this personalized information into their interviews, and rehearse how they will answer anticipated interview questions. Rehearsal can make the performance go more smoothly because it provides a pre-formed script, boosts self-confidence if the rehearsal goes well, and reduces the disruptive effects of social anxiety (e.g., Bandura, 1997). Furthermore, planning and rehearsing a performance can not only improve the clarity of the verbal components of a message but also their coordination with nonverbal behaviors. DePaulo (1992) concluded that people's posed nonverbal expressions, regardless of whether they accurately expressed existing emotions or involved faking emotions that were not being experienced, are more effective in conveying the desired impression to audiences than are people's spontaneous emotional expressions. Thus, planning one's presentation does not necessarily differentiate what is authentic from inauthentic and often results in more effective communication.

Acting skills play an important role in determining people's effectiveness in producing a desired impact on audiences. Normally, one thinks of actors as people who are good at seeming to be what they are not. High self-monitors, who tend to be good actors, are more effective at playing assigned roles than are low self-monitors, in that they are viewed as better fitting the role and being more believable in it (Elliott, 1979). However, communicating clearly and accurately also requires acting skill, even for conveying the truth and con-vincing an audience that it is the truth. People with better acting skills, as de-termined by their scores on the acting component of the Self-Monitoring Scale (Snyder, 1987), display smaller discrepancies between their own self-beliefs and their friends' ratings of their personal qualities (Cheek, 1982). They also are better able to send emotional expressions effectively to audi-ences than are poorer actors (Riggio & Friedman, 1982). Thus, it seems that better actors are more effective in accurately communicating their own pri-vate self-views and feelings to others than are poorer actors.

Audience Impact

Audiences play a vital role in influencing how people package infor-mation, regardless of whether the information is true or misleading. Mead (1934), Cooley (1902), and other symbolic interactionists proposed that the self exists only in relation to the selves of others. Self-regulation involves taking the role of others, anticipating their likely reactions to one's own pos-sible conduct, and adjusting one's behavior accordingly. Mead (1934) even proposed that thought itself, the most private and personal of activities, is social in character and takes the form of an inner dialogue, in which the self alternates between the roles of actor and audience, not a monologue. Social behavior occurs in the context of real or imagined audiences, whose exis-tence affects an actor's thoughts, feelings, and conduct. Indeed, social be-havior can be defined as behavior that takes into account other people (Higgins, 1992).

Audiences affect self-regulation in at least three ways. First, they affect the reward–cost contingencies in the situation. Audiences provide actors with opportunities to obtain desired outcomes such as approval, respect, and material rewards, as well as the portent of possible undesired outcomes such as disapproval, disrespect, and other punishments (Baumeister, 1982; Jones & Wortman, 1973; Leary, 1995; Rosenfeld et al., 1995; Schlenker, 1980; Tedeschi & Norman, 1985). People are therefore likely to shift their public conduct, often without awareness, in order to optimize their reward–cost ra-tios. People are particularly likely to shift their behavior to make a desired impression when the audience is significant (powerful, attractive, expert), larger in size, and more proximal psychologically (Leary, 1995; Nowak, Szamrej, & Latané, 1990; Schlenker, 1980).

Second, audiences can activate relevant identity images, goals, scripts, and evaluative orientations. For example, seeing a child may activate a set of roles and scripts dealing with parenthood and nurturance, or seeing an at-tractive member of the opposite sex may prime a romantic-quest script and a set of roles that the individual associates with making a good impression in dating situations. The impact of imagined audiences on the salience of al-ternative self-images was shown by Doherty, Van Wagenen, and Schlenker

(1991). They asked college students to visualize a variety of stimuli, such as cotton balls and bright red apples, supposedly so that their physiological responses to mental imagery could be measured. Toward the end of the visualization task, participants were asked to imagine either a parent, a best friend, or a romantic partner. After being disconnected from the recording apparatus, participants were asked, in the context of a different study, to rate themselves on a variety of traits. It was found that participants rated themselves as less independent (e.g., more obedient, cooperative, respectful) and as less sexual (e.g., sexy, passionate) when they had previously imagined a parent than when they had imagined a peer. These results illustrate James's (1890/1952) famous proposition that people have as many social selves as there are groups of audiences to be encountered. Different facets of self become salient not only when we are with others who are important to us (e.g., as when the college student returns home for the holidays and reverts to older roles rather than more current ones), but also when we simply imagine them. The individual's private thoughts and public self-presentations are then more likely to contain these audience-relevant images of self instead of alternative self-images or roles. Of course, there is no duplicity here. Humans are complex, with many facets of their personalities and self-concepts, some of which are even contradicting. The aspects that become salient at any point in time, and therefore become part of self-presentations, depend partly on the audience.

Priming a particular audience also influences people's standards for evaluating conduct. Baldwin and Holmes (1987) found that women evaluated a sexually permissive piece of fiction more negatively after visualizing one of their parents, who might be expected to disapprove, than after visualizing a campus friend, who might be more permissive. Similarly, Baldwin, Carrell, and Lopez (1990) asked students to evaluate themselves or their ideas after unconscious exposure to slides of disapproving or approving others. Their evaluations were more negative after exposure to the image of a disapproving significant other. Finally, Pennington and Schlenker (1999) asked students to serve as judges in what they believed was a judicial pilot program for the student honor court. They evaluated an alleged honor violation and recommended a verdict and sentence. It was found that participants were more punitive when they believed they would have to justify their decisions to either an honor court representative or an accusing professor who argued that the student should be punished than when they had to justify their decisions to the accused student who favored a lenient sentence. Furthermore, this impact was significant even for participants who learned, after they read the case but before they rendered a verdict, that the meeting with the particular audience was unavoidably canceled and could not take place. Thus, the mere anticipation of having to defend their position to an audience who favored a particular outcome produced an irrevocable shift in the evaluative framework people used to make their judgments.

Even emotional expressions, which are sometimes regarded as pure expressions of internal feelings, are shaped by real and imagined audiences. People smile more when they are imagining enjoyable situations in which they are with other people rather than alone (Fridlund et al., 1990) and are more facially expressive when experiencing emotions when others are present or are imagined to be near (Fridlund, 1991a, 1991b). Emotional expressions appear to be in part tools for communication and are not simply or uniquely private activities or expressions of what is inside.

Third, audiences are targets of communication, influencing how information is packaged. As was described earlier, effective communication requires that information be fitted to the audience's knowledge and value systems using ideas, examples, and evidence they can readily understand. People will shift their verbal and nonverbal communications to take into account the specific characteristics of the audience (DePaulo, 1992; Higgins, 1992). For example, adults speak differently depending on whether the audience consists of children, people with mental retardation, people from foreign countries, or other adults with backgrounds like their own (DePaulo & Coleman, 1986), and people can embed messages in their speeches that are decoded accurately by friends but not by strangers (Fleming, Darley, Hilton, & Kojetin, 1990).

Effective communication is not the spontaneous expression of any and all information that comes to mind about a topic. A "mind dump" is not being genuine; it is being egocentric, undisciplined, and unsocial. People learn during socialization that they must package their thoughts to communicate; that the uncensored expression of thoughts, especially those that might offend or shock others, is inappropriate; and that some types of packaging are more likely than others to help them accomplish their interpersonal goals. The failure to package thoughts for the benefit of audiences does not necessarily imply an honest or true expression of self and, at the extreme, could be a sign of disordered thinking that can characterize schizophrenia.

Are Some People Oblivious to Audiences?

For those who reason that the goal-directed control of information to audiences implies fraudulent behavior, and not everyone is fraudulent, then there must be people who do not take part in the "scam." In other words, are there some people who do not actively package and revise information to accomplish their interpersonal goals when interacting with others? To distinguish people who engage in self-presentation versus those who do not, two contrasting styles of self-regulation have been proposed (Buss & Briggs, 1984; Carver & Scheier, 1985). One style, epitomized by public self-consciousness, is characterized by a concern about how one appears to others and the motivation to make a positive impression. This style is associated with chameleon-like behavior, that is, people change their behavior to impress the salient audience. The second style, epitomized by private self-consciousness, is characterized by tuning out the social matrix, being oblivious to the expectations of others, and behaving so as to express inner qualities. This style is associated with greater cross-situational consistency in conduct. Buss and Briggs (1984) explicitly associated the former style with impression management and the latter style with authenticity and expressiveness. Do privately self-conscious people ignore audiences and resist packaging information in ways that help them create desired impressions? Are they invariably more truthful than people who are less privately self-conscious?

Research suggests that they, too, package information but have different interpersonal goals than those held by publicly self-conscious people. Schlenker and Weigold (1990) suggested that privately self-conscious people view themselves and want others to view them as autonomous, independent, and self-reliant. If privately self-conscious people prefer these identity images, they may monitor and control their social behavior to convey these images to others. This self-presentation agenda would produce the type of word–deed matching and cross-situational consistency that has been found in prior research. In initial support of this view, Schlenker and Weigold (1990) found that private self-consciousness was directly related to people's self-ratings of autonomy and personal identity, whereas public self-consciousness was directly related to self-ratings of being team players who get along with others and fit social expectations. Dispositional self-consciousness is thus not content free but is associated with particular types of preferred identities.

Next, Schlenker and Weigold (1990) tested whether privately self-conscious people will monitor and control their self-presentations to convey an image of autonomy to others. Will privately self-conscious people express their own opinions regardless of the impression it creates on others, or will they change their publicly reported opinions if so doing better allows them to appear autonomous? They paired participants with a discussion partner who initially seemed to regard them as either independent or dependent. The situation was also arranged so that participants were led to believe that reporting their actual attitudes, as measured at a prior session, would make them appear to be either similar to most college students, and hence somewhat conforming, or different from most college students, and hence independent. The results showed that the attitudes of both privately and publicly self-conscious participants were significantly influenced by the likely attributions of their partners, but in different ways. Those who were publicly self-conscious changed their reported attitudes to conform to the expectations of the partner. They made themselves appear to be more similar to others when the partner thought they were dependent and more different from others when the partner thought they were independent. In contrast, privately self-conscious participants changed their reported attitudes to protect their appearance of autonomy. They publicly shifted away from their private beliefs if the partner seemed to think they were dependent and expressing their real attitudes would have made them look dependent.

These results suggest that audiences matter for everyone, but not for the same reasons—different people have different self-presentation agendas when relating to others. Privately self-conscious people look to salient audiences to tell them if they are coming across as the type of person they want to be. In this sense, they are inner-directed but not oblivious to the opinions of others. If their self-presentation agendas are jeopardized, they, too, will misrepresent their attitudes to create the right impression. In contrast, publicly self-conscious people look to salient audiences to tell them who they should be; they then step into that role. In this sense, they are other-directed. Self-regulatory styles do not seem to be differentiated on the basis of whether or not people's self-presentations are influenced by others, rather, they are differentiated on the basis of how they are influenced by others. Audiences thus appear to be a vital component of the self-regulation process. People may sometimes monitor audiences' reactions less closely, be less willing to conform to certain audiences' expectations, and be less willing to subordinate their own desired identities and agendas in favor of those preferred by certain others. But this is far different from saying that people are oblivious to audiences.

Is it self-presentation when people use an audience to find out whether they are coming across as they want and then adjust their behavior accordingly? Our answer is an unequivocal yes. Doing so involves monitoring and controlling one's actions to create a desired impression of self on others, which is how self-presentation is usually defined.

Telling Stories: Narratives, Autobiographical Memory, and Self-Presentation

Critics who suggest that self-presentation is inherently duplicitous, because information is packaged for audiences rather than just expressed, often seem to assume that there is a clear, crystallized self, complete with well-formed memories of past experiences. If people are truthful, they simply access these experiences and report them faithfully. If they modify or package the information in a goal-directed fashion for audience consumption, then they are being duplicitous. However, research on memory, and especially on autobiographical memory, consistently reveals that experiences are not encoded in objective detail, stored faithfully over time, and accessed later as if reviewing a clear picture in memory. Instead, people reconstruct past events in memory, putting together stories about the past that are organized in part around themes, goals, and experiences from the present (Baumeister & Newman, 1994; Gergen & Gergen, 1988; Schacter, 1997; Singer & Salovey, 1993).

The concepts of narrative (or story), script, and schema have become widely used in psychology to represent ways in which people make sense of events, store them in memory, recall the past, and communicate information to others (Baumeister & Newman, 1994; Gergen & Gergen, 1988; Murray & Holmes, 1994; Neisser, 1980; Schank & Abelson, 1977; Singer & Salovey, 1993). These concepts, although differing in emphasis and specifics, share the idea that people impose patterns on complex realities to understand, predict, and control their experiences.

Neisser (1980) proposed that autobiographical memory is organized in a nested structure. Information about previous events in people's lives is stored at different levels of specificity or detail. At no time are we able to access all of the details. We often recall the more general details and assume that the smaller, related ones occurred. For example, we may recall driving to work and therefore assume that we used turn signals. Although in most cases this turns out to be true, it may not actually represent what happened on a particular occasion when we forgot to signal, nor may that detail even be stored in memory. This reconstructive nature of autobiographical memory allows for the selectivity that occurs in recalling and recognizing events as memories and enables people to deal in coherent ways with the enormous amounts of knowledge they have about themselves and the world. Neisser (1980) suggested that how much people "make up" versus "omit" from the past depends on both the individual's intentions and the situation at the time of recall. The smallest amount of elaboration in memory usually occurs when people are silently reminiscing for their own purposes, whereas more occurs when people must communicate their accounts to others. When talking to others, more "detailed and colorful accounts are effective if you want to impress an audience," but less detail and color are appropriate when testifying in court (p. 78). In any case, when remembering past events, people "smooth out" details and fill in gaps to create more coherent stories.

The factors that influence the recall of autobiographical memories are the same as those that affect the packaging and editing of information for public self-presentation. For example, memory for the past has been shown to be affected by social motives and interpersonal goals, as people recall incidents that support their power and affiliation motives (McAdams, 1982); by expectations, as people remember more positive self-evaluative information when expecting success rather than failure (Mischel, Ebbesen, & Zeiss, 1976); by currently salient self-images, as people quickly recall information consistent with those images (Klein & Kihlstrom, 1986; Markus & Sentis, 1982); by traits known to be admired by an audience, as people selectively recall information that will most likely impress the audience (Sanitioso, Kunda, & Fong, 1990); by audience consensus about an event, as people say they also remembered (actually false) facts that were supposedly recalled by a consensus of other witnesses (Betz, Skowronski, & Ostrom, 1993); and by leading questions, as people integrate false information into their memories based on the phrasing of an interrogator's questions (Loftus, Feldman, & Dashiell, 1997).

Sanitioso et al. (1990) illustrated the power of identity concerns in influencing what people remember as true about themselves. They gave participants information as to whether extraversion or introversion was the better trait to possess. It was found that participants recalled faster and listed more personal events from memory that supported whichever trait had been portrayed as the more socially desirable one. Similarly, people recalled donating more money to charity, voting more often, raising more intelligent children (Cannell & Kahn, 1968), and doing better in school (Bahrick, Hall, & Berger, 1996) than objective records suggested. Mothers even misrecalled such important life events as when their children stopped bottle feeding, when they were toilet trained, and when they took their first steps, even only one to three years after the event actually occurred (Robbins, 1963). Much of this recall was in the direction of what experts dictated at the time were the appropriate ages for children to complete the events.

Overall, research on the reconstructive nature of memory shows that current agendas, identities, and audiences shape recall of personal experiences. It thus seems to be an oversimplification to suggest that people will simply enter a social situation and be able to express an authentic self or recount prior personal events in a socially pristine fashion, as if a social vacuum existed. Desired identities, current agendas, and salient audiences influence how information is packaged, and such packaging does not imply that the resulting self-presentation is inherently duplicitous.

Internalizing Self-Presentations: Saying Is (or Can Be) Believing

The actor's public self-presentations, which may initially have been intended largely to create a desired impact on others, may come to influence the actor's subsequent private self-assessments. Early social theorists like Cooley (1902) and Mead (1934) proposed that the self is constructed through social interaction, as people come to view themselves partly in terms of the roles they publicly enact and other people's reactions to them. Consistent with this view, research shows that people's strategic self-presentations will produce changes in their subsequent self-appraisals, as people change their global self-evaluations (Gergen, 1965; Jones et al., 1981; Rhodewalt & Agustsdottir, 1986) and the corresponding contents of their self-beliefs (McKillop, Berzonsky, & Schlenker, 1992; Schlenker, Dlugolecki, & Doherty, 1994; Schlenker & Trudeau, 1990; Tice, 1992) to become more like the public roles they played.

People are more likely to internalize their self-presentations when their actions appear to be representative of self. The appearance of representativeness is created when people freely chose to play the role or are asked to draw on their own prior personal experiences when enacting the role rather than on experiences that are obviously taken from the life of someone else (Jones et al., 1981; Rhodewalt & Agustsdottir, 1986; Schlenker & Trudeau, 1990; Tice, 1992). There are limits to how extreme role-playing can be before the actor rejects it as unrepresentative. Roles that are greatly discrepant from clear prior self-beliefs are not internalized; people reject them as "not me" (Schlenker & Trudeau, 1990). However, if the role is only somewhat discrepant from clear prior self-beliefs, or if self-beliefs are less clearly formed on the dimension, people will shift their private self-beliefs in the direction of the role (Schlenker & Trudeau, 1990). Furthermore, social validation is important in perceiving representativeness. People are more likely to internalize public portrayals that are met with approval and acceptance from others (Gergen, 1965). Thus, to the extent that people label their own public actions as self-representative or have the label applied by others, they become more likely to see themselves in corresponding ways.

Role or identity enactments have a more powerful impact on private self-beliefs when they carry with them a public commitment, as compared to when they are privately performed with few or no public repercussions. Tice (1992) found that self-characterizations produced more change in self-conceptions if they were enacted publicly rather than privately. Furthermore, public behavior produced more change if it was freely selected, drew on episodes of one's own past rather than on the obvious pasts of others, and involved expected future interactions with the audience. Schlenker et al. (1994) found that having people think about past experiences that were consistent with specific roles did not affect later self-beliefs, but having people play the role publicly produced shifts in self-appraisals. In another study, Schlenker et al. (1994) had participants role play a desirable identity. Those whose characterizations were made during an actual interview or who made a public commitment to portray that identity in an upcoming interview later shifted their self-beliefs to become more like the person they portrayed. In contrast, those who learned that they would not have to portray that identity because the interview was canceled, and those whose portrayals were private, did not change their self-beliefs. These findings indicate that public commitment has a powerful shaping effect on private self-beliefs.

Public self-presentations can not only produce corresponding changes in self-beliefs, they can also produce changes in behavior in new situations with different audiences (Tice, 1992; Schlenker et al., 1994). Participants who presented themselves as more extraverted rather than introverted (Tice, 1992) or who portrayed themselves as more sociable (Schlenker et al., 1994), acted in a more extraverted, sociable way when later meeting a new person. Thus, self-presentations can produce carry-over effects that linger beyond the initial interaction. If one wants to become a certain type of person, one should try to publicly act like that type of person. Eventually, if the portrayal is unmarred by out-of-character incidents and audience feedback appears to be accepting, one is likely to become it.

As this research suggests, authenticity is not a static concept. Self-presentations that once may have been tentatively proffered and tenuously documented can become true as the actor gains confidence playing the role and receives feedback suggesting that others accept the portrayal. Thus, the somewhat shy student who wants to become more outgoing can, through hard work, perseverance, and public commitment to new self-presentations, gradually become, in his or her own mind and in social reality, more extraverted.

Truth in Packaging

The theme of this section is that packaging information to achieve goals is independent of truthfulness or sincerity. Packaging can be guided by the goal of aiding the audience by imparting truth, as in the case of the teacher who wants to impart useful information to students, or by the goal of selfishly manipulating the audience, as in the caricature of the deceptive used-car salesperson. Stories or narratives can be true or false in their major themes as well as in the factual detail that is communicated to support them. Sometimes true stories contain unintended errors of factual detail, and lies contain just enough true facts to make them appear credible. To determine deceit, one must look to the motives of the actor and the extent to which the message corresponds with information that can be independently assessed, not to whether information is packaged for consumption by audiences.

Information may be packaged in nearly unlimited ways to make desired points. This is not to suggest, however, that all is appearance without substance or that any and all interpretations of reality are equally valid. Reality imposes constraints on what can be credibly claimed. There are rules for determining the truthfulness of an assertion and comparing claims to accomplishments and characteristics. Goffman (1959, p. 13) noted that society is organized on the principle that people who have certain social characteristics have a "moral right" to expect that others will "value and treat" them in the appropriate fashion and, correspondingly, that people have a duty to be what they claim to be. People are socialized to match their words and their deeds and to tell the truth. Society cannot function if deceit on substantive matters is tolerated.

A reputation for honesty is an important interpersonal asset. People react negatively to those whose words and deeds deviate (Schlenker & Leary, 1982a). Furthermore, when presenting themselves to others, people demonstrate an appreciation of the importance of consistency between words and deeds. People present themselves consistently with publicly known information about them, even though they may exaggerate their claims when potentially contradictory information can be hidden from public view (Baumeister & Jones, 1978; Schlenker, 1975). Reality, in the form of publicly known information and independently verifiable facts, provides constraints on what people can credibly claim.

People do not have free reign to package information in any and all ways that serve their self-interests. People are accountable to others for being what they claim to be, and they risk social censure and sometimes legal peril for deceit. However, deceit is determined by judgments of the actor's motives and whether independently verifiable information supports or refutes the claims. The packaging of information for consumption by audiences, in and of itself, tells us nothing about the actor's truthfulness.

IS IMPRESSION MANAGEMENT AN INHERENTLY SELFISH ACTIVITY?

The concept of impression management sometimes evokes images of selfish, superficial, manipulative individuals whose goal is to jockey for personal advantage in the social world, even if it means misleading or exploiting others. Much of the research on impression management has focused on how people will shift their attitudes and self-descriptions to secure some personal advantage, such as social approval, better interpersonal evaluations, or pay raises (see Baumeister, 1982; Leary, 1995; Rosenfeld et al., 1995; Schlenker, 1980; Schlenker & Weigold, 1992; Tedeschi & Norman, 1985), so it is perhaps not surprising that many researchers tend to think of impression management as selfish conduct. In our view, impression management is like any other social activity in that it can be guided by a variety of goals, some of which seem to derive from concerns about others.

People often use impression management to help others sustain the images they would like to convey, thereby maintaining harmonious and smoothly flowing social interactions. Goffman (1959) discussed how people help others "save face" when confronted by embarrassing incidents or threats to identity. Similarly, politeness theory (Brown & Levinson, 1987) indicates that people consider not only their own face needs when verbally accounting for their actions, but also the needs of the recipient of the action. Folkes (1982), for example, showed that when people reject another person, as when refusing a date, they provide excuses that focus on external attributions such as illness to protect the self-esteem of the other. Similarly, people's lies often seem motivated by the desire to protect the feelings of the recipient (DePaulo, Kashy, Kirkendol, Wyer, & Epstein, 1996). Thus, people's self-presentations and impression management activities are often tailored to accommodate the sensibilities of others.

People also seem to go beyond merely accommodating the feelings of others and will use strategic impression management to help others, especially their friends. Jennie Jerome Churchill, the charming and popular American-born mother of Winston Churchill, once advised, "Treat your friends as you do your pictures, and place them in their best light" (Churchill, 1916). Her advice reminds us of the importance of social support in relationships. Through displays of appreciation, approval, respect, and encouragement, people cement relationships, build friendships, and provide each other with a host of benefits. As Schlenker and Britt (1999a, 1999b) discussed, such support can help recipients by boosting their self-efficacy and self-esteem; by generating positive moods or dispelling negative ones; by inspiring them to new accomplishments; by enhancing or protecting their reputations; and, ultimately, by facilitating their goals in social and business life. Social support through beneficial impression management may be one of the more important and more frequently used forms of help in everyday life, and it is usually greatly appreciated by its recipient. The social support literature documents the importance of social support, especially identity-affirming support, for the psychological well-being and interpersonal success of recipients (see Schlenker & Britt, 1999a, 1999b). However, the research literature has not given much attention to the provision of support as a goal-oriented strategy. Who offers support to whom, when, and why?

Although the impression management literature has discussed benefitting others, such as by complimenting them or providing assistance, the focus has been on the anticipated consequences for self, not for the other person. For instance, people will flatter others and do favors for them to obtain personal advantages such as better evaluations and pay raises (Jones & Wortman, 1973; Wayne & Kacmar, 1991), provide assistance to others as a way of compensating for their own threatened public images after transgressions (Tedeschi & Riordan, 1981), or praise others with whom they are associated in order to bask in reflected glory (Cialdini, Finch, & De Nicholas, 1990). We propose that impression management also can be guided by concerns for others. The distinction between prosocial behavior that appears to be guided by concerns about self versus concerns about others has been made in both the helping literature (Batson, 1995) and the literature on close relationships (Aron, Aron, Tudor, & Nelson, 1991; Clark & Reis, 1988), and this distinction can be readily applied to impression management.

Research supports the proposition that people will strategically control information to help friends make a desired impression on significant others. Schlenker and Britt (1999a) had participants describe a friend to an individual of the opposite sex whom the friend supposedly regarded as very attractive or very unattractive and whose ideal date was either extraverted or introverted. Participants portrayed their friend consistently with the qualities preferred by the attractive audience, thereby communicating that their friend was the type of person the attractive other would find desirable. However, they portrayed their friend inconsistently with the qualities preferred by the unattractive audience, thereby communicating that their friend was "not your type" and helping the friend avoid unwelcome entanglements. In both cases, participants portrayed their friend in a way that the friend would seemingly have most preferred to be seen, given the qualities and preferences of the audience. Furthermore, the situation was arranged so that there were no obvious, direct advantages to the participants themselves for helping their friend. Although their portrayals of their friend supposedly were seen by the attractive or unattractive audience, they did not expect to meet that audience, nor did they expect that their descriptions would ever be seen by or discussed with their friend. Thus, their descriptions were publicly available to the target audience but were confidential in relation to the friend.

In a second experiment, Schlenker and Britt (1999a) had participants describe a friend or stranger to a researcher who was evaluating this partner's cognitive skills. For half of the participants, the partner was expected to go through a face-to-face interview with the researcher and receive evaluative feedback, so the partner had a high social need to make a good impression. For the remaining participants, the partner was expected not to be interviewed directly and not to receive evaluative feedback, so the researcher's evaluation had virtually no social impact on the partner. As hypothesized, participants described the partner as having the best cognitive skills when the partner was a friend who had a high social need to make a good impression on the researcher. Descriptions of the partner's cognitive skills were less positive when the friend did not have a social need to create a good impression or when the partner was a stranger regardless of social need. These strategic shifts occurred even though there was no obvious personal advantage to the participants for helping a friend in social need. The situation had been arranged so that the participants' descriptions would not be seen by or discussed with the partner, and the partner supposedly would not be told that the participant played any role whatsoever in the evaluation process.

In a third experiment, Schlenker and Britt (1999b) used a similar procedure and again found that participants' descriptions of a partner were more positive when they believed a friend would go through a face-to-face interview about an important cognitive skill, as compared to when no face-to-face interview of the friend was anticipated, the skill was unimportant, or the partner was a stranger. These effects were pronounced only for (a) participants who were high as compared to low in empathy and (b) those who previously reported greater liking and caring for their friend as compared to those whose liking and caring were below the sample median.

The facts that beneficial impression management is greater for those who have greater empathy or who feel a stronger bond to a friend are consistent with the idea that this strategic behavior is motivated by a concern for the welfare of the other and not simply or exclusively for one's own welfare. Empathy has long been described as a foundation, if not the foundation, of moral conduct (Batson, 1995; Wilson, 1993). In the 18th century, the Scottish Moral Philosophers emphasized the importance of communication and sympathy (empathy) in understanding society (Stryker, 1981). In *The Theory of Moral Sentiments*, Adam Smith (1759/1976) argued that moral sentiments derive from sympathy, or people's capacity and inclination to imagine themselves in the place of others and vicariously experience their thoughts and feelings. The capacity to take into account the perspective of others and envision their reactions permits human communication, which is the foundation of human association. Sympathy (empathy) also provides a means and motivation to procure the good will of others. Smith argued that because one's own welfare depends in large measure on the good will of others, people must be concerned with the welfare of those others and be able to anticipate how they are likely to feel and react in different situations. By trying to procure the good will of others, people mutually benefit themselves and others. Research provides ample support for the hypothesis that greater empathy is associated with greater helping (Batson, 1995; Krebs, 1970).

The work of Mead (1934) and other symbolic interactionists, who viewed role-taking and role-playing skills as cornerstones of social conduct, extended the ideas of the Scottish Moral Philosophers. Symbolic interactionism, in turn, influenced the dramaturgical approach (Goffman, 1959), which was a seminal inspiration for current work on impression management. There is a certain irony in the realization that the intellectual roots of impression management, which is often characterized as being illicit and superficial, and moral conduct, which is precisely the opposite, can be traced to the same ideas and intellectual tributaries. Impression management and moral behavior involve putting oneself in the place of others, anticipating their experiences and reactions, and regulating one's conduct in a way that might generate good will. There is no reason to argue that impression management cannot be motivated by the full range of human goals, including the more admirable ones. Recognizing that the strategic control of information can be used for prosocial purposes and be motivated by socially laudable goals restores balance to the concept.

CONCLUSION

We opened the chapter with three questions about impression management and self-presentation that are often answered in ways that limit the range or applicability of these concepts and inhibit conceptual development. We offered alternative answers. First, we proposed that impression management and self-presentation are not restricted to highly evaluative or unusual social situations, such as first dates and job interviews, nor are they used only by people who are manipulative social chameleons. Impression management and self-presentation are pervasive features of social behavior. Although self-presentation can be used to gain approval and achieve valuable interpersonal goals, it also is a fundamental component of all social transactions. In order to interact, people must define the situation by selecting the relevant social scripts and the roles each will play. Self-presentation communicates people's definitions of their identities, motives, and orientation toward the relationship. Once identities are established, each participant has a moral obligation to behave consistently with the identity he or she projected and to respect the other's identity by treating him or her appropriately. Even in long-term relationships, the self-presentation process continues as people perpetuate key aspects of their own identities, negotiate new aspects to change with the times, and provide strategic support for the identities of close others.

Much of the time, self-presentation goes on in the background, without awareness and via habit-molded patterns of behavior, automatically guided by scripts that permit people to focus their attention on more immediate, challenging problems. When the audience or situation becomes highly important, unusual, or problematic, self-presentation shifts to the foreground, as people become conscious of the impression they are making and exert cognitive effort to plan, monitor, and control their actions. Although it is these latter situations that are often regarded as those that define self-presentation, we argued that it is inappropriate and problematic to restrict the concept in this way.

Second, we proposed that impression management and self-presentation are not inherently duplicitous or pretentious. People must simplify and package the world when they recall and reconstruct their personal histories and communicate information to others. The packaging process, which involves memory reconstruction and edited communications, is influenced by the actor's agendas and the salient audience. The fact that information is packaged does not lead to the conclusion that the actor is deceitful by changing stories from one situation to another or is pretentious by constructing stories that create a desired impression on others. Deceit and pretension are determined by the motives of the actor, not by the existence of edited, packaged information. It takes as much self-presentation skill to communicate accurate, truthful information that creates the desired impact on others as it does to tell lies that try to take advantage of others.

Third, we proposed that impression management and self-presentation should not be regarded simply as selfish, manipulative activities. Some conceptual analyses of impression management have defined the concept in terms of specific selfish motives, such as the motives to acquire power or approval. In contrast, we argued that people's goals are diverse, and impression management can be used to facilitate a wide range of agendas. It can be used strategically to educate as well as to propagandize and to help friends in social need and not just benefit the self. Providing social support by constructing and maintaining desirable identities for others may be one of the more common forms of help-giving in daily life and one of the most graciously appreciated by the recipient.

The concepts of impression management and self-presentation contribute to the view that people are agents who actively construct, maintain, and protect their social environments. People try to influence others and

arrange events so as to produce more beneficial, less threatening surround-
ings. People's abilities to influence others and navigate their social worlds effectively can be regarded as vital components of intelligence (Cantor &
Kihlstrom, 1987) and as critical to evolutionary adaptiveness and reproductive success (Hogan & Hogan, 1991). Social influence is exercised in large
measure by controlling information in ways that lead others to form desired
impressions and draw desired conclusions. People's prosperity depends on
the good will of others, and one achieves good will in part by being the kind
of person and doing the kinds of things that people admire and appreciate.
Impression management and self-presentation are not bit players on the
stage of social psychology's concepts. They are leading characters in permit-
ting us to understand and explain social behavior.

REFERENCES

Aloise-Young, P. A. (1993). The development of self-presentation: Self-promotion
in 6- to 10-year-old children. *Social Cognition, 11*, 201–222.

Aron, A., Aron, E. N., Tudor, M., & Nelson, G. (1991). Close relationships as including other in the self. *Journal of Personality and Social Psychology, 60*,
241–253.

Bahrick, H. P., Hall, L. K. & Berger, S. A. (1996). Accuracy and distortion in memory for high school grades. *Psychological Science, 7*, 265–271.

Baldwin, M. W., Carrell, S. E., & Lopez, D. F. (1990). Priming relational schemas:
My advisor and the pope are watching me from the back of my mind. *Journal
of Experimental Social Psychology, 26*, 435–454.

Baldwin, M. W., & Holmes, J. G. (1987). Salient private audiences and awareness
of the self. *Journal of Personality and Social Psychology, 52*, 1087–1098.

Bandura, A. (1997). *Self-efficacy: The exercise of control.* New York: Freeman.

Bargh, J. A. (1989). Conditional automaticity: Varieties of automatic influence in
social perception and cognition. In J. Uleman & J. A. Bargh (Eds.), *Unintended
thought* (pp. 3–51). New York: Guilford Press.

Batson, C. D. (1995). Prosocial motivation: Why do we help others? In A. Tesser
(Ed.), *Advanced social psychology* (pp. 333–381). New York: McGraw-Hill.

Baumeister, R. F. (1982). A self-presentational view of social phenomena. *Psychological Bulletin, 91*, 3–26.

Baumeister, R. F., Hutton, D. G., & Tice, D. M. (1989). Cognitive processes during
deliberate self-presentation: How self-presenters alter and misinterpret the behavior of their interaction partners. *Journal of Experimental Social Psychology,
25*, 59–78.

Baumeister, R. F., & Jones, E. E. (1978). When self-presentation is constrained by
the target's knowledge: Consistency and compensation. *Journal of Personality
and Social Psychology, 36*, 608–618.

Baumeister, R. F., & Newman, L. S. (1994). How stories make sense of personal experiences: Motives that shape autobiographical narratives. *Personality and Social Psychology Bulletin, 20,* 676–690.

Betz, A. L., Skowronski, J. J., & Ostrom, T. M. (1993). Shared realities: Social influence and episodic memory. *Social Cognition, 14,* 113–140.

Brodt, S. E., & Zimbardo, P. G. (1981). Modifying shyness-related social behavior through symptom misattribution. *Journal of Personality and Social Psychology, 41,* 437–449.

Brown, J. D. (1998). *The self.* New York: McGraw-Hill.

Brown, P., & Levinson, S. C. (1987). *Politeness: Some universals in language usage.* Cambridge, England: Cambridge University Press.

Buss, A. H., & Briggs, S. R. (1984). Drama and the self in social interaction. *Journal of Personality and Social Psychology, 47,* 1310–1324.

Cannell, C. F., & Kahn, R. L. (1968). Interviewing. In G. Lindzey & E. Aronson (Eds.), *The handbook of social psychology* (2nd ed., Vol. 2, pp. 526–595). Reading, MA: Addison-Wesley.

Cantor, N., & Kihlstrom, J. (1987). *Personality and social intelligence.* Englewood Cliffs, NJ: Prentice-Hall.

Carver, C. S., & Scheier, M. F. (1981). *Attention and self-regulation: A control-theory approach to human behavior.* New York: Springer-Verlag.

Carver, C. S., & Scheier, M. F. (1985). Aspects of self and the control of behavior. In B. R. Schlenker (Ed.), *The self and social life* (pp. 146–174). New York: McGraw-Hill.

Cheek, J. M. (1982). Aggregation, moderator variables, and the validity of personality tests: A peer-rating study. *Journal of Personality and Social Psychology, 43,* 1254–1269.

Cheek, J. M., & Hogan, R. (1983). Self-concepts, self-presentations, and moral judgments. In J. Suls & A. G. Greenwald (Eds.), *Psychological perspectives on the self* (Vol. 2, pp. 249–273). Hillsdale, NJ: Erlbaum.

Churchill, J. J. (1916). *Small talks on big subjects.* London: Pearson.

Cialdini, R. B., Finch, J. F., & De Nicholas, M. E. (1990). Strategic self-presentation: The indirect route. In M. J. Cody & M. L. McLaughlin (Eds.), *The psychology of tactical communication* (pp. 194–206). Bristol, PA: Multilingual Matters Ltd.

Cialdini, R. B., Levy, A., Herman, C. P., Kozlowski, L. T., & Petty, R. E. (1976). Elastic shifts of opinion: Determinants of direction and durability. *Journal of Personality and Social Psychology, 34,* 663–672.

Clark, M. S., & Reis, H. T. (1988). Interpersonal processes in close relationships. *Annual Review of Psychology, 39,* 609–672.

Cooley, C. H. (1902). *Human nature and the social order.* New York: Scribner.

DePaulo, B. M. (1992). Nonverbal behavior and self-presentation. *Psychological Bulletin, 111,* 203–243.

DePaulo, B. M., & Coleman, L. M. (1986). Talking to children, foreigners, and retarded adults. *Journal of Personality and Social Psychology, 51,* 945–959.

DePaulo, B. M., Kashy, D. A., Kirkendol, S. E., Wyer, M. M., & Epstein, J. A. (1996). Lying in everyday life. *Journal of Personality and Social Psychology, 70,* 979–995.

Doherty, K., Van Wagenen, T. J., & Schlenker, B. R. (1991, August). *Imagined audiences influence self-identifications.* Paper presented at the 98th Annual Meetings of the American Psychological Association, San Francisco.

Elkind, D. (1980). Strategic interactions in adolescence. In J. Adelson (Ed.), *Handbook of adolescent psychology* (pp. 432–444). New York: Wiley.

Elliott, G. C. (1979). Some effects of deception and level of self-monitoring on planning and reacting to self-presentation. *Journal of Personality and Social Psychology, 37,* 1282–1292.

Fiske, S. T., & Taylor, S. E. (1991). *Social cognition* (2nd ed.). New York: McGraw-Hill.

Fleming, J. H., Darley, J. M., Hilton, J. L., & Kojetin, B. A. (1990). Multiple audience problem: A strategic communication perspective on social perception. *Journal of Personality and Social Psychology, 58,* 593–609.

Folkes, V. S. (1982). Communicating the cause of social rejection. *Journal of Experimental Social Psychology, 18,* 235–252.

Fridlund, A. J. (1991a). Evolution and facial action in reflex, social motive, and paralanguage, *Biological Psychology, 32,* 3–100.

Fridlund, A. J. (1991b). The sociability of solitary smiling: Potentiation by an implicit audience. *Journal of Personality and Social Psychology, 60,* 229–240.

Fridlund, A. J., Sabini, J. P., Hedlund, L. E., Schaut, J. A., Shenker, J. I., & Knauer, M. J. (1990). Audience effects on solitary faces during imagery: Displaying to the people in your head. *Journal of Nonverbal Behavior, 14,* 113–137.

Friedlander, M. L., & Schwartz, G. S. (1985). Toward a theory of strategic self-presentation in counseling and psychotherapy. *Journal of Consulting Psychology, 32,* 483–501.

Gergen, K. J. (1965). Interaction goals and personalistic feedback as factors affecting the presentation of self. *Journal of Personality and Social Psychology, 1,* 413–424.

Gergen, K. J., & Gergen, M. M. (1988). Narrative and the self as relationship. In L. Berkowitz (Ed.), *Advances in experimental social psychology* (Vol. 21, pp. 17–56). New York: Academic Press.

Gilbert, D. T., & Osborne, R. E. (1989). Thinking backward: Some curable and incurable consequences of cognitive busyness. *Journal of Personality and Social Psychology, 57,* 940–949.

Goffman, E. (1959). *The presentation of self in everyday life.* New York: Doubleday.

Greenwald, A. G. (1980). The totalitarian ego: Fabrication and revision of personal history. *American Psychologist, 35,* 603–618.

Hatch, J. A. (1987). Impression management in kindergarten classrooms: An analysis of children's face-work in peer interactions. *Anthropology & Education Quarterly, 18,* 100–115.

Higgins, E. T. (1992). Achieving "shared reality" in the communication game: A social action that creates meaning. *Journal of Language and Social Psychology, 11*, 107–131.

Hogan, R. (1982). A socioanalytic theory of personality. In M. Page (Ed.), *Nebraska symposium on motivation* (Vol. 29, pp. 55–89). Lincoln: University of Nebraska Press.

Hogan, R., & Hogan, J. (1991). Personality and status. In D. G. Gilbert & J. J. Conley (Eds.), *Personality, social skills, and psychopathology: An individual differences approach* (pp. 137–154). New York: Plenum Press.

James, W. (1952). *The principles of psychology*. Chicago: Encyclopaedia Britannica. (Original work published 1890)

Jones, E. E. (1964). *Ingratiation*. New York: Appleton-Century-Crofts.

Jones, E. E. (1990). *Interpersonal perception*. New York: Freeman.

Jones, E. E., & Pittman, T. S. (1982). Toward a general theory of strategic self-presentation. In J. Suls (Ed.), *Psychological perspectives on the self* (Vol. 1, pp. 231–262). Hillsdale, NJ: Erlbaum.

Jones, E. E., Rhodewalt, F., Berglas, S., & Skelton, J. A. (1981). Effects of strategic self-presentation on subsequent self-esteem. *Journal of Personality and Social Psychology, 41*, 407–421.

Jones, E. E., & Wortman, C. (1973). *Ingratiation: An attributional approach*. Morristown, NJ: General Learning Press.

Kelly, A. E., & McKillop, K. J. (1996). Consequences of revealing personal secrets. *Psychological Bulletin, 120*, 450–465.

Klein, J. F., & Kihlstrom, J. F. (1986). Elaboration, organization, and the self-reference effect in memory. *Journal of Experimental Psychology: General, 115*, 26–38.

Krebs, D. (1970). Altruism—An examination of the concept and a review of the literature. *Psychological Bulletin, 73*, 258–302.

Leary, M. R. (1986). The impact of interactional impediments on social anxiety and self-presentation. *Journal of Experimental Social Psychology, 22*, 122–135.

Leary, M. R. (1995). *Self-presentation: Impression management and interpersonal behavior*. Madison, WI: Brown & Benchmark.

Loftus, E. F., Feldman, J., & Dashiell, R. (1997). The reality of illusory memories. In D. L. Schacter (Ed.), *Memory distortion: How minds, brains, and societies reconstruct the past* (pp. 47–68). Cambridge, MA: Harvard University Press.

Markus, H., & Sentis, K. (1982). The self in social information processing. In J. Suls (Ed.), *Psychological perspectives on the self* (Vol. 1, pp. 41–70). Hillsdale, NJ: Erlbaum.

McAdams, D. P. (1982). Experiences in intimacy and power: Relationships between social motives and autobiographical memory. *Journal of Personality and Social Psychology, 42*, 292–302.

McCall, G. J., & Simmons, J. F. (1978). *Identities and interactions* (Rev. ed.). New York: Free Press.

McKillop, K. J., Jr., Berzonsky, M. D., & Schlenker, B. R. (1992). The impact of self-presentations on self-beliefs: Effects of social identity and self-presentational context. *Journal of Personality, 60,* 789–808.

Mead, G. H. (1934). *Mind, self, and society.* Chicago: University of Chicago Press.

Mischel, W., Ebbesen, E. B., & Zeiss, A. R. (1976). Determinants of selective memory about the self. *Journal of Consulting and Clinical Psychology, 44,* 92–103.

Murray, S. L., & Holmes, J. G. (1994). Storytelling in close relationships: The construction of confidence. *Personality and Social Psychology Bulletin, 20,* 650–663.

Neisser, U. (1980). Nested structure in autobiographical memory. In D. C. Rubin (Ed.), *Autobiographical memory* (pp. 71–81). New York: Cambridge University Press.

Nowak, A., Szamrej, J., & Latané, B. (1990). From private attitude to public opinion: A dynamic theory of social impact. *Psychological Review, 97,* 362–376.

Paulhus, D. L. (1988). *Automatic and controlled self-presentation.* Paper presented at the meeting of the American Psychological Association, Atlanta.

Paulhus, D. L. (1993). Bypassing the will: The automatization of affirmations. In D. M. Wegener & J. W. Pennebaker (Eds.), *Handbook of mental control* (pp. 573–587). Englewood Cliff, NJ: Prentice-Hall.

Paulhus, D. L., Graf, P., & van Selst, M. (1989). Attentional load increases the positivity of self-presentation. *Social Cognition, 7,* 389–400.

Paulhus, D. L., & Levitt, K. (1987). Desirable responding triggered by affect: Automatic egotism? *Journal of Personality and Social Psychology, 52,* 245–259.

Pennington, J. W., & Schlenker, B. R. (1999). Accountability for consequential decisions: Justifying moral judgments to audiences. *Personality and Social Psychology Bulletin, 25,* 1067–1081.

Pontari, B. A., & Schlenker, B. R. (in press). The influence of cognitive load on self-presentation: Can cognitive business help as well as harm social performance? *Journal of Personality and Social Psychology.*

Rhodewalt, F., & Agustsdottir, S. (1986). The effects of self-presentation on the phenomenal self. *Journal of Personality and Social Psychology, 50,* 47–55.

Riggio, R. E., & Friedman, H. W. (1982). The interrelationship of self-monitoring factors, personality traits, and nonverbal social skills. *Journal of Nonverbal Behavior, 7,* 33–45.

Robbins, L. C. (1963). The accuracy of parental recall of aspects of child development and of child rearing practices. *Journal of Abnormal Social Psychology, 66,* 261–270.

Rosenfeld, P., Giacalone, R. A., & Riordan, C. A. (1995). *Impression management in organizations.* New York: Routledge.

Sanitioso, R., Kunda, Z., & Fong, G. T. (1990). Motivated recruitment of autobiographical memories. *Journal of Personality and Social Psychology, 59,* 229–241.

Schacter, D. L. (Ed.) (1997). *Memory distortion: How minds, brains, and societies reconstruct the past.* Cambridge, MA: Harvard University Press.

Schank, R., & Abelson, R. (1977). *Scripts, plans, goals, and understanding*. Hillsdale, NJ: Erlbaum.

Schlenker, B. R. (1975). Self-presentation: Managing the impression of consistency when reality interferes with self-enhancement. *Journal of Personality and Social Psychology, 32*, 1030–1037.

Schlenker, B. R. (1980). *Impression management: The self-concept, social identity, and interpersonal relations*. Monterey, CA: Brooks/Cole.

Schlenker, B. R. (1985). Identity and self-identification. In B. R. Schlenker (Ed.), *The self and social life* (pp. 65–99). New York: McGraw-Hill.

Schlenker, B. R. (1987). Threats to identity: Self-identification and social stress. In C. R. Snyder & C. E. Ford (Eds.), *Coping with negative life events: Clinical and social psychological perspectives* (pp. 273–321). New York: Plenum Press.

Schlenker, B. R., & Britt, T. W. (1999a). Beneficial impression management: Strategically controlling information to help friends. *Journal of Personality and Social Psychology, 76*, 559–573.

Schlenker, B. R., & Britt, T. W. (1999b). *Strategically controlling information to help friends: Effects of empathy and friendship strength on beneficial impression management*. Manuscript submitted for publication, University of Florida, Gainesville.

Schlenker, B. R., Britt, T. W., & Pennington, J. W. (1996). Impression regulation and management: A theory of self-identification. In R. M. Sorrentino & E. T. Higgins (Eds.), *Handbook of motivation and cognition: The interpersonal context* (Vol. 3, pp. 118–147). New York: Guilford Press.

Schlenker, B. R., Dlugolecki, D. W., & Doherty, K. J. (1994). The impact of self-presentations on self-appraisals and behaviors: The power of public commitment. *Personality and Social Psychology Bulletin, 20*, 20–33.

Schlenker, B. R., & Leary, M. R. (1982a). Audiences' reactions to self-enhancing, self-denigrating, and accurate self-presentations. *Journal of Experimental Social Psychology, 18*, 89–104.

Schlenker, B. R., & Leary, M. R. (1982b). Social anxiety and self-presentation: A conceptualization and model. *Psychological Bulletin, 92*, 641–669.

Schlenker, B. R., & Trudeau, J. V. (1990). The impact of self-presentations on private self-beliefs: Effects of prior self-beliefs and misattribution. *Journal of Personality and Social Psychology, 58*, 22–32.

Schlenker, B. R., & Weigold, M. F. (1989). Goals and the self-identification process. In L. Pervin (Ed.), *Goals concepts in personality and social psychology* (pp. 243–290). Hillsdale, NJ: Erlbaum.

Schlenker, B. R., & Weigold, M. F. (1990). Self-consciousness and self-presentation: Being autonomous versus appearing autonomous. *Journal of Personality and Social Psychology, 59*, 820–828.

Schlenker, B. R., & Weigold, M. F. (1992). Interpersonal processes involving impression regulation and management. *Annual Review of Psychology, 43*, 133–168.

Singer, J. A., & Salovey, P. (1993). *The remembered self: Emotion and memory in personality*. New York: Free Press.

Smith, A. (1976). *The theory of moral sentiments*. In D. D. Raphael & A. L. Macfie (Eds.). Oxford: Clarendon Press. (Original work published 1759)

Snyder, M. (1987). *Public appearances/Private realities: The psychology of self-monitoring*. New York: Freeman.

Stryker, S. (1981). Symbolic interactionism: Themes and variations. In M. Rosenberg & R. H. Turner (Eds.), *Social psychology: Sociological perspectives* (pp. 1–29). New York: Basic Books.

Tedeschi, J. T., & Norman, N. (1985). Social power, self-presentation, and the self. In B. R. Schlenker (Ed.), *The self and social life* (pp. 293–321). New York: McGraw-Hill.

Tedeschi, J. T., & Riordan, C. A. (1981). Impression management and prosocial behavior following transgression. In J. T. Tedeschi (Ed.), *Impression management theory and social psychological research* (pp. 223–244). New York: Academic Press.

Tetlock, P. E. (1992). The impact of accountability on judgment and choice: Toward a social contingency model. In M. P. Zanna (Ed.), *Advances in experimental social psychology* (Vol. 25, pp. 331–376). New York: Academic Press.

Tice, D. M. (1992). Self-concept change and self-presentation: The looking glass self is also a magnifying glass. *Journal of Personality and Social Psychology, 63*, 435–451.

Tice, D. M., Butler, J. L., Muraven, M. B., & Stillwell, A. M. (1995). When modesty prevails: Differential favorability of self-presentation to friends and strangers. *Journal of Personality and Social Psychology, 69*, 1120–1138.

Wayne, S. J., & Kacmar, K. M. (1991). The effects of impression management on the performance appraisal process. *Organizational Behavior and Human Decision Processes, 48*, 70–88.

Wilson, J. Q. (1993). *The moral sense*. New York: Free Press.

AUTHOR INDEX

INDEX

Intelligence (*continued*)
theories of (experiment on role models and self-perception), 157–58
International Society for Self and Identity (ISSI), x–xi
Interpersonal membership, 9, 10
Intrinsic dynamics, of mental system, 42–43
Introverts, self-presentation aided by distracting tasks for, 209–10
Irrational beliefs, and cognitive load, 44n

James, William, 4, 6, 206

Landscapes, of stream of self-reflection, 45–50
Learned helplessness, as ego depletion, 27–28
Learning motives, 101, 104–5
as malfunctioning, 111
Leary, Mark, x
Level of abstraction, and cognitive dissonance theory, 134–35
Looking-glass self, 5, 173
and romantic relationships, 173, 175–80, 182–84, 188–90, 192–93

Mead, George Herbert, 4–5
Memory, autobiographical, 217–18
Mental effort, 17
Mental health, coherent integrated self as hallmark of, 69
Mill, James, 3
Mill, John Stuart, 3
Mood
and cognitive dissonance, 130
and ego depletion, 24–25
and self-regulation, 16–17
Moral conduct
empathy as foundation of, 223–24
and impression management, 224
Motivation. *See also* Self-evaluation motives and ego depletion (conservation motives), 18–20, 24, 26, 29
proximal and distal (discrepancy reduction), 136–38

Multiple agendas, 203–4
Muscle model of self-control, 11, 12–13, 21. *See also* Energy model of self

Narratives, in self-presentation, 216–18
Nonlinear dynamical systems, 36, 60

Objectified self, 92
Organization, of self-structure, 70, 81

Perceived regard, and dependency regulation, 177–93
Personal efficacy, and self-verification motive, 105–6
Phi statistic, 71, 74, 76, 81
Plans, 203
Politeness theory, 221
Psychological Perspectives on the Self (ed. Suls), xi
Public self, 100

Qindlen, Anna, 147

Reflected glory, 124, 166–67
Reflected selves, in romantic relationships, 182. *See also* Romantic relationships
Reflexive consciousness, 9, 10
Reflexive potential, of symbolic self, 93
Relevance, in role models' effect on self-perception, 148–49
analogy to determine, 168
and career-matched role models (Study 1), 151–51, 166
Representational aspect, of symbolic self, 92
Research
on self, x, xi, 5–6
on self-concept, 51
self-presentation as contaminant in, 200
on self-structure, 78–82, 84
Rogers, Carl, 5
Role enactments, 218–19
Role models' effect on self-perceptions, 147–48

ABOUT THE EDITORS

Abraham Tesser

Abraham Tesser completed his doctorate in social psychology at Purdue University in 1967. He took faculty position at the University of Georgia where he directed the Institute for Behavioral Research from 1984 to 1994 and is currently professor emeritus. Tesser has been a visiting Fellow at Yale University, Princeton University, the Center for Advanced Study in the Behavioral Sciences, and the Ohio State University. He has served the discipline as an associate editor of the *Personality and Social Psychology Bulletin* and as an editor of the *Journal of Personality and Social Psychology*. Tesser is currently the president of the Society for Personality and Social Psychology, Division 8 of the American Psychological Association. Tesser has published on self-esteem, attitudes, thought and ruminative processes, interpersonal communication, and attraction. This research has been consistently funded by the National Science Foundation and the National Institute of Mental Health (NIHM). Tesser is a recipient of an NIMH National Research Service Aware, and NIMH Research Scientist Award, and the William A. Owens Award for creative research.

Richard B. Felson

Richard B. Felson is professor of crime, law and justice, and sociology at Pennsylvania State University. He received his doctorate at Indiana University in 1977, and was on the faculty at the State University of New York at Albany until recently. His research is concerned with determinants of the self-concept and situational factors in violence. He is the author of numerous articles and is the co-author (with James Tedeschi) of *Violence, Aggression and Coercive Actions* (APA Books, 1994).

Jerry M. Suls

Jerry Suls received his doctorate from Temple University in 1973. Before joining the faculty at the University of Iowa in 1990, he taught at Georgetown University and the State University of New York at Albany. As a social and health psychologist, Dr. Suls's main research interests concern social influence, self-evaluation, and adaptation to chronic illness. He has published over one hundred and twenty articles and chapters and edited or co-edited seven books. He has been the recipient of grants from the National Institutes of Health, National Science Foundation, and the American Heart Association. From 1990 to 1996, he was an associate editor of *Journal of Personality and Social Psychology: Interpersonal Relations and Group Process*; currently, he is editor of *Personality and Social Psychology Bulletin*.